TAKE AWAY ROMANIA

ROMANIA EXPLAINED TO MY FRIENDS ABROAD

Cătălin Gruia

Text copyright © 2016 Cătălin Gruia

All rights reserved. No part of this book may be reproduced in any form or by an electronic or mechanical means, including information storage and retrieval systems, without permission in writing from the publisher, except by a reviewer who may quote brief passages in a review.
www.catalingruia.com

This book is a collection of essays about Romania. It includes abridged versions of my five kindle books below.
The Rise and Fall of Saxon Transylvania
Romanian Gypsies
The Man They Killed on Christmas Day
What About Dracula? Romania's Schizophrenic Dilemma
Who Were The Dacians?

37-Minutes Publishing
First Printing, January 2014
Cover Design by Tudor Smalenic
Photo Cover by Catalin Gruia

Translated by Andreea Geambasu, Monica Seceta, Adriana Hoanca, Cristina Popa, Silviu Constantin, Anca Barbulescu, Adriana Hoanca, Domnica Macri, Cristina Mitocariu, Ilinca Anghelescu, Alexandra Popescu
Editing and Proofreading by Alexandra Popescu
ISBN-13:978-1495231872
ISBN-10:1495231879

For all my friends abroad.

CONTENTS

1. WHAT ABOUT DRACULA? 1
2. THE FIRST ROMANIAN MUMMY 33
3. THE RISE AND FALL OF SAXON TRANSYLVANIA 35
4. ANGRY CAROL-SINGERS 68
5. THE MAN THEY KILLED ON CHRISTMAS DAY 70
6. THE NUTCRACKER 99
7. ROMANIAN GYPSIES 101
8. THE GRAPES OF HOPE 127
9. KADIS FOR THE ROMANIAN JEWS 142
10. WHO WERE THE DACIANS? 143
11. THE CIUC SCOUTS' BIG GAME 167
12. BACK IN THE SADDLE 180
13. THE LANGUAGE OF THE FOLK COSTUME 185
14. THE TREASURE IN OUR BACKYARD 187
15. THE PIPE OF THE MOTI 195
16. PETROVAN'S RED LIST 197
17. THE JOURNEY OF A ROYAL HEART 201
18. ANA ASLAN'S ELIXIR 202
19. THE AVATARS OF OBOR MARKET 211
20. THE LEU AND ITS MANY FACES 213
21. BELLADONNA'S CULT 217
22. ROMANIAN … ESCU 219
23. WHO IS NR TWO IN ROMANIA? 221
24. WHAT'S IN A NAME? 224
25. ROMANIA'S SOILS 225
26. LIFE BEYOND THE WALLS 231
27. A LIBRARY OF STONES 234
28. THE OTHER SOCCER 235
29. THE LOST WORLD OF MAGURA-GORGANA 240
30. THE YEAR OF PARKS 248

INTRO

Dear Reader, you should know from the very beginning this is not an exhaustive, academic paper on Romania; nor is it a travel guide of Romania. I'm a simple journalist and this is just my own private Romania – a subjective puzzle of all the things I know from experience to be interesting for foreign tourists.

I've been working for the Romanian edition of **National Geographic** for over 13 years. Mostly because of my job I've met many foreigners – either when they visited Romania or when I went abroad. I guess now I've got more friends from the other side of the Earth than from my native land. I've learned a lot from them and from trying to answer their questions:

Do Romanians consider Ceausescu a good or a bad dictator?
Are Gypsies dangerous?
Where do vampires come from?
Why did the Saxons leave Transylvania?
How dangerous is it to ride a bicycle in Bucharest?
Why do most Romanian surnames end in escu?
Where can I find Gerovital?
Recommendations, must-see places?

And so on... I had to research and prepare myself each and every time, for every curiosity they had. After a while, some of these studies became the essays I've collected in this book.

I'm a fan of Montaigne's Essays whose model I've tried to emulate. Now I'm bold enough to think that if you want a bite of Romania and for whatever reason you don't have the stomach or the time to sample it here – for a month, a year or a lifetime – this is exactly the book you need!

CHAPTER 1
WHAT ABOUT DRACULA?

Romania's schizophrenic dilemma.

Vlad Dracula III. Kunsthistorisches Museum Wien.

A distinguished and slightly bored gentleman, with short white hair and heavy rimmed glasses stood in the crowd waiting in the arrivals terminal at Henri Coanda International Airport in Otopeni. Speaking perfect English with a Bela Lugosi twang, Nicolae Paduraru, former chair of the *Transylvanian Society of Dracula* (TSD), smiled when he caught sight of his American guests who had paid for a Dracula tour in Romania: 'Welcome to Bucharest! There's no need to worry right now; however, tomorrow we're going up into Transylvania'.

It was already dark when Josh, Carly, Allaina and Kevin – four

American tourists thrilled that they had finally reached the land of vampires – occupied their seats on the minibus that was going to take them accros Dracula's country. 'Are we going to see any wolves?' Josh asked.

For Paduraru, the same episode took place several times a year – and for about 20 years since Dracula's legend become part of his life, as he went from disbelief to rapid learning, experimental tours with foreign guests, and finally to the establishment, in 1991, of the TSD, a sort of mediator in the Dracula problem between Romania and the West. *The Transylvanian Society of Dracula* is a cultural organization that studies both the fictional count and the historical prince Dracula. The Romanian branch of the Society includes historians, ethnologists, tour operators and other researchers interested in the Dracula phenomenon. There are also branches in Canada, USA, Sweden, Germany, Russia and Italy.

It was drizzling, the wipers screeched across the windshield, wiping away bits of the introduction lecture Paduraru offered to his tourists. 'In fact', he said, 'you are here thanks to an Irish writer, Bram Stoker, author of 18 novels and numerous short stories – mostly literary romance of doubtful taste – who is remembered for Dracula, a novel he published in 1897, translated into almost every language'.

Embodied and adapted countless times in literary works, films, plays, ballet shows, commercials, cartoons, computer games or music, the vampire Count has gained an independent existence, becoming one of the most famous figures in cultural history. The ubiquitous character, able to change appearances like Proteus, was adapted to various audiences: there's a Dracula for children, one for adults, as well as a classic, modern, postmodern, business and humorous version. One of the side effects of Dracula's success was that a perfectly real province has been transformed into a mythical realm: Transylvania become associated, worldwide, with vampires – 'a cursed spot, from this cursed land, where the devil and his children still walk with earthly feet!'

II. On a cold December afternoon, in a noisy café near the

University of Bucharest, Duncan Light, a British professor who came to Romania on a one year grant to study the Dracula-based tourism industry, dismantled every piece of the mechanism which has turned Transylvania into vampire land. (A few years later, Duncan Light wrote *The Dracula Dilemma: Tourism, Identity and the State in Romania*.) 'Stoker's working notes, discovered in the mid 1970s at the Rosenbach Museum of Philadelphia – three sets of 80 pages each, containing abstracts, information and photographs – account for the way Dracula was written and show that the Irish writer initially had no idea about Vlad (the Impaler) or Transylvania, and was actually thinking about a certain Count Vampyr from Styria, eastern Austria', said professor Light. He changed his mind in 1885 after reading in the **Nineteenth Century Magazine** the article *Transylvanian Superstition* about a land where most species of demons, fairies, witches and goblins supposedly found safe haven after the progress of science had banished them from other parts of Europe. The author – Emily de Laszowska Gerard – was the English wife of a Hungarian cavalry brigade commander who spent two years in Transylvania.

The story of Dracula starts and ends in Transylvania. Although only six out of 27 chapters take place here, the effect is overwhelming. Time has proven that Stoker stumbled upon the perfect location for a lost world. He wasn't the first one, though. Other authors such as Alexandre Dumas, in *Les milles et un fantomes* (1849) or Jules Verne, in his *Carpathian Castle* (1892) had located their stories in a mysterious, supernatural Transylvania. But it was Stoker who – due to the success of his book and its extraordinary impact on western culture – has reinforced this connection.

Stoker seriously toiled on Dracula for almost seven years. He took notes on shipwrecks, tomb inscriptions, weather data, train schedules, the behavior of zoo animals, a theory of dreams, treating certain injuries and alleged vampire attacks in New York.

He went through writings from which he extracted information on the fear of death, burial customs, werewolves, sea superstitions, mesmerism, Transylvania or the prince Dracula. The novel is not as much the product of Stoker's imagination as it is a cocktail of all these different ingredients. The initial title of the novel, replaced with Dracula literally in the last minute was *The Undead.*

Since he never visited the place himself, Stoker invented Transylvania in the way he believed a vampire's home should look like, compiling information from books written by British officials who had visited Transylvania and had written in disdain about a barbaric, full of superstition land. The details of Harker's journey through Transylvania, such as the robber steaks, the Golden Mediasch wine, the description of folk wear, the Gypsies, the settled Szekelys on the frontier, the leiterwagen, the houses with the blank gable end to the road were all inspired from Andrew F. Crosse's book, *Round About the Carpathians*. Through *On the Track of Transylvania* by Major E. C. Johnson, he learned about the national dish mamaliga, discovered the four Transylvanian nationalities: Magyars, Saxons, Szekelys and Wallachs and studied details about the Szekelys' history, the Slovaks of Transylvania, as well as the crosses at crossroads. In *Transylvania: Its products and Its People* by Charles Boner, he found the name Borgo Pass, as well as a description of Mittel land and of the fires in Bestride.

Hollywood was also responsible for Dracula's history. In 1931 America discovered the character and hundreds of films have been made ever since. 'Many people first heard of Transylvania in Dracula films or books. So they associated it with a remote, dark and sinister place, alive with vampires. Without any knowledge or personal experience of Transylvania, many saw the province as the fictional land where vampires are born. Many still believe that Transylvania isn't real. And when they find out it is, they only picture vampires and Dracula', said Duncan Light.

Radu Florescu and Raymond McNally (authors of *In Search of Dracula*, 1972) went to the Rosenbach Museum in Philadelphia to examine a German pamphlet about Vlad the Impaler. Here, they came across *Bram Stoker's Original Foundation Notes & Data for his Dracula*. These notes had been auctioned by Sotheby's in London in 1913 and bought by Rosenbach in 1970.

III. Although Dracula was a global hit, the Count remained practically unknown in his own country until recently. Romanian villagers in remote areas have still not heard of him. Vampire literature was prohibited here as a sample of western decadence and Dracula was translated into Romanian only after the fall of communism. Nicolae Paduraru was one of few Romanians who had heard of Stokers' character in the1970s. As a literature student who occasionally worked as a tourist guide, Paduraru remembers a Daily Mirror journalist who showed up at Otopeni all flushed and sweaty, waving a copy of *In Search of Dracula*: 'Look, it's just out of the printing press. Take me to Dracula's castle at once. I want to be the first to get there'. Since no one knew where that castle might be, the Englishman pointed to a spot on the map.

On a misty morning, they reached Vlad Tepes's ghostly castle in Poienari. 'Although a few obscure articles published in the 1960s had pointed out the connection, the fusion between the fictional Count and the historic figure of the Prince began in 1972, with the publishing of *In Search of Dracula*, a bestseller by Radu Florescu and Raymond McNally, two historians who argued that Vlad had inspired Stoker's vampire. 'The speculation soon became a matter of common-sense. Stoker decided to name his character Dracula after reading *An Account of the Principalities of Wallachia and Moldova* (1820) by William Wilkinson, former British consul in Bucharest. A phrase captured his imagination: In the Wallachian language, Dracula means devil – said writer Elisabeth Miller. Wilkinson had included in his book a few vague mentions about a lord named Dracula, who had fought against the Turks in the 15th century. There was no mention of Vlad or his passion for impaling. Nor do any of these facts appear anywhere in Stoker's novel. The Irish author just borrowed the name'.

'It's amazing how this name – Dracula – generated, five centuries later, two totally opposite myths: the vampire and the ideal Romanian ruler, Vlad Tepes', said historian Lucian Boia.

When the first Dracula world congress took place in Romania in 1995, national newspapers buried the event and its participants –

academy members and serious researchers – under a mountain of contempt, labeling it a collection of 'vampirologists' interested only in their vampires and not in Romania's true history. The congress triggered an avalanche of articles, summarized best in an editorial by writer Octavian Paler. In his opinion, 'we live in Dracula's country whether we like it or not, and we soothe our pride, hurt by foreigners' indifference and ignorance, by showing the world there's one domain in which we have no competition: vampires. Dracula is not a Romanian legend – Paler wrote – it's a myth that has been forced upon us. But since the madness is now global, why shouldn't we turn Dracula into a tour operator?'

The fact that Stoker's vampire originated from Transylvania brought frustration to many Romanians. A theory launched by historian Vasile Barsan, popular for some time, pointed towards a Hungarian conspiracy against Vlad Tepes – allegedly organized in the 15th century by king Matthias Corvinus; a vampiric touch was added later on in the 19th century by Armenius Vambery, a Hungarian scholar and spy, and supposed informer for Stoker; finally, in the 20th century the Hungarian-born actor Bela Lugosi played a memorable part as Dracula. The truth is that, at the time when Bram Stoker wrote his novel, Transylvania was not part of Romania, but of the Austro-Hungarian Empire, Romania and its people playing a minor role.

'There are a few geographic references such as Galati, Bucharest, Prut and Siret rivers; a Romanian sailor on Demeter, the ship that brings Count Dracula to England; another few Romanian crew members aboard Empress Catherine that brings Dracula back home. The Count declared himself part of the Szekely community and a descendant of Attila. In his discussion with Harker, he even used his country's tradition of placing the surname first, a characteristic of the Hungarian language', said writer Elisabeth Miller.

IV. In 1408, Holy Roman emperor Sigismund summoned several vassal princes to Nuremberg, where he made them Knights of the Order of the Dragon. Among them was Vlad II, who, proud of his new title, called himself 'Dracul', a term derived from the Latin 'draco' (dragon). The nickname was used by his son, Vlad Dracula III, as a surname (Dracula meaning 'the son of the Dragon'). Ottoman chroniclers in late 15th century named him Vlad Tepes – the Impaler (*Kaziklu Bey*). Romanian historians used this name although there is no proof Vlad ever called himself that way. On the contrary, the existing documents and letters bear the Dracula signature. Semantics also played a role: the word *dracul* has lost the original meaning of dragon and in modern Romanian stands for *devil*. The fact that Stoker named his vampire *Dracula* reinforced the Romanians' preference for Vlad's other name – Tepes.

Vlad the Impaler Dracula was born in Sighisoara in 1431. When he was five he moved to Targoviste when his father became the ruler of Wallachia. At around 11, he was sent as a hostage along with his younger brother, Radu, to Sultan Murad II as a guarantee that his father Vlad Dracul will be loyal to the Turks. At 17, after his father was murdered and his elder brother Mircea was buried alive, the sultan sent him back to Wallachia as ruling prince.

He lost power in about two months and spent the next eight years in exile plotting to recover his throne. He returned for the second time to rule Wallachia in 1456. His reign lasted six years. After the war with the Turks in 1462 he ran across the mountains in Transylvania when he was imprisoned for the next twelve years by king Matthias Corvinus. In 1476, after he accepted to embrace Catholicism, the Hungarian king released him and Vlad got back his Wallachian throne for the third time. He was killed in battle two months later.

Almost all written information about Vlad – especially German pamphlets printed between 1485 and 1500, but also Turkish chronicles detailing the Wallachian military campaign in 1461-1462 or the Slavic manuscripts of the 1480s (*Skazanie Drakule Voevode*) discovered in Russian archives – describe him as a psychopathic tyrant who went as far as cutting off mothers' breasts and filling the cavities with the heads of their babies before impaling the women.

For the Transylvanian Saxons he was the Devil. According to a German pamphlet published by Ambrosius Hubler, in 1499, at

Nuremberg, Dracula the Voivode was a bloodthirsty man who impaled people, roasted them and boiled their heads in a kettle; he also skinned people and chopped them like cabbages. He also roasted children, forcing their mothers to eat their offsprings. These are only a few of the horrible acts the tract mentions.

Antonius Bonfinius, chronicler of king Matthias Corvinus of Hungary, who imprisoned Dracula for twelve years after being overthrown by the Turks, described the Impaler as being 'a man of unheard cruelty and justice… He behaved with such harshness in this barbarous country that everybody's belongings were safe, even in the middle of the forest'. 'When he set out against the Turks, he told his army: Whoever is afraid of death will not come with me, but will remain here', say Russian stories which consider him a brave warrior, but condemn him for abandoning the Orthodox Church. He was a minor prince in a small country. He ruled for only six years (and stayed in prisons almost at least twice as much) and failed in all his projects. So how did he become a legend in his own time and remained one throughout the centuries? In a 17th century chronicle of Wallachia, Vlad appears quite inconspicuous. His myth was built only in the 19th century, when Romania was beginning to take shape. After centuries of following the eastern model, Romania suddenly turned around and, in just a few generations, embraced the western model. Romanian historiography felt the need to justify itself before this West: we are such a backward people because for centuries we have protected you from Ottoman invasions along the Danube and the Carpathians. Vlad the Impaler is one of the voivodes who fought the Turks. His rough justice seemed exemplary to a society that strived – and still does – to settle down. His atrocities were justified as state affairs. At the same time, Romanian literature was glorifying the Impaler. Mihai Eminescu, the famous national poet conjured him in memorable lyrics:

'*Cum nu vii tu, Tepes Doamne, ca punand mana pe ei,*
Sa-i imparti in doua cete, in smintiti si in misei,
Si in doua temniti large cu de-a sila sa-i aduni,

Sa dai foc la puscarie si la casa de nebuni'.

('Rise once more, o Tepes! Take and divide these men/As lunatics and rogues in two big tribes, and then/ In mighty, twin infirmaries by force both tribes intern,/ And with a single faggot prison and madhouse burn'.)

Another important stage in consolidating the myth of Vlad Tepes took place after the '70s, during Nicolae Ceausescu's regime. The medieval prince was praised in school books, statues of him were raised, restoration works started at his castle on the Arges river, books and articles on him were published.

'In this context, after the success of Florescu and McNally's book, Dracula became a story that Romanians had to confront', Paduraru explained. Officials from the Ministry of Tourism answered back: let's show them who Tepes really was; and tours focused on prince's life. Disappointed, foreigners who came in search of Dracula reacted as expected: we're not interested in your petty lord, we want our vampire. There was a very swift change of tone, and tours shifted to Romanian superstitions and lore connected to Stoker's novel. But after three or four days on trips like these, tourists and guides alike inevitably ended up being really scared.

'The problem seems to be our shallow rational mind that is only about 5,000 years old. Beneath it there are hundreds of thousands of years of fear – fear of the dark, of death, of accidents or illness – encoded in usually latent archetypes until dangerous circumstances or persistent reminders stir them', said Paduraru. In the end, tours combined the historical and the fictional Dracula. Today, there are more than 30 companies organizing vampire tours in Romania, most of them selling a mix of the two Draculas.

V. Expensive glasses and cutlery sparkling in the dark on elegant tables were in sharp contrast with the medieval walls. All of a sudden, the delicate background music exploded in a crescendo of thunder and owl hooting; the dim red light was drowned by a surreal smoke surrounding the chopped human heads decorating the chapel where we were having dinner. It was then that Dracula appeared. 'Welcome to my house!' he cried, his red eyes staring at me from his paper-white face; he then started to crawl along the dirty wall, up to his vertical coffin. Loudspeakers broke into a wild howl right next to my ear, while the vampire vanished into the coffin. Every Tuesday and Friday, actor Petre Moraru recites his vampire monologue walking among the tables at **Count Dracula Club** in Bucharest. Every now and then, a pretty girl has the chance of being dragged away and bit by the neck. Foreign guests adore the show, the atmosphere, and the food. Most of them become regular customers.

20 minutes earlier I was peacefully strolling down Calea Victoriei – admiring the beautiful façade of the **National Museum of History**. (It displays lots of mementos from Dracula's time, including a special room, i.e. 'Wallachia in the Time of Vlad the Impaler'). I turned left on French Street. The decaying unrenovated buildings were adding a romantic, Gothic touch to the place; French Street takes us to the **Palace Museum of the Old Royal Court**. In 1459, Prince Vlad III Dracula of Wallachia made the fortified settlement of Bucharest his capital. The remains of Vlad's palace and church are the city's oldest standing buildings. I soon got hungry and went to this Count Dracula Club (www.count-dracula.ro) and ordered the Renfield's Platter (Renfield is Jonathan Harker's predecessor in the Transylvanian Count's Castle, who goes mad after returning to England, is admitted to a madhouse and eats rats and flies). On the platter brought to us was a chicken breast displayed as a rat, with a red butter sauce and beetroot, whilst the entire dish was served on fries in a straw-like arrangement. Not to mention that I indulged in a round of Transformation cocktails at the bar.

Immediately after celebrating the Dracula Centenary in Los Angeles, August 1997, the Count Dracula Club was inaugurated in Bucharest during September. Designed as a theme club, the five rooms follow Bram Stoker's description of Dracula's Castle. Essentially The Count Dracula Club met the need of tourists, who were either beginning or ending their tours. Therefore, the Dracula-themed night in Bucharest offered a gateway for all tourists, even those who arrived for two or three days and had no time to visit the country.

'Over the years we had many distinguished guests, including the famous director Francis Ford Coppola, former U. S. ambassador to Romania James Rosapepe, Dumitru Prunariu – the first Romanian astronaut in space, and many others', said Count Dracula Club manager Mircea Poenaru. In general, Romanians come here only if they accompany a group of foreigners (just like we did). And most of them are not amused by the experience...

'With a legacy 254 movies, over 1000 books, thousands of articles, about 45,000 Dracula associations or fun clubs, it is absurd that a myth which can be used in so many ways abroad should be ignored in its own country', argued back in 2001 Dan Matei Agaton, at that time Minister of Tourism, who suggested that a Dracula Theme Park should be built in Sighisoara. The idea sprouted at a time when Romanian tourism reached its all-time low. The number of foreign tourists began to drop in 1985, and by 2002, the country attracted even fewer visitors than in 1989 when Ceausescu was dethroned and killed. The government of social-democrats tried to use Dracula to resuscitate the local tourism industry. The project met huge opposition and its supporters had to back off. Apart from Sighisoara, several other locations were suggested, such as Rasnov, Poienari, Brasov or Bran, but from one reason or another, they were all abandoned. Finally, the government asked for a project feasibility study project, which in 2003 concluded that the best location was Snagov. After the 2004 elections, the new administration declared itself uninterested in the project. Dracula Park is the quintessence of Romania's mixed feelings towards Dracula: opportunism and violent rejection. It is fair to say that Romania will continue to be associated with Dracula, whether we like it or not and maybe it's better to face the challenge head-on, and at least try to support the tourism industry. For those who think that way, Dracula is the type of merchandise ready to be commercialized. Dracula has the eye of the devil. His magic made possible that a communist-looking building be erected in the Borgo Pass and be dubbed as Dracula Castle Hotel, while a Dracula-based mythology with no real foundation could be created around a medieval castle, such as Bran. On the other hand, there are those, like Duncan Light, a researcher of the Dracula-based tourist industry in Romania after the '60s, who resist the whole Dracula Park concept.

'I'm not convinced that there is a demand to make such a park viable. I doubt that hundreds and thousands of western tourists will flock to Romania just for a new theme park. There's a niche market for Dracula. I would think that the serious and dedicated Dracula fans would shun the park and see it as something which trivializes their interest. I also doubt that more general tourists would be that interested in a theme park. Although Romania doesn't currently attract huge numbers of western tourists, those who do visit are either mass tourists (therefore looking for the beach or ski resorts rather than a theme park) or more affluent middle class cultural tourists who as a rule are the sort of people who don't go to theme parks. I also doubt that large numbers of Romanians will go there either. Romanians aren't terribly interested or enthusiastic about the vampire Dracula and I doubt that many of them could be bothered to pay to spend time at a Dracula theme park, even if it's built near Bucharest. So, economically, the whole idea is controversial.

Making a big theme park out of Dracula could just reinforce Romania's image of a rather strange place, not fully European, a backward, underdeveloped, even sinister land. It is sad, but true that Romania doesn't have a good image in the West (or at least in Britain). Many British people associate Romania to negative things: orphans, asylum-seekers, corruption, delayed political reforms, etc. Dracula is just one more thing which presents Romania in a negative way and seems to underline the country's Otherness or not quite European-ness. Personally, I don't think Romania needs Dracula as ambassador! I am pretty confident that the number of foreign tourists will steadily increase. In particular, Transylvania's amazing rural and cultural heritage is just waiting to be discovered', said Duncan Light.

VI. About five hundred years ago, a crowd of boyars punished for their disloyalty, left Targoviste to rebuild Poienari, Vlad's fortress. Following in their footsteps, our minibus reached Poienari only after sunset, when the mist descending from the mountains was blending in with the fog rising from the valleys and waters, filling the Arges Gorge. Encouraged by the snowfree concrete steps, we dared to climb the mountain, with the girls – Carly and Allaina – way ahead of us. When we got to the top the light was fading out. We entered the ruins, looking with horror in the abyss around us.

Prior to *In Search of Dracula* the world had no idea what Poienari was. This Dracula castle was an exaggerated concoction created by the two historians who argued that Bram Stoker had based his vampire on Vlad. Paduraru recounted once more that story how one day back in the 1970s, a journalist from Daily Mirror landed on Otopeni Airport, all flushed and sweaty, waving a copy of *In Search of Dracula*: He was the first journalist who came to photograph Poienari. But we were telling him that Dracula's castle was far away, in Transylvania! The man had to pinpoint the castle on the map, and this is how we finally discovered it.

Florescu gave Paduraru this explanation: 'We used Count Dracula and Vlad Tepes in order to promote Transylvania and Romania!' The good news was that in this way Dracula-tourism also extended into Wallachia, said Paduraru. Now we were able to show people more variety, whilst before that, the only thing they were interested in was Transylvania'.

Vlad's Castle was quite small compared to either Bran Castle or Hunedoara. It could not accommodate more than 300 people. The Turks attacked and captured it in 1462. Vlad made his escape to the north, through the mountains. Some of his successors used it as a mountain retreat, but it was gradually abandoned. In 1912 the towers of the castle still stood. On January 13, 1913 an earthquake caused the main tower to collapse into the river. A second earthquake in 1940 did further damage. In 1970, with a growing interest in Dracula, the Romanian government carried out a partial reconstruction and built a walkway up the mountain side to the entrance of the ruined castle.

The icy, slippery steps made our descent from Poienari fortress quite an adventure. In 1462, Prince Vlad was besieged here by the Ottomans. The local legend says that Vlad sent for help and advice in Aref village, across the hill. The Arefeans came at night and managed to take the prince all the way to Transylvania, across the high Carpathians. Vlad rewarded them with 16 mountains for pasture. We also spent the night in Aref. We were pretty tired, but a show had been prepared for us. Around a bonfire farmers told us the legends they remembered about Vlad; our conversation continued long into the night.

VII At **Bran Castle** where throngs of visitors are convinced that this is Dracula's home – we joined the colorful line of people slithering from the entrance, through the Spartan halls of the castle. (Paduraru bought entrance tickets for me, Josh, Carly, Allaina and Kevin, and said he won't go inside as one who has seen this castle far too many times…) As we were waiting for our turn to go inside I tried to replace Paduraru and make a short introduction for my American friends about this medieval castle standing high atop a steep cliff, guarding a strategic route between Transylvania and Wallachia.

The Teutonic Order began building a wooden fort in the early 13th century. At the time it was known as Dietrichstein and was later on destroyed in 1242 by the Mongols. On November 19th 1377, the Hungarian king Louis I of Anjou granted the people of Brasov the privilege of building the fortress. After finalizing the construction in 1382, the fortress became property of the Hungarian royalty, who brought here a garrison of mercenaries. Over time, Bran Castel changed many masters and has suffered many alterations – the latest being carried out by Queen Mary of Romania who turned it into her summer residence in the 1920s.

Bran became the American Castle of Dracula in 1960, as it 'looks very much like the vampires' castles in Hollywood movies' (TSD survey). It just happened like this. Another example is the region of Zhongdian (Tibet) which was renamed Shangri-La in 2002 to cater for tourists on the trail of James Hilton's book.

Once inside, the official guide took over and recounted preposterous stories about the Tepes-Dracula-Stoker trio which my American friends seemed to love. Upon exit, we had to face an army of merchants offering kitschy souvenirs at prices tailored for foreigners. Since we were in Bran anyway, we couldn't miss a visit to the **Museum of Horror**: an amazing shack of ghosts and monstrous creatures, which included a restaurant, designed for American and Japanese tourists. I came out of there half amused and half disgusted, as if I had emerged from a huge intestinal tract.

'You should not be so hard on Bran', Paduraru scolded me. This castle is a miracle for folklorists and cultural anthropologists alike. According to Narcis Ioan, former director of Bran Castle we are privileged to witness the creation of a myth in our contemporary times, as a historical objective has become a mythological one. Bran reputation does not rely on Queen Mary of Romania, but it is currently associated with Dracula. It all started with the tourists' almost unanimous desire for Bran to become Dracula's castle, although the guide keeps saying: 'There is no evidence of Tepes ever spending at least one single night here'. But it doesn't matter! This is about people's ancient wish to mark the boundaries of a realm where dreams may come true, and promises may become hard facts. When they left home, these tourists had promised themselves they were going to Romania to see Dracula's Castle, so they must definitely see it!

Bran – which has nothing to do with the historical prince or the literary vampire – become Dracula's Castele, having two major advantages over its competitors: 1) it is located right in the middle, between history (Poienari) and mythology (Hotel Castle Dracula in Borgo Pass); 2) it reflects the archetype of the castle fit for Dracula. Fans have created their own Dracula's Castle. Everything we can imagine exists, said Plato. So this is how our desire to discover Dracula's castle has actually created it.

Here is its short story, Paduraru went on: Romanian communism was in full swing in the 1960s, when a group of American tourists arrived in the Land of Dracula. They only had four days to cross Romania and reach Hungary, as the former Yugoslavia's tourism agency Compas had brought them from Bulgaria on a strict schedule: Day 1: We are in Bucharest. Day 2: Brasov-Bran, and so on. When they got to Bran castle, they named it Dracula's Castle, the only thing there that resembled the castle in the novel. Thus, this is how it all started, with the need to find and acknowledge a Hollywood idea in Romania. Bran's style is gothic, completely opposed to our other castles. This is the way we see Dracula's castle depicted in various Hollywood movies: a greystone construction, savage, somehow entirely different from Peles Castle. It was enough for a single group of tourists or journalists to launch this idea, and the rest is history.

Tourists have flooded Bran valley for several years now; house after house offering accommodation from the heart of Bran all the way up in the mountains. Smoking grills and cold beers welcome you in every yard. However, success can turn into degradation if you don't manage it properly. Bran is a mere conglomerate of villas that have turned the place ugly. I foresee a dark future for Bran and Moeciu, where is precisely the genuine part that got destroyed. Accommodation offers are much better around the castle.

After this we had lunch at Hanul Bran (www.hanulbran.ro) – opposite to the castle. (Here you can have lunch on the terrace and admire the castle. Ask the owners to show you the back annex, their joy and pride). Before continuing the journey we returned to the museum yard where a few stalls were selling selected folk art pieces: hand-made embroideries, wooden carvings, jewels and traditional musical instruments. Paduraru said we shouldn't miss the **Village Museum in Bran**. And he was right again: It's small, going from the bottom of the Bran valley to its left, but a really special place.

VIII On my desk at home where I'm currently writing, a square ceramic bottle towers above souvenirs brought from all over the world. It has exactly the same shape as the house where Vlad Dracula was born in 1431.

Once again twilight was getting closer when we reached our next stop. Since we were rather thirsty, we headed straight to the **Alchemy Bar**, opened in the cellar of the house where Vlad the Impaler was born, in Sighisoara. We were invited to sample Harker's special menu, as mentioned in the novel. In Alchemy Bar, you can sample age-old concoctions such as: Four Boards, Paracelsus,

Cognac of the Big Bear, Six-Six, WWII, The Beast and the Beauty, or the Count's favorite wines (New Moon, Full Moon, Moon Sonata). Later on that evening, we made friends with a high school student who was playing in a rock band with some of his friends. He invited us to his place, to listen to their music. His mother cooked for us, and all of us smoked heavily. We didn't want to ever leave that place...

Sighisoara is one town where I'd love to live in. The citadel has remained pretty much unchanged since the times when Vlad was strolling around on its cobbled streets. It is the best-preserved 15th century European fortified town, and a World Heritage site. Located on the Tarnava Mare River, the town was built by Saxons between the 12th and 17th century. Eleven towers guard Sighisoara's walls, among them the Tailors' Tower and the Shoemakers' Tower.

From the top of the Clock Tower, I was looking down at the Old Town and its red-tiledroofs, admiring the well-preserved Saxon houses lining the narrow streets. Merchants and craftsmen still go about their business today – just like they did centuries ago. Sighisoara's charming hotels, restaurants, and historic attractions make it one of the few citadels in the world where life still untouched within within the fortified walls.

IX Under a candle's flickering light, the old woman gave me some sour milk and polenta, served in chipped clay plates. We were sitting at a low three-legged table. The night was already falling when, dead tired, we knocked on her window. My initial target had been the nearby Marotinu de Sus (in Oltenia), where, several years ago, some villagers had each been sentenced to six months in prison for desecrating graves. They had been described – not only by the international, but also by the local media – as vampire slayers. After all the problems they had encountered with the State Attorney's Office, due to the massive media coverage, they did not even want to talk to me. I meekly left; the car broke and night caught me there, in Prunisor village, asking for shelter in this decaying shack, in a godforsaken village in Oltenia. At first, the old woman refused to open the door. She thought the strigoi, the Romanian vampire, was calling her. As she told me later, she was convinced that her dead husband had turned into a strigoi and was tormenting her at night. She had exhumed him several times and pierced his chest with a stake, but with no results. In a final and desperate attempt, she even tried to burn his heart down, but the heart would not burn in her stove. The woman eventually cut it in four, and threw the pieces down the toilet. How could I have not believed her?

I was about four when I witnessed the digging up of an undead in a village in the Danubian plain, where I grew up. It was midnight, full moon, scores of people at the cemetery; and a white stallion that had been made to walk across the grave. I couldn't get past the compact, black phalanx of old women, standing in rows around the grave. News was passed on from the two men who were down in the grave to drive the stake in: they found the dead man with blood around his mouth (he'd bitten his own hand) and his face turned downward...

These things still happen in today's Romania more often than you'd think. The belief in strigoi is extremely powerful in the traditional part of Romania and my fascination with vampires goes as far back as my early childhood. In Romanian mythology the strigoi can be dead or alive. The dead ones are spirits who keep haunting the living because their funeral rituals were faultily conducted, or they went astray on their way to the other world, or they were strigoi during their lifetime. These dead strigoi 'eat their family members one by one, or eat only their heart and suck their blood', writes folklorist Simion Marian.

According to the folklorist Aurel Candrea, a strigoi can also be a living being if, 'all day long it attends to his own business, just like everyone else, but at night, as soon as he or she falls asleep, the soul leaves the body and wanders off to meet other ghosts. The souls of these strigoi ... kill children and suck their blood, steal milk from cattle and rob the fruits of the harvest'. According to Aurel Candrea: 'when one of these creatures, who is believed to be a ghost, dies, a red-hot roasting stick is stabbed, or impaled, into its heart so that the soul may never get out of the grave and may no longer be able to torment people at night. '

Folklorist Agnes Murgoci wrote in 1926 about the tests that determined whether any dead man is a vampire:

1. His household, family, his livestock, and even the livestock of the entire village, die off quickly.

2. He comes back at night and speaks to the family. He may eat what he finds and knock down things, or he may help with the housework and cut wood. Female vampires also come back to their children.

3. The priest reads a service at the grave. If the occurring evil does not cease, it is a bad sign.

4. A hole about the size of a coin may be found near the tombstone of the dead. This indicates the presence of a vampire, as they come out of graves by just such holes.

5. Even during daytime a white horse will not walk over the grave of a vampire, but will stand still, snorting and neighing.

6. A gander, similarly, will not walk over a vampire's grave.

7. If it's a vampire and the corpse is exhumed, it may present the following characteristics:

   a. a red face, even months and years after the burial,

   b. his or her face turned downwards,

   c. a foot forced into a corner of the grave or coffin.

   d. if its relatives have died, the mouth will be red with blood. If it has only spoilt and ruined things at home, and eaten what it could find, the mouth will be covered with maize meal.

X Back in Bucharest, on a Friday evening, I was stepping out of the crowds endlessly parading in front of McDonalds; I entered the old mansion house that hosts the Institute for Folklore and Ethnography as into yet another world of obscurity. I waited half an hour for director Sabina Ispas, enough to review my notes on the history of vampires. Some 250 years ago, vampires used to be taken very seriously in this part of the world. Entire eastern European villages were abandoned by their dwellers scared of vampires. These hysterics are recorded in the official documents of the time. In 1718, when Austria annexed the Serbian kingdom following the peace of Passarowitz, Serbian practices regarding vampires quickly drew the attention of the imperial authorities. In 1725, an official report from the Vienna State Archives mentioned for the first time a case of vampirism investigated post-mortem: Peter Plogojowitz.

According to writer Margot Rauch, on July 21st, 1725 the *Weinerisches Diarium* paper published a letter from the imperial provisor Frombald to the court of Vienna, in which he reports events from Kisolova, Gradisca district. Nine people had suddenly died in only eight days, and all of them told right before dying how Peter Plogojowitz, who died almost three months earlier, 'lay over them and strangled them in their sleep'. When the villagers dug up Peter in the presence of the priest, they found his body intact, except for the nose – he had not rotted at all and his mouth was full of fresh blood. The vast majority of such reports mention situations that occurred in Hungary, Poland, Moravia, Silesia and Serbia. The first treatises on vampires – like the one published in 1750 by French bishop Dom Augustine Calmet – hardly mention the territories that make up Romania today.

The absence of written records does not mean that the Romanian territory did not experience such things, but it probably has to do with the lack of a genuine bureaucratic apparatus of the rulers here. The existing documents are almost unknown. But here is what Father Matei, an archpriest in Plasii de Jos (Valcea county), wrote to his bishop in 1837: 'I must report to Your Holiness that some of my flock, acquiring evil habit, every time one of them gets a languish in his heart or head, goes and – without any notice to the priest or archpriest – gets drunk, grabs hoes, pickaxes and shovels, goes into the churchyard and unearths the dead, saying those are ghosts that threaten people's lives, filling the churchyards with tunnels and holes and exhuming the dead..'. The answer to the bishop's demand for harsh punishment was: 'Regarding the content of Your Holiness's address, we inform you that we ordered tour people of Oltet and Cerne to keep the guilty ones under arrest for three days, with only bread and water; the others shall receive 50 cane beatings, if they're men. The women, being weaker, shall receive 25 beatings and shall vouch to renounce the audacity of digging up the dead.'

'Over the last years, now that everyone has heard of Dracula and we all see Dracula movies on TV, the definition of the vampire has started to overlap that of the ghost (*strigoi*). In fact, these two representations of the undead are totally different both in shape and motivation – explained Sabina Ispas. While the vampire is a blood-eater because he wants to live a corporeal life, alongside humans, the ghost is, on the contrary, completely immaterial, a concentration of energy aimed at sanctioning people, with no specific ritual'.

The word 'vampire' is of Slavic origin and entered the Romanian language through French only in the 19th century. The Romanian word 'strigoi' (undead) is inherited from the Latin 'striga' meaning wizard.

Then what explains these differences in a relatively small space such as Southeastern Europe? Why do Romanians believe in the undead and Slavs have vampires?

'Romanians became Christians in the first centuries A.D., while the Southern Slavs did so only in the 9th century. Primitive Christianity is closer to Judaism. Yahweh has forbidden blood eating, because blood is life. Jews perform kosher slaughter. Romanians do not eat any blood-containing products. The Slavs converted to Christianity later. They probably made human sacrifices and were blood drinkers, but after their religious conversion, blood drinking became a sin. The vampire just wants to live by consuming the life-giving blood. In some areas, apart from believing in strigoi people also believe in moroi – copies of the Slavic vampires', said Sabina Ispas.

Most Romanian ethnologists I have talked to expressed the need to stress out the differences between vampires and ghosts. Hence I was rather puzzled when Nicole Paduraru told me that the vampire and the ghost are some kind of cousins. 'Superstition is a law protecting the individual and the community, a form of ancient wisdom, a code of regulations.The ghost or vampire is an archetype, guarding traditional custom. For instance, one superstition suggested don't let a cat jump over a dead body. Why? Because the dead man goes to the grave, while the cat and the germs in its fur stay in the house with you. If you don't comply with the custom, the vampire will get you!'

Transylvanian vampires are not the result of Stoker's imagination. Among the writer's notes there is an excerpt transcribed from Emily Gerard's article, *Transylvanian Superstition*. 'Every Romanian peasant believes in vampires or Nosferatu the way one believes in Heaven or Hell... A man killed by Nosferatu also becomes a vampire after death, and will continue to drain blood from innocent people until his spirit is exorcised, either by exhuming the corpse and staking it, or by shooting a gun at the coffin. In very difficult cases, it is recommended that the head should be detached from the body and the mouth be filled with garlic, or that the heart should be plucked out and burnt'. The word nosferatu, offered here as a synonym for vampire, does not exist in Romanian language. Probably Gerard – who obviously had no penchant for foreign words – heard people talking of necuratul, the 'unclean' – meaning the devil.

I wrote to Elisabeth Miller, asking her to clarify the discrepancy between foreign researchers who focus on similarities between ghosts and vampires, and Romanian ethnologists who point out the differences. 'I think it all boils down to semantics, resistance and misinterpretation. For modern Romanians, the word vampire refers to a supernatural being created by the western culture. Besides, there is a certain determination to reject any idea that Romania is a land of vampires and that the most famous vampire in the world bears the name of one of the country's national heroes', Miller wrote back.

XI There was quite a dispute the one I witnessed during the *Mysteries in the Life of Vlad the Impaler Dracula* symposium, held in 2005 in the town of Curtea de Arges.

'Nobody has the right to touch the memory of Vlad Tepes the Just! Romanian Princes are unbeatified saints', orated a gentleman, who introduced himself as Vasilescu from Bucharest. 'To counterbalance the western Dracula mythology, Romania should initiate a propaganda campaign and show the world the deeds and life of the real Vlad Tepes', historian Radu Vergatti told me.

'In the Saxon towns of Transylvania, impalement was already an officially established punishment in the 1400s. Saxons were the first to impale Vlad's men, and he answered in the same way. Punishments on the Romanian territory were some of the mildest. Even murder was settled with a fine and trials were held only with a jury and witnesses. The great cruelty wasn't in Eastern Europe, it was in the West', said historian Constantin Rezachievici.

'For us, westerners, Dracula is fiction, a mere game. Actually, we are not very interested in your Vlad Tepes. It is not us who make the connection between the historical character and the vampire Count; it is you who keep telling us about Tepes when we come to visit the places mentioned in Bram Stoker's novel', explained Charlotte Simsen, former chair of *The Dracula Society Quincy P. Morris* in the United States.

XII For visitors, Romania's schizophrenic reaction towards Dracula – a mixture of dignified rejection and opportunistic temptation – is hard to understand. Lucian Boia, the historian who perhaps gave Romania its most objective analysis, spent hours to describe a country where general dissatisfaction, historic delays and the frontier condition generate frustration.

Although on the map the Romanian territory is halfway between the Atlantic and the Urals, it has always been at the edge of great political and cultural ensembles. 'Here was a frontier of the Roman Empire, of the Byzantine Empire, then of the Ottoman Empire. The western civilization also stopped here. At the beginning of the modern age, three empires were coming together on the Romanian territory: the Ottoman, Habsburg and Russian empires. And Romanians are still on the edge, the edge of the European Union', said Lucian Boia. This constant frontier condition has isolated the country, but also opened it to influences from all directions. Relating to various, sometimes contradictory, foreign models – Byzantine and then Ottoman (in the Middle Ages), western (in the 19th century and first half of the 20th century), eastern (second half of the 20th century), and now western again – has generated an unstable, contradictory, yet coherent, Romanian history. The Romanian states were created only in the 14th century. Here, the middle ages began while in the West they were coming to an end. This historical delay – partially recovered only in the 19th and early 20th century – is fueling dissatisfaction and frustrations. Historical myths – for instance, that of Vlad the Impaler – are meant to compensate for failures of the present.

'This manner of glorifying one's own past and being bothered by everything other people say are part of the Romanians' current frustrations. Had we been a successful country, half as rich as Switzerland, had the Romanians been considered an important nation, they wouldn't even care about Dracula', said Lucian Boia. 'We would have liked to show the world someone like Michael the Brave, Mihai Eminescu or other representative figures. But no one is interested. Dracula is the one who entered the universal folklore and put Romania in the spotlight. It's not his fault that the country has a bad international image. After all, if you remove all the petty details, Dracula is an invitation for people everywhere to visit Romania'.

Vlad Tepes's mythological career is on the rise. Romanian president Traian Basescu declared during his 2004 campaign that his favorite prince is Tepes and invited 'corrupt' politicians to the stakes trusted in Victoriei Square (hosting the government headquarters) after his election. 'Romanians should not be afraid of the vampire mythology; they should rather fear the Vlad Tepes myth. Genuine democracy is incompatible with such extravagant methods. Ceausescu also took advantage of the nation's penchant towards the personalization – both real and symbolic – of power. After the communist era, Romanians have constantly been searching for a savior: in Iliescu, in Constantinescu and, in Basescu they have sought the authoritarian president able to look after us. Romanians should be aware of their inclination towards authoritarianism and paternalism, and try to temperate it', said historian Lucian Boia.

XIII 120 years ago, in Bram Stoker's Dracula, a young English solicitor named Jonathan Harker embarked on a train journey from London to 'the post-town of Bistritz'– to reach Dracula Castle in

Borgo Pass, northern Transylvania, and finalize a property deal with Count Dracula. The county of Bistrita-Nasaud, nestled between Rodnei, Caliman and Suhard Mountains in northern Romania, is an archetypal Transylvania of beetling crags and dark forests. In Bistritz (Bistrita), Harker dined on Robber's Steak and drank Golden Mediasch wine at the **Golden Krone Inn**, before continuing his journey. Harker left a detailed description of his dinner at the Golden Krone, thus we were able to sample the same dishes and wines. By sunset, we arrived at **Dracula Castle**, near Borgo Pass. We reached our destination through Pasul Tihuta, a point near the summit of the crossing, on a road leading south into the soaring mountains.

Around me, I could see foreign tourists happy to have finally arrived at Dracula's Castle; however, I was pretty disappointed. Built in the 1980s, the castle looked more like a communist block of flats dreaming of one day becoming a castle. It also had a higher point called 'tower'. However, all in all, I can say that it was really nice to sip your morning coffee up on the terrace, admiring the surrounding valleys and forests. Sometimes, the fog up there gets so thick and whitish, that you feel like you're floating, high up in the clouds.

The following afternoon, we encouraged each other to step in the private cemetery of Dracula's Castle Hotel, and descended in the underground Chamber of the Coffin, together with a noisy group of American tourists. As soon as we entered the cellar (with its painted walls depicting scenes from the novel Dracula) everybody grew silent as the grave. The performance that went on in the chamber was not exactly for my taste, but it gave an awful scare to our foreign guests. Lights went out all of a sudden. The lid of the coffin slowly opened, with a lugubrious screech, while an entity made its escape running away and leaving everybody stupefied. Later on, I heard the hotel employees whispering that it was just a monkey – specially trained to run out of the coffin. We could not see a thing, except the omnipresent Darkness. Startled people panting next to you in dim lights distracted your attention, while the strange creature was running around...

We went out to get some air, and walked around until we stumbled upon a cabin with huge shepherd dogs calmed down by a sturdy man. Just a few steps away from our hotel, at *Tasuleasa Association* headquarters, some down-to-earth Germans host workshops where they teach kids how to protect the environment and care for their community. The Association is part of the Knights of Saint John's Order, descendants of the distinguished Knights Templar.

XIV The man to whom we owe The Hotel Castle Dracula – Paduraru begun telling us a new story – was Alexandru Misiuga, a most unhappy communist head of a county tourism division. What did he have back there, in Bistrita Nasaud? Only Geoagiu Bai, a resort with some monstrous hotels accommodating up to 800 guests. He filled them any way he could, with syndicate-supported holiday-makers, retired people and God knows what else. In 1958, when international tourism started blooming in Romania, he met his first western tourists. They were all holding the same book, Dracula, and kept bombarding him with questions. And he simply had no idea what they were talking about. One way or the other, Misiuga finally got the book, read it and understood that Stoker had offered him a fabulous gift. Well, who on Earth would go all the way to Bistrita Nasaud? So Misiuga mustered all his courage and went to see the County Prime-Secretary, an important communist official who had an office across the street from him. He told him: Prime-Secretary, Sir! We need this hotel in our county, because this is what Bram Stoker's novel Dracula said and everybody coming here is asking about the Golden Crown restaurant. Thus a few grumblings later, they decided to approve his project and this is how a new hotel materialized in Bistrita, in 1973: The Golden Crown. What a delight for the members of the Dracula Society in London, who used to come here on an annual basis, back in the 1970s! (Each fall, the British people from the Dracula Society arrived here to hold their annual banquet similar to the one described in the book. During the celebration there was always one unoccupied chair, with Count Dracula's cape draped over it.) After the success of the Golden Crown, Misiuga decided to go even further. He crossed the street once again, to talk to the Prime-Secretary, and told him that he wanted a hotel in the shape of a castle, built in Borgo Pass, resembling the one in the novel: a complete ruin on the outside, but a five-star beauty on the inside.

Misiuga took his argument all the way from Bistrita to Bucharest, to show the Tourism Minister himself what a beauty of a castle-ruin he had planned. He had even made a matchstick model of the castle-to-be. But the big tourism boss in Bucharest chased Misiuga out of his office: 'Go stuff your ruin!' he said. That project would have been a huge investment made in the middle of nowhere, about 45 kilometers away from anything else, with no running water, no power, and no sewage system. Misiuga finally succeeded however, with Ceausescu's help, whom he managed to meet one day while he was out hunting in Borgo Pass. Ceausescu agreed, but nobody had told him the construction was actually supposed to be called 'Dracula's Castle'. It only seemed to be some sort of a hotel. Those years were tainted by Ceausescu's hunger for hard currency and his desire to promote Romania abroad. It was enough to mention in your paperwork that your project was to generate hard currency revenues amounting to I don't know how much... and you had huge chances to succeed! Misiuga brilliantly played this card. They already had regular visits from Great Britain – big buses of 20-30 people, all following Stoker's book, all members of the Dracula Society in London, accompanied by writer Bruce Whitman and Paduraru. This provided a direct support to Misiuga's project.

But what was there to see in Bistrita County, back in the 1970s? Absolutely nothing! So let's build something to accommodate the British! In the end, Misiuga triumphed. He did not get his ruin, but a hotel designed by architect Codrea Marinescu, who did not see Hotel Castle Dracula as a communist block of flats, but as an archetype of Transylvanian castles. Therefore this is how seven years later, in the exact location Stocker had indicated in his novel, close to the border between Transylvania and Moldavia, the communists built a hotel at an altitude of 1,116 meters, dedicated to vampire Dracula.

XV During their few days in Romania, our American tourists who came in search of Dracula discovered and fell in love with this country. They were always at ease and carefree, taking loads of pictures of green leaves and grey buildings, derelict fences and bank posts alike, amazed by how cheap everything was, delighted by every cat, dog or pig they set their eyes on, outspoken enemies of the fork and knife, but always ready to pile up everything on their plate into a sandwich. I already miss them. I'd like to think they also changed somehow during those days that we spent together: Carly – always in love, always reading from Stoker's novel – seemed even more of an introvert when we parted; Josh – a future Hercules – actually developed a taste for rare steaks (after initial protests); Allaina – the spontaneous one, ecstatic whenever she saw an animal, no matter if it was a dog or a pig – gave me a big kiss; and Kevin – the shy and withdrawn one, most often watching the world through the lens of his camera, as though he was using it like a shield against everything around – took one last photo of me...

Not all the places they visited were connected to Dracula. But Nicolae Paduraru was one of the best tourist guides in Romania, an expert in getting people in touch with the spirit of the places visited, able to tell a story about every hamlet, every mountain top, every glass of wine, knowing when to scare and when to entertain or when to comfort with small talk and when to get serious.

'Imagine – he said just before we said good-bye– imagine that it's raining cats and dogs; on a deserted street two men resentfully are walking side by side, avoiding each other's sight, their eyes filled with hatred: Count Dracula and Prince Vlad. They're marching together through the rain just because an unseen hand is holding above them an umbrella'.

Whose is it? I exclaimed to myself. Isn't it ours...?

XVI SIDEBAR: Your own search of Dracula

According to a Transylvanian Society of Dracula survey, eight of ten Americans believe Transylvania doesn't exist. They think it's some sort of Shambala or Disneyland. But Transylvania is a real province of Romania and I'd like to use Dracula as an invitation for anyone who'd like to discover this beautiful country. Below is some basic information that might help if you come here in your own search of Dracula.

Bucharest

You'll most probably land in Bucharest, Romania's capital, on Henri Coanda International Airport – Romania's busiest international airport, located 16.5 km northwest of Bucharest, within Otopeni city limits. There are quite a few good hotels in this city. Most foreign friends I know stay at Rembrandt Hotel. (www. rembrandt.ro.)

Bucharest is the city Prince Vlad Dracula III founded. Nearby, Snagov is where he is supposed to be buried. For me Bucharest is not a beauty and I don't recommend spending more than two days here. But while you're here, make sure you don't miss these experiences:

⬜ Enjoy special dishes at Dracula Restaurant inspired by Bram Stoker's Dracula (Count Dracula Club, www.count-dracula.ro)

⬜ See the ruins of the Princely Palace and the vaults built by Prince Vlad Dracula. (Curtea Veche Museum, Bucharest; fee.)

⬜ See the second largest building on earth, the House of the People, currently the Palace of the Parliament, built by the late communist dictator Nicolae Ceausescu.

⬜ The Romanian Peasant Museum is an option especially if you're there before a major holiday; make sure you take a look at the fairs organized in the museum's garden, where craftspeople and farmers from all over the country come to sell their goods. Take a 'bite' of Romanian cuisine – sample traditional cakes, jams and of course, wine and 'palinca'.

⬜ Check out Carturesti library, which offers a lot of art and architecture books, many in English, and gives you the chance to quench your thirst with a cup of tea in a bohemian setting. Also, for an English-only book collection, go to Anthony Frost Bookstore.

⬜ Lipscani district hosts a lot of junk, secondhand and antique shops. Make time to get lost on its streets and explore all of them. More than the objects, you'll love the atmosphere.

Targoviste
This city was Vlad Dracula's capital. The ruins here are quite massive and many of them are linked directly to Vlad's reign. The palace is the site of many atrocities attributed to Dracula. It is near this city that he set up the forest of impaled to frighten the army of Sultan Murad the Conqueror.

The Royal Court, Targoviste, the museum includes the Royal Residence, the Great Royal Church, the Small Royal Church and Chindia Tower; Fee.

Poienari
You'll have to climb 1400 steps to get to this small, partially restored fortress. The panorama makes you understand why this fortress was a strategic point for the Impaler. Legend has it that his wife flung herself out of the window of Poienari castle to avoid being captured by the Turks. Vlad Dracula rebuilt Poienari fortress in 1459 with the hands of enslaved traitor boyars from Targoviste.

Poienari Fortress, Capatanenii Pamanteni Village.
www.exploringromania.com/poienari.html

Aref
Foreign tourists come to Aref to listen to stories of the elders, as told by 30 farmers around a bonfire, dressed in folk costumes from Vlad's time; ancient songs and folk dances are interlaced with awesome legends. Besieged by the Ottomans at Poienari in 1462, Vlad sent for help in neighboring Aref. The Arefeans managed to take prince Vlad out of the encirclement and hurried along the river, ever higher in the Carpathians, till Transylvania came into sight.

In Aref village – guest houses available. Check the accommodation section at www.restromania.com/About/About-CurteaDeArges.htm

Our recommendation is the Tomescus – a family of peasants with strong initiative. You can also take home some genuine souvenirs: hand-made traditional blouses, hand-embroidered handkerchiefs and napkins or home-made plum brandy.

Bran Castle

At Castle entrance we'll find Dracula kitsch gadgets sold to tourists from all over the world. Built in 1377 to defend the Transylvanian end of the Pass, this is the 'American Dracula Castle' (since 1960), as it 'looks very much like the vampires' castles in the Hollywood movies' (TSD survey). In reality, this Castle has nothing to do with neither the fictional, nor the historical Dracula. Bran meets the expectations of western tourists with its collections of vampires and dark fairies brought from abroad. But if you want to take home something genuine, don't hesitate to buy fermented cheese wrapped in fir-tree bark, smoked cheese or hand-knitted woolly hats, gloves and thick jumpers that do not read Dracula or Transylvania.

Bran Castle, www.brancastlemuseum.ro/indexfrm_en.htm; Fee
House of Terror, 502A Principala Street, Bran; Fee

Sighisoara

The place might give you an idea of the atmosphere surrounding the steps of little Dracula. In the middle of Transylvania lays the best-preserved 15th century fortified town in Europe – Sighisoara, birthplace of the historical prince Vlad the Impaler Dracula.

Alchemy Bar, Sighisoara, in the house where Vlad Dracula was born

Bistrita-Nasaud

One can also find easily scenes, people and landscapes as those described by Jonathan Harker in his voyage through Transylvania. You can carefully follow Harker's steps – and look at medieval Bistrita through his eyes. Harker left a description of his dinner at the Golden Krone. You can go to today's Golden Krone (Golden Crown, four Petru Rares Square, Bistrita, http: //www.hotel-coroana-de-aur.ro. Singles from 160 RON) and try the dishes yourselves. Valleys of Bistrita County are still hosting small communities with simple lifestyles. You can cross villages, rivers mentioned in Dracula, and then start the climb into Borgo Pass. Bram Stoker put his Dracula Castle in the spectacular Borgo Pass, 45 km away from Bistrita. The farmhouses here are so spread, that each has its own, private cemetery – living and dead within whispering distance.

Hotel Dracula Castle (Hotel Castle Dracula, 427363 Piatra Fantanele, in Borgo Pass, www.hotelcasteldracula.ro; Singles from 175 RON) is a communist imitation of the Romanian castle built in the 80's for American tourists. After all this traveling you can finally rest here in the coffin placed in the cellar. In Borgo Pass, next to the castle, a little bit lower than the terrace created for the parking lot, several stalls offer cheap Hungarian and Chinese merchandise. Inside the hotel you can find shops selling Romanian folk art. Don't hesitate to buy The Plum-Brandy of Domnita Radulovici.

Marotinu de Sus, Oltenia
The graveyard of Marotinu de Sus looks like a typical cemetery from a horror Holywoodian movie, with its crosses covered in lichens, skewed in the wind… In January 2004, Toma Petre's relatives engraved his body in the cemetery of Marotinu de Sus, ripped his heart out, burned it to ashes, mixed it with water and drank it. Police put six people under investigation for what the western media called a vampire slaying.

CHAPTER 2

THE FIRST ROMANIAN MUMMY

A century old enigma solved.

In 1908, professor Mina Minovici, the founder of the **Forensic Institute** in Bucharest, mummified the body of an old beggar. The mummy spent most of the following 95 years in a window case at the Institute. During all that time, legends spread among the generations of medical teachers and students regarding the supposed existence of internal organs inside the mummy and certain secrets of conservation, that professor Minovici had allegedly learned in the years he had spent in Egypt. Dr. Cristian Curca is the one who managed to solve the mystery. 'We have made several investigations, a computed tomography, an endoscopy and a toxicological exam, as well as a detailed search through the archives of the Institute', he said.

Surprisingly, the tests show that all internal organs are still inside the mummy, in their natural position. The only incision was made on the right thigh, in order to open the circumflex artery of the thigh where the embalming substance was injected. According to dr. Curca, two methods have been successfully combined: embalming and mummification. The preservation has been efficient mainly because of artificial dehydration, indicating that we are talking about a real mummy, not simply an embalmed body.

The myth of Professor Minovici's secret was built on ignorance and on the belief that his preservation method was lost. But the 'magic formula' was there, in plain writing, in the Institute's archives: the composition of the embalming fluid (*two liters of 40% formalin, 250 ml of glycerol and 250 ml of 96 degrees ethylic alcohol*) had been passed on to disciples and published in the press as early as 1938.

CHAPTER 3
SAXON TRASYLVANIA

The rise and fall of an civilization.

Illustration: RADU OLTEAN

Underdeveloped country seeking investors – this was the slogan of Eastern Europe after the fall of Communism. Like flowers competing for pollinators, its states outdid each other in advertising economic privileges and legislative facilities to attract western investors. The different governments that took turns in the last 15 years in the Victoria Palace in Bucharest did not bother to go beyond mere declarations of good intentions; but, while TV channels broadcast their formal speeches, the exodus was underway for the most enterprising part of the population, the only one related to the West: Transylvania's German guests. Eight hundred years earlier, the first Magyar kings wanted to develop a newly conquered land. They, too, needed western human capital, which they attracted with the most generous set of privileges of their time.

Saxons came, worked, and built in Transylvania a civilization that reached its peak in the 16th century. For them, prosperity went hand in hand with autonomy. Starting with the 19th century, when history took a nationalist turn, the misfortunes of Saxons came one after the other, culminating in deportations to Siberia, confiscation of property, Communist nationalism and post-revolutionary chaos. Today, they are an endangered people. Of those left in Transylvania, most are old people who want to die in their homeland. The rest have returned to the West, in search of the same thing that had brought their ancestors to Romania: authonomy and economic prosperity....

I. All the Birthlers had gathered in the kitchen. There was a strong smell of cheese. The father, the imposing Herr Alexandru Adalbert Birthler, was passing large pieces of unsalted, fresh cheese through a tiny grinder and merrily nibbling on the crumbs. Frau Lidia-Elena Birthler was commenting the news of the day in righteous horror: some wrongdoers from Glodeni village had vandalized the benches placed on the Mures riverbank by their son Klaus and other volunteers in the *Fata de Mures (Mures's Face) Association*. The father did most of the talking, about how life sometimes knocks you upside the head and how the unfounded optimism of 'ignorant children' can be a trap. The children were present, across the table: Klaus Birthler and Georgiana Branea, architects in their 30s, founders of the Fata de Mures Association. It's been three years since they started to dedicate their weekends to specific activities on the Mures bank, through which they seek to raise awareness of the values of the area among the locals. Georgiana's black eyes were smoldering: 'Don't they understand we're doing all this for them?!' After a while, shy, fair-skinned Klaus whispered: 'Maybe it was our fault after all, maybe we didn't get the point across'.

The Birthlers are one of the ten or twelve families of Germans left in the once-Saxon Reghin (Sächsisch-Regen). Our discussion gradually turns to history. (The Saxons are probably the world's most history-obsessed people: they wrote over 6,000 works on their history and that of Transylvania – in relation to a population that, at its demographic peak, in the period between the two world wars, had 200,000 members.)

The Birthlers were speaking Romanian, out of consideration towards me, since I don't speak German. Only Klaus sometimes dotted the conversation with German words, giving the cue to his father who continued it, still turning the grinder handle.

The Colonization: The Promised Land
Like managers with vacancies in the organizational chart, the first Hungarian kings invited guests from the West to develop a Transylvania that was in the process of being conquered.

II. For nearly two years, I traded Bucharest for a country cabin in Mures. Throughout this time, taking advantage of my travels in the footsteps of the Saxons, I discovered in Transylvania a foreign country. Attempting to reconstruct the final, Transylvanian leg of the journey of the first German colonists, I set out from Alba Iulia (*Karlsburg*) to Sibiu (*Hermannstadt*), still uncertain as to what pushed these people forth. What made German peasant Hezelo from Markstein (considered the first Saxon mentioned by name) sell all his possessions to the Klosterrath monastery in 1148 and leave for Hungary, an unknown land at the edge of the civilized world? Knights participating in the second crusade crossed Hungary in 1147, on their way to Palestine. One of them, chronicler Otto von Freising, described it as the land of opportunity. And still...

Starting from the 11th century, the Holy Roman Empire – particularly its western part, the Netherlands and Flanders of today – was the leading power in Europe. Technological innovations in agriculture, crafts and mining had brought about an economic boom. The seventy towns in the area between the Rhine and Elbe became three thousand in the 13th century. The population doubled, reaching about twelve million. Due to the new agricultural methods, it took fewer farmers to work the fields. With the economy, the noblemen's claims grew, too. Craftsmen, subject to feudal lords, were burdened by taxes. Their yearning for land and freedom fueled the German migration towards the East. It began in the heart of the country, with deforestations and drainage, and kept spreading to Bohemia, Poland, Lithuania,

Moravia, Slovenia, Hungary or Transylvania. Most emigrants were poor peasants, lesser, ruined nobles and their subject craftsmen.

III. Just as a manager with vacant positions in the organization chart contracts a recruiting company to find the right people, rulers who wanted to colonize a land used the services of a professional locator. He would travel along selected routes, with summoning documents bearing the rights promised to colonists in the destination territory; on his way back, he would lead the group to the assigned land and sometimes – if he was wealthy enough to support the colony's finances in the first years (as a loan) – become the administrator of the future settlement. The feudal lord granted him a number of plots of land and economic privileges. Although there were several waves of immigration to Transylvania over more than two centuries, the colonization was always planned. The colonists reached Hungary following the Danube. Then they crossed the Tisa River. Those who went upstream along the Mures were assigned lands from the ruler's property, in southern Transylvania, on a strip from Orastie to Baraolt, limited to the North by the rivers Tarnava Mare and Tarnava Mica; those who went up the Somes River reached the Bistrita (*Bistritz*) area, where most Saxon villages would become vassals to the secular or clerical nobility. According to historian Thomas Nagler, 'the Episcopal polity in Alba Iulia and – starting in the second half of the 12th century – the one in Sibiu may have acted as receiving centers. Groups were probably taken over at the border and led to the place they were going to colonize; the chiefs ('greavi', chosen from among the colonists, or clerics, with whom the colonization conditions would also have been negotiated) must have covered the route between their homeland and Transylvania several times'.

IV. The Magyars terrorized the West for over half a century. Their looting forays seemed unstoppable until 955, when Holy Roman emperor Otto the Great crushed them in the battle of Lechfeld. The Hungarians abandoned their preying expeditions and formed a state, taking after their vanquishers. They turned their expansion to the

South-West, to the Adriatic Sea, and to the East, where Transylvania loomed as a natural fortress, with the Carpathian Mountains as walls. They conquered it between the 10th and 12th centuries, gradually pushing their frontier eastwards. The new 'crown lands' left by the border-dwelling Szekelys, who moved along with the frontier, had to be exploited. Hungarian kings invited 'guests' from the West to settle on the lands inhabited by conquered Romanians, Cumans, Pecheneg and Slavs and to develop them. They were promised an enclave free from the domination of nobility and from vassalage, subject only to the king. All countries in Central and Eastern Europe were competing for German colonists. Hungary, which lay furthest into the unknown, raised the stakes by offering the most extensive privileges of its time: **personal freedom, land property that could be passed on as inheritance, the right to change lots, local administration and jurisdiction, Church autonomy and calculable taxes**. These privileges would be recorded in writing in 1224 by King Andrew II. But the champion of Transylvanian colonization was his grandfather, king Géza II (1141-1162), who succeeded in attracting Flemish, German and Walloon 'guests'. The Magyar chancellery called them Saxons – a name having nothing to do with their land of origin, but rather with a legal statute. 'In medieval Hungary, Saxons were the holders of privileges which had initially been granted to miners in Saxony, thanks to their rare skill', says historian Konrad Gundisch.

V. I traveled from Brasov to Targu Mures and back again about twenty times before I learned to see it. From the car speeding on the highway, the silhouette of the ruined fortress in Feldioara, barely outlined on a hilltop, appears as a mirage wrapped in the dark fog rising from the waters of the Olt River. I made a habit of stopping by the village for a visit to the fortress. Lately, it's actually become crowded, ever since construction began at a large sewage treatment plant at the foot of the hill.

The first Saxon colonists in Feldioara have been unearthed from the small square between the rectory and the Evangelical Church. Local tradition has it that they entered the Tara Barsei region from Rupea, the settlement over the hill, fraying a path with their axes through the Bogata forest. The German name of Feldioara (meaning 'earth fortress' in Hungarian) is Marienburg – Virgin Mary's Fortress – after the patron saint of the order of Teutonic knights brought to Tara Barsei around 1211 to defend the southern reaches of the Hungarian kingdom.

Archaeologist Adrian Ionita and his team studied 127 tombs here. The dead were wrapped in gauze and laid, without a coffin, in holes with steps leading down, dug in the shape and size of the human body, with a niche for the head. Here lie two or three generations – from the last years of reign of king Géza II to the coming of the Teutonic order.'Analogies with cemeteries in western Europe and Transylvania – areas of Saxon colonization – show that the necropolis in Feldioara belonged to the first wave of German colonists come to Transylvania around the mid-12th century', says Ionita. 'Here they formed an autarchic, egalitarian community'.

Saxons brought the habit of planned settlements to Transylvania. The Flemish-type village became widespread, with homesteads lined up on two rows along one street or square. According to architect Hermann Fabini, 'ever since these settlements were founded, there was a tendency to reduce the distance between homesteads as much as possible, for joint, effective action against outside dangers.' Each settler got an equal share of the field – split into three areas (for crop rotation over a three-year cycle). Villages were small, around 25 families. Their population rarely exceeded 100. One *sesie* (lot) had as much as 42 acres. Wheat, oats, barley and rye were grown. Forests, meadows and waters were used jointly.

'The Saxons, a people of resolute, steady and unhurried will, chose the land where they would raise their houses and dig their graves based on deeply pondered criteria; they cautiously tasted the water, weighed the light and carefully measured the thickness of the topsoil; they were wary of exceedingly steep heights and tested the direction of the winds with flags and nostrils', wrote philosopher Lucian Blaga in *The Trilogy of Culture*. In troubled times, in a foreign country at the edge of the world, Saxons learned to live in their communities much like bees in their hives. Individual freedom was sacrificed to the interests of the group that ruled almost all aspects of life and death, of work and play, of rest and faith. Any deviation – as little as swearing, expressing a superstition, lying, drinking or poor hygiene – was punished. Coming from lands with an advanced agriculture, Saxons brought to Transylvania the seeds of economic development. They introduced three-year crop rotation, lot measurement, cereal cultivation, the plow beam with mobile crosspiece, water and windmills etc. The new, more efficient tools accelerated deforestation, the expansion of arable land and increased production. Animals, water and wind power came to the aid of human labor. The 159 mills mentioned in 14th century documents reflect the improved cereal yield.Archeological discoveries illustrate the development of crafts and trade. The agricultural progress and strict specialization of crafts enhanced each other. Trade became a profitable occupation, stimulated by the Saxons' right to hold tax-free fairs and travel with their goods without paying customs.

VI. It seemed that nothing could stand in the way of the Mongols, united under Genghis Khan. They conquered China (starting 1211) and the Russian principalities of Kiev and Halych (1223) then fell upon Europe (1241). The Hungarian army was obliterated at Mohi, the Magyar kingdom fell into ruin, and one quarter of the population was massacred. The campaign was abandoned when news came of the death of great Khan Ögedei, in 1242. Batu Khan returned home, to the heart of Asia, to defend his right to the throne. After this unprecedented invasion, described in *Carmen Miserabile* by Church official Rogerius from Oradea, many names of settlements, from Rodnei Pass to Oradea, from Tara Barsei to Alba Iulia, disappear from the records. After 1241, colonization began again, supported by king Béla IV, to repopulate deserted areas. Decades and centuries followed, each with its own share of pillage by Tatars, Turks, Wallachians, Magyars, Austrians or mercenary armies; but the Saxon civilization in Transylvania reinvented itself, sheltered by sturdy walls, in towns (such as Sibiu, Brasov, Cluj, Bistrita,

Sighisoara, Medias etc.) and in over 250 villages with fortified churches. On a tower in Senereus, a Saxon village in Mures I found a Latin text which etched itself in my memory: *O quam beata res publica, o quam felix comunitas, quae temporae pacis considerant bella* (How fortunate the country, how happy the community, that in times of peace keeps war in mind). My wife, Adina, insisted to take me to the villagers' citadel in Rasnov to see this motto made real, in the eagle's nest where she used to play as a child. In the centre of town, she pulled me into an alleyway: let me show you a secret shortcut, through the wood. At the end of the passageway there was a narrow path. Ten minutes of climbing irregular steps to the top. The unchiseled stone and brick fortress is surrounded by steep inclines to the South, West, and North.

'When I was little, I used to come here at least once a week. The ruins were covered in grass – no entrance fee and no tourists', my wife said. From the ticket booth, we were taken over by guide Gabriel Guteanu – a slender young man in Bermudas, who looked more like a DJ (I couldn't take my eyes off his plucked eyebrows). A few workers on scaffolding were working on the wall on the eastern side, where we started our tour. The fortress is undergoing renovation; after retrieving it from an Italian licensee who wanted to turn it into a pension, the town administration strives to return it to its former glory. Mayor Adrian Vestea turned out to have made a lucky bet: the 200,000 ticket buyers (at two Euros a ticket) make the Rasnov citadel one of the most visited Romanian destinations in 2011.

VII. According to historian Thomas Nagler, in the 13th century, through inspired regional management policies, the Magyars had recovered the handicap that separated them from the West: they were a European kingdom with a population of two million, an ethnic melting pot. The first results had been visible for a century: in 1186, king Béla III (1172-1196) asked for the hand of Marie of France, daughter to French king Louis VII. Béla sent the king of France a list of all the income sources of the kingdom. The document, kept in the National Library in Paris, mentions among other things the 15,000 silver marks cashed in each year by the king from his guests. The sum, though probably exaggerated, shows that the Saxons were thriving and that their settlement proved to be a profitable business.

The Rise: Sibiu, Grand Square, no. 8

The Hecht House was the home of a great medieval merchant. It is neither the most beautiful, nor the largest and oldest one in Sibiu. But its metamorphoses and the line of former owners shape the story of the rise of the Transylvanian Saxons.

VIII. A walk through Hermannstadt (Sibiu) is a trip through both space – the charming labyrinth of narrow streets, communicating courtyards, stone pavements with drains – and time – in a medieval workshop-town, shackled by hundreds of internal regulations. As a foreigner lost in this colorful stone honeycomb crisscrossed by little cobbled streets, I'm looking for the house at no. 8, Piata Mare – the Great Square. Hecht House used to be the home of a great medieval trader.

From Elisabethgasse I turn into Brutarilor Street – the Bakers' street, where women used to carry the baskets of leavened dough to the baker's. I pass the Potters' street and get to the Leather Dressers' street. The craftsmen who had workshops here would sell their goods on Tuesdays and Fridays in the Small Square. On the Dyers' street (a continuation of the Leather Dressers' street) there used to be a small stream feeding the craftsmen's workshops. Near the Dyeing workshop, the Leather Dressers' Tower was once painted red. The corner of Wine Street and Tower Street was the place of the Wine Fair, where Sibiu townsmen would bring their cattle to graze during sieges. In the Huet Square, I circle around the Evangelical church, then enter the upper part of town through an alleyway that used to belong to the shoemakers' guild. The Great Square was where fairs, festivities, trials and executions used to be held – and also where the town's rich men lived. Among them, three foreigners – Oswald Wenzel, Nikolaus de Wagio and Christophorus Italicus of Florence – were commissioned to manage the Hermannstadt

Mint in 1456. Their company also obtained rights on the gold and silver mined in Transylvania. No. nine was the house of Oswald Wenzel, mayor in the 1450s, originally from Bohemia. Next door was Nikolaus de Wagio, a second-generation Sibiu townsman. His father, Italian banker Matthäus Baldi, came to live in Sibiu in the last quarter of the 15th century, managing salt mining in Ocna Sibiului, and administrating the Mint in Sibiu. He had houses in the towns of Abrud and Aiud and, since 1408, this residence in the Great Square. His closest neighbor was Mint chief Markus, whose house at no. eight was probably purchased around 1443 by the other member of the trio, Christophorus Italicus of Florence. In the following years, the tide of business took Christophorus to Cluj and then Baia Mare. His son, Paulus Italicus, now owner of the house at no. 8, sold it for 1,000 guilders, on the 1st of June 1472, to Georg Hecht, licensee of the mining exploitation in Baia de Aries and of the Sibiu Mint, owner of all customs points in Transylvania for the trade with Moldova and Walachia.

How had Sibiu come to be such a cosmopolitan place, attracting entrepreneurs from everywhere to make excellent business in Transylvania?

IX. The first colonists who settled here, around the middle of the 12th century, founded a town twice as big as its neighbors. In less than 100 years, Sibiu became the political and administrative center of the union of colonists, from Orastie to Tinutul Secuiesc. Between 1225 and 1229, due to a land reform ordered by king Carol I Robert, the former Sibiu County was split into seven seats (administrative units): Orastie, Sebes, Miercurea, Cincu, Nocrich, Sighisoara, Rupea, headed by the main seat, Sibiu. Four times, the town moulted, growing out of its walls.

In the early 13th century, Sibiu was little more than a bigger village, with fortifications around Huet Square; in the first half of the 14th century, the second ring of walls was built to include the Small Square. In the second half, the walls were extended around the higher part of town, and at the end of the 15th century a fourth enclosure appeared, meant to defend the lower town, up to the neighborhood of the Cibin River. The Mongol invasion in 1241-1242 caused an upheaval in South-

Eastern Europe, but it created a state of affairs from which Saxon towns benefitted. Hungary was one step away from leaving the game; the Cuman rule to the South of the Carpathians was gone. It was in this power void that the principalities of Tara Romaneasca and Moldova were born. Saxon craftsmen used the two new countries both as sources of raw materials and as markets for their goods (weapons, tools or luxury items). Saxon merchants grew involved in the transit trade connecting Black Sea ports to north-eastern Europe and the lower Danube to the south-west. With the retail system secured, merchants increased their production.

X. From the very beginning, Hermannstadt was led by people who had money and intended to make even more. The first to get rich were the greavi (small nobility) who had founded settlements – taking their share of the gains from milling, the sale of spirits, slaughterhouses, selling land in town, then long-distance trading. In the following centuries, they were repeatedly replaced at the town hall by a new elite of non-noble entrepreneurs who made fortunes from wholesale and long-distance trading, mining and the administration of various royal sources of income (salt, customs, coin minting). They all proved to be masters at lobbying: they constantly fought to extend and protect trade, making a competition out of collecting economic exemptions and privileges from Hungarian kings. Between 1351 and 1400 only, the Magyar chancellery issued over 40 documents referring exclusively to the situation of Sibiu traders.

XI. A tax ledger from around 1475, when Georg Hecht bought the house at no. 8, lists the 896 house owners in town. Taxation was proportional to the taxpayers' wealth. The only people owing more than one silver mark (1 mark = 16 lots = four guilders) were 17 patricians – most of them neighbors of Hecht in the Great Square. Members of the city council – formed of four high clerks: the mayor, the vilic (responsible with public buildings and infrastructure) the royal judge and the seat judge, aided by twelve counselors – were chosen from among only 40-50 high-ranking families. Next were retailers and rich craftsmen – about 200 of them, who had made a fortune selling goods out of their workshops. As early as 1376, Sibiu had 19 guilds with 25 crafts. Hermannstadt worked like a large multi-skilled company, each guild a trade union of sorts for one type of craftsmen who, instead of competing, chose to help each other.

In 1480, the town had 920 family heads and 368 tenants – over 6,000 people in all.

XII. On the 6th of February 1486, at the request of Sibiu mayor Thomas Altenberger, king Matthias Corvinus extended the validity of the Andrean privilege (initially granted by king Andrew II, in 1224, to Saxons in the Sibiu country) over all free Saxon settlements. Thus, the Saxon Universitas was formed – a Parliament of sorts for free Germans in Transylvania. According to historian Konrad Gundisch, 'the representatives of Saxon seats and districts assembled in Sibiu, usually on Saint Catherine's day, to decide on the correct allocation of tax duties, on prices for goods, on common units of measurement, on guild statutes, on the regulation of all aspects of daily public life, but also on important political issues'.

Five years later, merchant Georg Hecht, of Great Square, no. 8, became mayor of Sibiu. It was a prosperous time for the town – and for the house at no. 8, where improvements and renovations were made; its Gothic archways date from that period. The guilds of tailors and shoemakers built new headquarters (on the locations of today's Catholic parish house and Podul Minciunilor, the Bridge of Lies). Construction was finished on the steeple of the parish church of Saint Mary. In 1494, the first pharmacy in town is documented.

During Hecht's mandate, the Turks invaded Transylvania and pillaged the countryside around Sibiu. The mayor, at the head of the army, gave chase and defeated them at Turnu Rosu. Hecht had also led the Saxon cavalry in 1479, in the victory obtained by Pál Kinizsi and István Báthory, ruler of Transylvania, at Campul Painii, against the Turks led by Ali Kodsha. After Georg Hecht's death, in 1496, his son, Johann – Luther's main supporter in Sibiu – inherited the house. It held the first Reformationist services (before Brasov citizen Johannes

Honterus introduced the Reformation in Transylvania, in 1543).

It was a time of great changes in Transylvania. The Turks defeated Hungary at Mohács (1526). The heart of the country became a pashaluk (1541). Transylvania remained an autonomous principality under Ottoman suzerainty until 1688. The three privileged groups – Magyar nobility, Saxons and Székelys – ruled the country with equal rights. They chose the prince; they were represented in his councils and had the power of veto against decisions of the Diet that could harm their interests. This is seen as a flourishing time for the Saxon self-administration in the Universitas of the Nation.

In 1584, the house at no. 8 was bought by Johann Waida, one of Sibiu's most famous mayors. For the next 237 years, the house remained in the property of the Waida family. They were responsible for many updates seen to this day, such as the Renaissance-style gate. After a long time during which Saxon Comites lived here, in 1821 the Saxon Universitas purchased Hecht House for 20,000 guldens. Repairs amounted to another 12,260 guldens; the floor plan, shape of the roof and aspect of the façade were changed. Currently, there are homes and shops in Hecht House.

The Decline: Pandora's Box
The star of the Saxons began to fade in the 18th century, when they failed to obtain the 23rd validation of their privileges. In the era of nationalism, they dealt with a new kind of ruler – the nation state – who was determined to assimilate them at any cost.

XIII. I returned to Reghin, where architect Klaus Birthler had put together his family tree. The oldest documented ancestor is Samuel Birthler (1818-1887).

It was about the same time that Joseph II of Austria opened Pandora's Box to the Saxons. A kindly, enlightened autocrat, the emperor issued 6,000 edicts and 11,000 new laws through which he attempted, with dismal results, to regulate his subjects' happiness based on rational principles and to turn his hydra of an empire into a modern centralized state. One of these edicts gave Transylvania a new administrative partition into eleven counties, canceling out the autonomies of privileged peoples. The Habsburgs had recognized the Saxon privileges when they took over Transylvania, through the *Diploma Leopoldinum* (1691). Though the edict was partly revoked in the year of the emperor's death, the history of Transylvanian Saxons had already taken a new course. Their star started to fade in the 18th century, when they failed to obtain the twenty-third reconfirmation of their privileges. In the age of nationalism, they were faced with a new leader – the national state – determined to assimilate them at any cost.

XIV Hungary annexed Transylvania after the rebellion in 1848-1849; Romanians and Saxons stayed faithful to Vienna. Székelys resorted to reprisals: Reghin and several neighboring villages were burned. (This is why Klaus can't find his roots beyond 1848...). For the Saxons, it was a time of 'Hungarification'. Hungarian became the official language (1868), guilds were forbidden for being obsolete (1872), the 'royal territory' of the Universitas of the Saxon Nation was abolished (in 1876, when the Saxons lost much of their common assets). Dissatisfaction with the Hungarian government and the customs war between Romania and Austria-Hungary (1886-1893), which plunged Saxon towns into a deep economic crisis, gave rise to a wave of emigration: 10% of the 200,000 Saxons left for the U.S.A. or Romania.

Once Transylvania became part of Romania, Hungarification was replaced by Romanization. In the Greater Romania of 1918, Saxons from Ardeal, together with Swabians from Banat and Germans from the pre-1918 Romanian kingdom, Bucovina and Bessarabia, formed the most numerous Germanic community in South-Eastern Europe: 800,000 people. But there was more harm yet to come out of the Box... During the agricultural reform in 1921, almost 15,000 acres were seized from Saxon citizens and over 18,500 acres from Saxon communes, while the Evangelical Church and the Saxon Universitas lost over half of their lands. Financing for education and church – the two fundamental institutions of the Saxons – was deeply affected. The next blow was the decision made by the Bucharest government to impose a 1:2 rate for the exchange of Hungarian koronas into

Romanian lei that melted away all Transylvanians' savings, but hit the Saxons particularly hard, as they were wealthier. Starting 1925, the end-of-school examination was held in Romanian only.

XV. The transition from the periphery of a great European Empire to the center of a Balkan country caught the Saxons unprepared; still, they knew how to reinvent themselves, and their economy had another attempt at a comeback. Two thirds of them were peasants. Half of the almost 38,000 Saxon households owned less than 15 acres of land. After the Unification, the Saxons realized they couldn't face the competition of the farmers to the south of the Carpathians, who produced more abundant crops sold at much lower prices, which covered internal demand and left a surplus to export. On the verge of bankruptcy, the Saxons came up with a new revolution: industrializing agriculture.

They brought from Germany farming machines, selected seeds and breeds, fertilizers, new methods for farming and fighting pests. They reoriented themselves towards more profitable fields: animal farming, industrial plants (soy, sunflower, hop, potatoes), medicinal plants, vegetables and fruit. Education played a key role. Itinerant teachers held conferences in village after village to spread new knowledge and new technologies. In 1929, a school of agriculture was founded in Sibiu – holding short classes in winter. The results were quick to show. In the early 20th century, three quarters of the Saxon communes exploited their lands together. The new, industrialized agriculture – particularly in Sibiu, Tarnava Mare and Brasov – yielded wheat and maize crops more than 100% above the country average. In 1925, agronomist Gheorghe Ionescu-Sisesti summarized the situation as follows: 'Saxons are the best agriculture and cattle farmers of all the nationalities of the Romanian provinces united in 1918'.

XV Although they stood for only 1.37% of the country population, the Saxons' total investment into industry amounted to about seven billion lei in 1934, one third of the Romanian state budget; 10% of the money deposited in Romanian banks was entrusted to the over 40 Saxon banks, of which the General Savings House in Brasov (1825) is thought to be the first of its kind in Romania. In 1943, the Germans had 420 enterprises totaling 22,000 workers (12.3% of the national sum total), that accounted for 27% of Romania's industrial production.

The Saxon press boomed in the years between the two world wars: Sibiu alone had three such daily newspapers at the same time, plus other cultural or specialized publications. Circulation was low (five to six thousand for daily newspapers), but issues reached the entire European German-speaking area.

Having been a privileged ethnic group until 1867, Saxons did not take well to becoming a minority constantly thrown against the ropes first by the Hungarian national state, then by the Romanian one; 'in 1930, they chose to form their own nation, against the state in which they lived', explains historian Cornelius R. Zach. Disappointed with the Bucharest government, most Saxons embraced the Renewal movement, a form of nationalist-socialist protest. In the beginning, many saw a savior in Hitler. In September 1941, during a sermon, Vicar Friedrich Müller declared the *Heil Hitler* salute to be tantamount to a prayer. Soon, however, 'decision was taken from the hands of the community and reserved for a small leading elite and, later for the Central Office for Ethnic Germans in Berlin. With their proud sense of identity, Saxons were thus degraded to becoming mere instruments', says Zach.

While Germany was riding its wave of glory, Saxons lived well, too. Bishop Viktor Glondys, an adversary of the national-socialist ideology, wrote in his diary in 1941: 'No one has dared to stand up against the Renewal Movement, not only because they were afraid that Germany would see them as an adversary of national-socialism, but also because, without this movement, the Saxon people would be deprived of the money from Germany'. There were hopeful talks of an autonomous Transylvania under German protectorate. But Hitler had other plans: on August 30th 1940, in Vienna, he decided to split Transylvania between Romania and Hungary. North-Western Transylvania and its 34,000 Saxons were annexed by Hungary.

XVI Starting September 1940, Berlin appointed young Saxon Andreas Schmidt as the head of the Ethnic German Group in Romania. He succeeded in spreading Nazism to the majority of Germans in Romania, who had now become a war accessory of the Third Reich. After the invasion of the U.S.S.R., ethnic Germans from Germany's satellite states became a reserve for the German army. 70.000 Romanian Germans joined the SS or the Wehrmacht and contributed to the German war industry. 26,000 of them were Saxon. When Romania turned the weapons against Germany, they were all declared to be defectors. By Hitler's personal appointment, General Arthur Phelps became Transylvania's SS and police chief. One of his orders: taking any measure necessary to save the Germans in Transylvania and Banat. He only succeeded in evacuating the Saxons in northern Ardeal. Opinion leaders of the Southern Saxons opposed his attempts. 'Those who stir without reason hurt the heritage of their forefathers and their holy duty towards their children', said, in an interview in September 1944, lawyer Hans Otto Roth, who had become an unofficial leader of the German population in Romania.

In the North, the evacuation followed a careful plan. German officers returned from the eastern front insisted that the Russians would massacre any German they find in their way. General hysteria ensued. On the 17th of September 1944, in Lechinita, Bistrita County, the bells no longer called the 1,100 Saxons to Sunday morning mass. It was the evacuation signal. The convoys left in perfect order, led by German soldiers. The same ritual was repeated everywhere: a short religious service, a common prayer and, at the bell's signal, the start.

Klaus' grandfather, Josef Birthler, a mechanic foreman in Reghin, was one of the 30,000 Saxons evacuated from the town – 95% of the population. The value of the abandoned properties amounted to about 500 million dollars in gold, at the value in 1944.

XVII In the Rasnov house that used to belong to his parents, with his ears straining to hear the antique radio the size of an altar, with family photos and badges for icons, the old man is listening to morning mass on a German radio station. His lips are sunken in and surrounded by vertical lines so deep that his mouth looks like a grouchy zipper. But don't be fooled by appearances. If you get to know him, old man Hans

(Gagas Johann) becomes a witty guy who, at 93, still 'loves girls' and plays some mean drums in Fanfara Tarii Barsei, the area's brass band.

Even while deported to the U.S.S.R., in the Donbass camp, where his peers lived for three years 'like cattle', he would dispel the prison mood for a while by playing the drum he had fashioned 'out of a preserve tin, a spring and a piece of wire'. Old man Hans fought in the Romanian army during the Second World War. He spent eleven months in the first line of the Caucasus front. It made no difference. After the war, both he and his wife were deported to the U.S.S.R. along with 70,000 German ethnics in Romania. 14,000 died due to hard labor and shortages. 'They were innocent, all of them'.

The Saxons evacuated from northern Ardeal lived through an ordeal of their own, orchestrated by their Romanian fellow countrymen. In the weeks after the 13th of September 1944, when the last German and Hungarian soldiers withdrew from northern Ardeal, Saxon households were looted by neighboring Gypsies and Romanians, who stole everything they could. In villages like Ghinda, Chirales or Tarpiu, some had taken the habit of moving from one absentee house (a term used by Romanian authorities for the departed Saxons) to the next every few days. Between October 1944 and the autumn of 1945, the Romanian authorities reinstalled in northern Ardeal brought 2156 families of Romanian colonists in the towns and villages deserted by Saxons. The agricultural reform on the 23rd of March 1945 took the lands away from German ethnics. One quarter of the evacuees were overtaken by the Red Army on Reich territory and sent back to Transylvania during the summer and autumn of 1945.

Their fear of a Russian massacre turned out to be unfounded. Rudolf Schuller, curator of the Evangelical church in Bistrita, told of colonel Serbakov, the Russian military commander: 'He showed none of the hatred towards Germans which Romanians displayed'. In some areas, Romanians beat up their neighbors when they returned.

According to *Report no. 635/August 24th 1945* issued by the Gendarmerie of Nasaud County, the mayor in Tarpiu robbed the Saxons who returned to the village. *Order no. 7499/May 26th 1945*, as issued by the general police headquarters: 'take measures to see that all German citizens departed with the German troops and returning to their homes be arrested and sent to camp'. Unwanted by those who had gotten hold of their fortunes, Saxons were styled as 'traitors of their motherland who leeched on the Romanian nation'. Ioan Popu, who had only recently been appointed chief of the Nasaud prefecture in June 1945 and who grew to be known as the Saxon Eater, sent a confidential note, *no. 8999/ July 5th 1945*, to the Ministry of Home Affairs, requesting the deportation of the Saxons returned to the Bistrita area and living, at the time, in a camp in another part of the country, 'so that they give up any thought that they will ever return to their properties, where we have settled citizens with a right to own the land'.

All German ethnics were sent to labor camps as 'community service', far from their places of origin. Klaus' grandfather, Josef Birthler, had a different experience. After the evacuation, he only made it to Budapest, where he was badly injured by a grenade. He lay in a hospital, struggling between life and death. He fell in love with the Hungarian pharmacy attendant who looked after him, but in the end the love for the Mures's banks (the family curse, as Birthler senior calls it) was stronger and grandpa Josef returned, later but still during the Saxon persecution. He changed his name to that of his Hungarian grandmother and declared himself Hungarian.

XVIII The situation only started to lighten in 1948. Most labor prisoners were set free. Reparatory measures were attempted in the 1950s: the survivors returned to their hometowns, got back their right to vote and attend German schools and were given back their churches. But more misfortune was waiting in Pandora's Box. An all-powerful communist state was established in Romania, with increasing nationalist tendencies after the 1960s. For Saxons, it meant discrimination, uncertainty, hindrances, prison, and displacement to the Baragan plain. It was also when the paid Saxon exodus began. At the height of its economic boom, West Germany needed labor. Its authorities initiated protocols with all eastern European countries with German minorities. According to Florian Banu, researcher at the National Council for the Study of Securitate Archives (CNSAS), secret negotiations between Romania and Germany resulted in over 200,000 German ethnics leaving the country between 1962 and 1989. One Saxon graduate thus 'exported' brought 3,000 $ to the country treasury. One student=1,500 $.

After the fall of Ceausescu's regime, the borders were open and, in only two years (between 1990 and 1992), the huge majority of Germans in Romania (another 160,000) left the county freely.

XIX At the top of the roofed stairway at the entrance of the fortified church in the Sarosul pe Tarnava village, I asked the guard how many Saxons still live in the village. 'Three families. All of them old people'. How does one feel about the turn of the wheel of history for his ancestors, who in the 14th century started to raise here a stone fortress of the Church, meant to last a thousand years?

I was walking through the empty church like a ghost, weighed down by burdening thoughts. The air was heavy with the scent of the black locust tree blooms. Could it have been worse? Certainly! According to historian Ernst Wagner, 'Romania does not look so bad if we compare its attitude towards German ethnics to that of other eastern European countries, such as Poland or Czechoslovakia'.

The Birthlers signed up for emigration in the '80s. They were written in somewhere near the bottom of the list and never made it out. Around 1992, they did visit their relatives in Germany, but 'we wouldn't stay…' After 1990, with the massive exodus of the Saxons, their houses were given to other locals – Romanian and Gypsy. The Saxons moved to the Diaspora: 200,000 live in Germany, about 20,000 in Austria, 30,000 in the U.S., 8,000 in Canada. Rohtraut Wittstock, chief editor of *Allgemeine Deusche Zeitung für Rumänien*, estimates that there are only 15,000 Saxons left in Romania – most of them elderly. And a few idealistic young people like Klaus, who feel connected with this land.

I said goodbye to Klaus on a rainy Saturday, after helping him build a pontoon on *Canalul Morii* in Reghin. The town's anniversary was coming up the following day and Klaus, ever the optimist and ever in love with the Mures, was preparing boating lessons for the local children. 'Have you noticed that most Romanians build their houses facing away from the river? In other countries, having your address next to a body of water is an honor… We must learn to turn our faces back to the Mures'.

Key dates in the 800 years history of Saxons in Transylvania
- 1141-1162 – king Géza II invites 'guests' from Western Europe to defend and develop the new 'king's land' in Transylvania.
- 1211-1225 – The Teutonic knights are settled in Tara Barsei to secure the Southern frontier of the Magyar kingdom.
- 1224 – The Diploma Andreanum establishes the rights and obligations of German colonists.
- 1241-1242 – A Mongol mega-invasion devastates south-eastern Europe. Many Saxon settlements are razed to the ground.
- 1325 – The Saxon rebellion against the ruler of Ardeal is suppressed. The seat constitution is instated.
- 1395 – First Ottoman attack on Tara Barsei.
- 1486 – King Matthias Corvinus confirms the unity of Saxons on the lands of the crown (Universitas Saxonum).
- 1526 – The battle of Mohács; the central part of the Hungarian kingdom becomes a pashaluk.
- 1541 – The first Saxon secondary school is inaugurated in Brasov. In the early 16th century, each Saxon village had a school.
- 1542 – The Transylvanian Diet recognizes the suzerainty of the Ottoman Porte.
- 1542 – Johannes Honterus introduces the Reformation in Brasov and Tara Barsei.
- 1547 – Ecclesiastic regulations for all Saxons in Ardeal. Saxons become Lutherans.
- 1595-1606 – Troubled years for Transylvania. Rudolf II of Habsburg wants the Ardeal, recently conquered by Mihai Viteazu, initially in the name of the emperor.
- 1557-1568 – Religious tolerance in Transylvania.
- 1572 – Saxons adopt the Augsburg Confession. Biertan becomes the seat of the Evangelical Lutheran bishop.
- 1583 – Private civil law is introduced for Transylvanian Saxons.
- 1689 (April) – The great fire in Brasov. Saint Mary's Church

becomes the Black Church.
- 1734 – Lutherans from central Austria are displaced to Transylvania by force.
- 1774-1787 – Samuel von Brukenthal, counselor of Empress Maria Theresa, becomes governor of Transylvania.
- 1780-1790 – Joseph II attempts to impose enlightened reforms from the top down in the Habsburg Empire.
- 1835 – The General Savings House opens in Brasov.
- 1845 – The Transylvanian Saxon Agricultural Association is founded.
- 1848 – The revolution in Vienna reaches Transylvania. Romanians and Saxons remain on the side of the emperor; civil war ensues, and Reghin is torched.
- 1867 – The dual, Austrian-Hungarian state is formed; Transylvania is annexed to the Magyar half of the empire.
- 1872 – The first meeting of all Saxons in Transylvania is held in Medias.
- 1876 – Definitive annulment of the crown domain; new administrative land division.
- 1885 – Dr. Carl Wolff founds the first Raiffeisen-type consumer cooperative.
- 1918 – The Declaration of Alba Iulia: Transylvanian Romanians proclaim their unification with Romania.
- 1919 – The Union of Germans in Romania is founded.
- 1921 – The first agricultural reform in Transylvania.
- 1940 – Romania loses Bassarabia, northern Bukovina and northern Ardeal to the U.S.S.R. and Hungary.
- 1941 – Romania enters the war against U.S.S.R. on Germany's side.
- 1942-1943 – An agreement is established between Germany, Hungary and Romania on the enrollment of ethnic Germans in the Wehrmacht.
- 1944 (August 23rd) – Romania capitulates and declares war against its former allies.
- September 6-19 1944 – Saxons are evacuated from northern

- Ardeal.
- 1945 – German ethnics are deported to labor camps in the U.S.S.R. Their lands are expropriated as part of a second agricultural reform.
- 1947-June 1948 – The law for the nationalization of production capacities is passed. In August 1948, schools (even religious schools) are also nationalized – a hard blow for Saxon churches.
- 1949 – The Evangelical Church of Augustan Confession in Romania adopts its new Internal Regulations; the Union of Transylvanian Saxons Living in Germany is founded.
- 1950 – German ethnics in Romania regain their right to vote.
- 1951 – Many people from Banat, including about 10,000 Swabians, are sent to the Romanian Plain by forced evacuation.
- 1956 – German ethnics are given back their houses together with their new occupants. Saxons only have the right to live in one or two rooms of their homes.
- 1978 – An agreement is established between Chancellor Schmidt and Ceausescu for the emigration of ethnic Germans, with the purpose of reuniting families.
- 1981 – Deep economic crisis in Romania. Even bare necessities are very hard to come by.
- 1989 – Fall of the Ceausescu regime. Founding of the Democratic Forum of Germans in Romania.
- 1990-1992 – Mass emigration. Most Saxons return to the West.
- 1996 – The number of parishioners of the Evangelical Church of Augustan Confession in Romania is 17,867 (only two decades earlier, there were ten times as many).

Tourism Today: Romania's German Heritage
16 Saxon Discoveries in Transylvania.

Tombs and moss and grass and ancient slabs and cobbled alleys and centuries-old trees are placed in a flowing, snaking pattern, following the lines of nature, in a terraced cemetery stretching over 11 acres on Sighisoara's highest hill. I had been in the citadel several times before, but I had never climbed up here. The wind was blowing gently; the world seemed enchanted in the Cemetery on the Hill, floating in a dawn-of-the-world kind of peace and quiet. Eager to find out more about this unbelievable place, as soon as I left it I headed straight to a stern-looking lady in front of the Evangelical Church, a couple of steps from the cemetery's iron gate.

That's how I learned – from Lenuta Orban, wife of the grounds manager who lives right there, in the Ropemakers' Tower, like in a fairytale house – the history of the biggest and oldest (dating from 1704) Saxon cemetery. Such random encounters with extraordinary locals are the salt and pepper of successful travels and bring about the most unexpected revelations. Lately I've chanced upon many revelations and random encounters. After 800 years the Saxons returned to the West, seeking the same thing that had brought their ancestors here: liberty and economic prosperity. Their heritage, however, remains and calls us to discover it. For your next Transylvanian escapade, I have asked a few well-informed fellow travelers to recommend to you a Saxon discovery.

Hikes In The Heart Of Transylvania

Illustrator **Radu Oltean** discovered in 1991 the picturesque charm of hiking from one Saxon village to another, from one valley to the next, over the low, densely forested mountains. Gentle, friendly slopes, woods, crossing fields of corn, alfalfa or potatoes, hills still terraced from the work done on the old abandoned vineyards, deer, storks and short distances between places of interest drew the attention of groups of enthusiasts who, in the last few years, have started to promote trips (on foot or by bike) in the area.

Recently, itineraries have been marked and detailed maps have been printed. The Tarnava Mare valley and the Hartibaciu valley draw the boundaries of the biggest forested hill area in Transylvania, which has survived due to the local regulations of the Saxon villages (in the pre-communist decades) and the respect for the communal forest land of each village. The tiny valleys hide beautiful Saxon settlements, visible from afar thanks to the spires of the mediaeval churches, rising like donjons.

Rhubarb Jam From Hambarul Alimentar

'If you take a tour of Transylvanian fortified churches, you simply have to stop in Saschiz, a Saxon village about 20 kilometres from Sighisoara on road DN13, with a 15th century citadel included on the UNESCO World Heritage list', recommends photographer **Bogdan Croitoru**. 'Saschiz also discretely preserves some small secrets that may hide unsuspected joys. In 2009, Prince Charles visited Saschiz for the inauguration of a processing centre for the area's farmers, called Hambarul Alimentar – the Food Barn. This production unit, actually an old, repurposed Saxon barn, is authorized to retail in Romania and abroad, supporting small regional producers who use traditional methods, first trained through a course organized by the Royal Society for Public Health.

The Barners sell to tourists, visitors of fairs with traditional products and especially British clients (Royal Family included) jams, pickles, fine blue cheeses, plant-based products, cakes, bread, drinks and oils. One highly sought-after Saxon delicacy is rhubarb jam. Thought to have been brought to Germany from Asia around the half of the 16th century, it is highly likely that rhubarb reached Transylvania thanks to Saxon traders. Rhubarb jam is refreshing, slightly tart. The parts of the plant must be carefully chosen, as the leaves contain toxic oxalic acid; rather than going through the trouble of making it at home, go buy it from a Saxon housewife. It reinvigorates you, it regulates digestion and puts wings where you remembered your shoulder blades to be'.

More details at: Tourist Info Center, ADEPT Foundation, str. Principala no. 166, Saschiz, jud. Mures 547510 Romania, phone no.: 40 (0)265 711635

The St. Michael Church Hill, Cisnadie

'Exhausted after 20 hours of driving straight from Amsterdam, I parked in Cisnadioara and, with my last sliver of energy, climbed up the hill to the old St. Michael (Sf. Mihail) church', says National Geographic Netherlands editor **Pancras Dijk**. 'At sunset, I felt as though I had been transported to the 12th century, having found a beautifully restored church that looked like mass was about to start in it, with walls ready to withstand any Ottoman or Tatar threat. Spread all over the plateau, many perfectly round boulders stood witness to the titanic task young men were required to fulfill in order to be recognized as adults: rolling one of these stone balls all the way from the valley to the top. But all these testimonies of the past were silent. There was not a man in sight. It looked like not just the Saxons, but the rest of mankind had deserted this hill, too. Meanwhile, I've travelled high and low in Transylvania in search of its Saxon heritage. On the last day, in the Rucar-Bran area, I drove to Cisnadie to buy a genuine Cisnadie carpet. I couldn't help myself – I covered the extra few kilometers to visit the church a second time. By some quirk of fate, it was also the time when the sun was setting over the enchanting scenery. I could hardly believe my eyes: this time, the church and the plateau were full of artists, poets, musicians, spectators, both young and old, many of them from Sibiu. The event I was witnessing was called Exodus, but in fact I was quite happy to find that life had returned there. The Exodus had breathed life back into the history of this sacred hill – and it had given it a future, too'.

The Shortcut To The Rasnov Citadel

'Just 15 minutes from the historic town center lies the place I love more than any other in Rasnov, the place where I take anyone visiting our country for the first time: the citadel', says **Adina Branciulescu**, coordinator of the Beau Monde magazine. 'There are two routes leading to it: the comfortable one, by car, branching off from the road to Poiana Brasov, and the slightly more difficult one, on foot – which I prefer by far. From the centre of Rasnov, you go through the passageway cutting through a Saxon building, the old culture centers, and you find yourself at the edge of the forest. The climb is easy and pleasant, and the view – more and more beautiful as you go. You can see the geometrically aligned streets, bordered by Saxon houses with tile roofs, the Evangelical Church, the Codlea hill, the mountains, forests and neighboring towns. Until recently, I used to come here just for the pleasure of the walk, but in the mean time the citadel itself has become interesting, more spectacular with each passing year. It is renovated, it has guides, souvenir shops and it hosts festivals all year long: Life in the

Citadel, the Jousting Tournament of the Citadels, the Mediaeval Festival and the International Historic Film Festival.

From there, I would recommend going down the other side of the citadel: At the bottom you will find a hotel with a restaurant and well-tended sports courts – the locals call it Acapulco. Rest for a few minutes, then continue on to the Valea Cetatii cave. It's easy to find, the path there is marked, and if the day is hot the coolness of the cave will be welcome (you absolutely need a warm jacket, though)'.

PS: Thanks to the excellent acoustic qualities of the cave, symphonic music concerts take place there on Saturday afternoons www.pestera-valeacetatii.ro.

PSS.: In 1965, a hotel-restaurant was opened at the foot of the citadel hill, called by locals Acapulco because Fun in Acapulco, starring Elvis Presley, had been shown in local cinemas in the same period; in it, the main character dove from a cliff that resembled the one next to the hotel.

Transylvanian Brunch

'On the last Saturday of each month from April to September, the villages in the Hartibaciu-Tarnava Mare Plateau organize a culinary and cultural event', says **Alina Alexa** of the Association for Ecotourism in Romania (AER). 'In summary, each edition shows off the beauties of a village, an orchard, a traditional household, a historic monument or a community. The ingredients come from local households, and the recipes are the result of centuries of multiethnic cohabitation: from cheese specialties and Romanian soups to székelykáposzta and Saxon hanklich'.

The full program of Transylvanian Brunch is available at brunch.dordeduca.ro. 'After the feast, there's also a helping of culture: a hike, a ride on the rail-cycle draisine, a concert, a crafts workshop and so on, depending on what we find in the villages', says Cristian Cismaru of Reki Travel. 'To join the brunches, you have to make a reservation by e-mail to transilvanian.brunch@gal-mh.eu. There have been a lot of people interested lately – once we reach around 150-200 participants (depending on the location) we no longer take reservations, in order to preserve the quality of the event'.

The Procession Cross And Saxon Tales

'Go to the museum in the Evangelical Church in Cisnadie to see the procession cross, said to have been carried at the head of the Saxon trail when they came to Transylvania in the 12th century', urges architect **Klaus Birthler** from Reghin. 'The hill church in Cisnadioara is a Romanic basilica – the most faithful representation of the style that has been preserved in its original form. The other churches were extended and modified according to the styles of the respective times, based on the Romanic basilica plan.

The book *Sächsische Volksmärchen aus Siebenbürgen* (Popular Saxon Tales of Transylvania) by Josef Haltrich (probably influenced by the Grimm brothers, with whom he exchanged letters) include two tales: *The Wonder Tree* (Der Wunderbaum) and *The Swan-Woman* (Die Schwanenfrau).

www.siebenbuerger.de is the website of the Transylvanian Saxon community, a great communication and information platform maintained by Saxons who have emigrated. In Germany, Saxons who have left Transylvania meet once a year at Dinkelsbühl, in Bavaria. They form groups named after the Transylvanian villages of their parents, grandparents or great-grandparents'.

Woolen Socks From Viscri

'It's hidden like a dusty treasure at the end of a bumpy, unpaved road, among tall trees and fields that are either green or white, covered in dandelion fluff', says **Andreea Campeanu**, a stringer for Agence France-Presse. 'Viscri could be touristy, but it isn't, because it's far, hard to reach and has every intention to stay that way. Its houses with thick walls painted in vivid colors, lined along the wide, muddy road, are only reachable by brave cars and the horse-drawn wagons of the locals – the few remaining Saxons, a few Romanians and the Gypsies.

With the ash-colored fortress at the top of the hill, full of labyrinthine nooks, Viscri, in its simplicity, always offers the joy of discovery. Such as the surprise when, lined up over a big, Saxon-style wooden gate, you find handmade woolen socks, house slippers and small shoulder bags, alone and unguarded, maybe forgotten there by a village woman who ran inside to cook dinner, knowing how rarely buyers pass on her street'.

The Saxon Mountain Shelters

'In 1880, in Sibiu, the *Siebenbürgische Karpatenverein* (SKV) was founded – Romania's first large organization dedicated to nature exploration, research and protection and to tourism in the Carpathians. It was a National Geographic Society of sorts, only eight years older. (Right after the establishment of the NGS, collaboration with the SKV was initiated.) The SKV built over 60 mountain shelters in the Southern Carpathians, some of which are still standing at Balea, Curmatura, Omu, Suru, Barcaciu, Negoiu and so on. In 1945, the communists dissolved the SKV and nationalized the mountain shelters. A few Saxons from Germany re-founded it in 1996', says **Cristian Lascu**, editor at large, National Geographic România.

Saxon Ceramics And Baumstriezel

'Buy Saxon vases and plates', advises **Madalina Nan**, tour operator. 'Apart from traditional costumes, ceramics are another element that defines the Saxon community in Transylvania. Ceramic vases or mugs with floral motifs, sometimes accompanied by the emblem of their regions of origin, are omnipresent in Saxon houses or churches. Pottery was an art in the Saxon community. The first potters' guilds date back to 1376. They required craftsmen to undergo rigorous training and produce very high quality ceramics of great artistic value. Also, a cultural recommendation: the Saxon equivalent of the delicious *kürtôskalács* (Saxon breadroll) is leavened dough baked in the hearth, on an open flame, originating in South-Eastern Transylvania. The raised dough is gently rolled out, cut into strips and laid in a spiral around wooden rollers. The baumstriezel is then glazed with melted butter and sugar, then left to bake… and the result is a delicious dessert that, much like the Romanian cozonac (yeasted sweet bread), is never absent from any Saxon holiday'.

A Village Called Biertan

'20 years ago I watched in fascination, on Deutsche Welle TV, a documentary about a centuries-old church, with a mechanism to secrete away riches, and about long-forgotten traditions for making spouses get along again', says travel blogger **Cezar Dumitru**. (www.imperatortravel.ro). Then, at the end, I was stupefied to find out that special place was in Romania, in an out-of-the-way Saxon village on a secondary road close to Sighisoara. Years later, I discovered that little-used road myself, snaking between fairytale hills to a village called Biertan, or Birthälm, in German. In vineyard country, in the heart of a traditional Saxon village, you are greeted from afar by the famous fortified church, Romania's first monument included in the UNESCO World Heritage list. Biertan lost administrative centre statute to Medias, so it was given the right to host the Saxon episcopate, which remained there for over three centuries – that explains the size of the fortified church in the village. You can get to the Gothic church at the top of the hill by climbing a flight of stairs shaded by a wooden roof much like the one in Sighisoara. The Evangelical church, austere, opposed to Catholic luxuries, is one of Romania's Gothic wonders. But what really makes it stand out is the door to the sacristy, where, behind a complex system made up of no less than 19 locks, created in 1515 by local craftsmen, the Episcopal treasure was kept. Another thing not to miss is the cell in the eastern bastion, where arguing couples who wanted to divorce were imprisoned for two weeks, with one plate, one spoon, one mug and one bed. Of all the couples that were subject to the experience, only one still wanted to divorce – the rest made up'.

The Evangelical Church In Herina

'Only 16 kilometers away from Bistrita, on the crown of a hill next to Herina village, Romania's best preserved Romanic church rises proudly', says university assistant **Gabriela Cocea**. 'The exterior, painted in immaculate white, impresses through the austerity of its lines, through the unfinished symmetry of its two uneven towers (that, on a smaller scale, remind the famous cathedral in Chartres). If you want to go in, ask around for Brighite Budacan, who holds the key; at any rate, it's best to try and visit around noon, when you are most likely to find her in the church, looking after the holy place with the Saxons' ancestral diligence. Once inside, you will notice the interior looks more like an unusual art gallery: the walls and the white columns bear the works of a Transylvanian artist – a different one each year. This year, the church is decorated with the tapestry and embroidery works of artist Zoe Vida Porumb. Don't forget to look for the mural piece preserved to the left of the simple wooden altar, or the stone face on the base of one of the columns. Mass is no longer held in the church, and the Saxon population has gradually left the area, with only five Saxons still living in the village. One of them is our guide – ask and he will tell you, nostalgically, about how Saxon traditions still survive in the maelstrom of a century that threatens the entire rural civilization, regardless of its forebears'.

The Country Hotel

'I never forgot the white towers of the Harman citadel, standing stark against the postcard-blue sky, the wooden stairs leading to the old pantries, the shaded walkway from which you can watch, from a laid-back past, the village that looks forever frozen in a Sunday', says **Roxana Farca**, travel writer for LumeaMare.ro. 'It's the kind of peace you only find in Austria or Germany. Close to the citadel I met Marcela Cosnean, who created in her B&B, The Country Hotel, a home into which you wish you could move for good, as long as the host can stay around too.

Marcela is an amazing cook and is not afraid to challenge you with unusual recipes and combinations you've never tried before. Conversations flow merrily, the delicacies on the table vanish in a blink, and the good wine keeps them company. You will enjoy the most restful sleep in the home-sewn linen sheets. We took home with us the memory of the morning sun gliding in through the windows, playing in the colors of the homemade jams, Marcela's energizing laughter in our ears and the white image of the citadel under our eyelids – a place so serene in times that are otherwise undeservedly troubled'.

The Apprentice House

'I was in highschool when the first apprentices came to Sibiu to live in the Apprentice House in Huet Square no. 3', remembers **Ana Benga**, German kindergarten teacher, who studied at the German Pedagogy

Highschool in Sibiu. 'Afterwards, apprentices kept coming to Sibiu – particularly young Austrians, Germans and Swiss, less than 25 years old, who must carry out their practice in various places of the world. By custom, they have a few rules to observe: wearing their traditional costume, not communicating with their families, not working for money etc. The minimum duration of their voyage is two or three years and a day and it must be established before departure. Usually, Sibiu is visited by bricklayer, carpenter and stonemason apprentices who, throughout the years, have worked for the renovation and restoring of many houses in Sibiu. You can recognize them by their compulsory traditional attire, specific to each guild, and you often find them near the Evangelical church that owns the Apprentice House (that is located in the Stairs Tower connecting the upper city to the lower city and has hosted travelling apprentices for centuries). In 2007, the Casa Calfelor (Apprentice House) Association was founded. If you meet any travelling apprentices around town, strike up a conversation (they speak English) and find out about the history and secrets of their craft'.

www.casacalfelor.eu/ro/despre-noi/

The Calnic Citadel

'Next time you're on European road E60 connecting Sibiu to Sebes, take a short detour to Calnic – says **Razvan Pascu** (www.razvanpascu.ro), tourism blogger and consultant – to experience the peace, order and feeling of «normality» exuded by the citadel that, since 1999, is part of the UNESCO World Heritage. Initially, Calnic was the residence of a Transylvanian count, later turned into a fortification for the village. That may be precisely why it was kept so well, while its picturesque quality is due to the locals' care for the citadel. I have rarely seen people repairing windows in citadels (many of them don't even have any left), or video surveillance, or a well-tended, functional chapel that, on top of everything else, welcomes tourists with the sounds of an organ (recorded, it's true, but it's the atmosphere that matters)'.

Dupa Ziduri, In Brasov

'Take a romantic walk at sunset on the *Dupa Ziduri* (Behind the

Walls) Alley – says stomatologist **Diana Tret** from Brasov. On one side you have the forest, on the other the city walls… All you can hear is the rustle of the trees and the gurgle of the Graft/Spurcata stream. The walk will introduce you to the city's outer fortifications: you will pass by the Black Tower (that got its name after it was struck by lightning twice), the White Tower, that was assigned for defense to the pewter and brass workers' guild, and the Graft Bastion, hosting a section of the Brasov County History Museum, with information on the guilds' role in the defense of the city'.

Pieces Of History In Sacele

'Let yourself be charmed by a break in Sacele, a village with typical Saxon architecture, an old Catholic church (presently a monument), partly renovated, beautifully perched on the top of a hill, many small Orthodox churches scattered throughout the village, and the air of a place outside time – advises journalist **Anca Popescu**. Wandering on the sloping, narrow streets, past the large, apparently impenetrable gates, you will eventually find an open gate, like an unspoken invitation. There you will find, like in a fairytale, what no one would expect to find behind the gates' old wood: flowers of all shapes and colors, old shady trees, the omnipresent grapevine arch and a fresh lawn. The smiling host will certainly offer you all you need – a good meal, a clean room, a lot of peace and quiet.

The forest by the village leads to Bunloc, where you can take the chairlift to take in the scenery; with a bit of luck, you'll see that it's also the favorite takeoff place for paragliders. You could try a double with an authorized instructor – I can assure the experience is well worth it!'

CHAPTER 4
ANGRY CAROL-SINGERS
Why Do the Hill And the Valley Fight Each Other at Ruginoasa?

At dawn, on the 31st of December, two groups of men, wearing costumes made of animal skins, fight each other like savages, with clubs, in Ruginoasa village, in Iasi county. Policemen supervise the fight. According to the locals, nobody has died in this fight in the last several years. After they chase away the defeated group by tapping the ground with their clubs, the winners go to the local bar to celebrate their victory. No one in the village knows the origins of this event. Sabina Ispas, director of the **Institute for Ethnography and Folklore**, believes this battle is a unique ethnographic accident blending several influences from the Slavic traditions and the Romanian groups of carol-singers and *calusari*. Traditionally, the function of carol-singers – who during the holidays used to turn into some kind of messengers – was to give a heavenly aura to the space around them, through their songs. In time, the villages gradually got larger and larger. The newcomers were usually settling in the valley, near the people living uphill, but the two groups could only have one set of divine messengers at a time. Probably at a certain moment, following some social prejudice, – usually the people uphill, the first owners of the land, were richer and refused to mingle with the newcomers – the people in Ruginoasa valley formed their own group.

The next step was probably influenced by the calusari tradition. 'Whenever two such groups met, they got into a huge fight that could end even in manslaughter', wrote Prince Dimitrie Cantemir around the beginning of the 18th century. The fact that these people dress in animal skins – a feature also found in the Slavic region – is undoubtedly of Slavic influence. This tradition has recently been enriched due to the media which considers this event a sensational show, the police forces sent here to keep the situation under control and the tourists who come to see the fighting.

CHAPTER 5

THE MAN THEY KILLED ON CHRISTMAS DAY

The life on Nicolae Ceausescu.

Collage from an omagial album.

This is the story of a state resident, for whom the world was a great village. His cottage happened to be Romania. For 24 years he led this country like an ambitious peasant, dreaming of turning an impoverished small holding into a rich farm.

He struggled to earn the respect of the people. Tired of depending on and borrowing money from his affluent neighbors, he tried to make it on his own. At first, he thought he would succeed. But he was sloppy and hasty. What others had, he wanted as well, without thinking too much about feasibility or necessity. If any other two world leaders fought, he would jump in to break them up. For a while he treated his people well – giving them many jobs and houses – but when things stopped going his way, he exploited them without mercy.

I A black dog licks at a puddle of blood in which two old people lie, executed on Christmas day in the Targoviste garrison. Following a kangaroo trial, a special tribunal sentenced them to death by shooting in December 1989 for 'serious crimes against the people of Romania. He died instantly. The woman died a minute later, after the execution squad's paratroop captain furiously emptied another round in her. Thus Nicolae and Elena Ceausescu's five-decade journey together ended, after they started from the bottom, seized power, and grew old while ruling the country. Adulated for all of his 24 years in power, during which he came to personify Romania, Ceausescu – dethroned and replaced by some of his former barons – was turned into a scapegoat for all the evils done to Romanians. During his regime, Ceausescu's image had been painted in sparkling white. Once he was killed – everything turned to pitch black. In the following pages I tried my best to paint a portrait in color, with all shades of grey included, combining the good and bad, the light and the dark extremes of the life of Nicolae Ceausescu.

II A short, stuttering kid left home at eleven to make something out of himself in Bucharest. His parents, peasants from Scornicesti, could barely put food on the table for their ten children. His father, Andruta, had three hectares of land, a few sheep, and would make ends meet by tailoring. 'He didn't take care of his kids; he stole, he drank, he was quick to fight, and he swore..'. said the old priest from Scornicesti. His mother was a submissive, hard-working woman. The family slept on benches along the walls of a two-room house. Corn mush was their staple food. Nicolae went to the village school for four years. The teacher taught simultaneous classes for different years in a one-room schoolhouse. The young Ceausescu did not have books and he often went to school barefoot. An outsider from early on, he did not have friends; he was anxious and unpredictable.

In a then cosmopolitan Bucharest – the first city he had seen – Nicolae moved in with his sister, Niculina Rusescu. Soon, he was sent to serve his apprenticeship at the workshop of shoemaker Alexandru Sandulescu, active member of the Romanian Communist Party (PCR), who initiated his apprentice in conspirative missions. Nicolae did not adapt to Bucharest. The switch from a world in which he couldn't find his place (his own village) to another in which he still couldn't find his place (the intimidating city) marked him. 'His initiation into the marginalized movement of the communists was his alternative solution for integrating into social life', says sociologist Pavel Campeanu, author of the book *Ceausescu: The Countdown. Historians of the Golden Age* never miss an opportunity to hyperbolize Ceausescu, the activist, as a 'young hero', arrested for the first time at the age of 15, and who, by the age of 26, had spent seven years in prison. The truth is that, in the 1930s, Nicolae was a rash, incompetent kid. 'I had never heard anything about him', says Constantin Parvulescu, one of the founders of the Romanian Communist Party (PCR). He would receive minor missions from his communist bosses. For example, in 1934 in Craiova, with three other young people, he caused a stir at the trial of a group of communists led by Gheorghe Gheorghiu Dej, who was at the time the leader of the Romanian Rail System union in Bucharest. Ceausescu and his comrades were arrested and beaten by the police. According to the testimony of Ion Gheorghe Maurer, who would become president of the Council of Ministers, Nicolae had been paid to distribute manifestos and petitions just as others were paid to sell newspapers.

Until the mid-1930s, Nicolae traveled on missions in Bucharest, Craiova, Campulung, or Ramnicu Valcea. He was arrested several times. His record was beginning to convey the image of a 'dangerous communist agitator' and 'distributor of communist and antifascist propaganda'. His first prison sentence: June 6, 1936, the court of Brasov – two years in prison, plus six months for defiance of the court, a 2000-lei fine, and a year of home detention in Scornicesti. The largest part of his sentence was served at Doftana. His fellow inmates say that the prisoner Ceausescu was envious, vengeful, and tough. But he knew how to get under people's skin. When he got out of prison, Ceausescu was no longer quite as anonymous. He became a leading member of the youth organization of the Romanian Workers' Party

(PMR). In Romania, there were about 700 free communists (led by Patrascanu, Foris, Parvulescu) and about 200 more imprisoned (the generation that had taken part in Dej's railway strike); a royal dictatorship has been instated, activist meetings were rare, money was scarce, member IDs and membership dues did not exist.

He was soon arrested again and sent to Jilava for three years for 'conspiring against the social order'. Ceausescu spent the war years in prisons and work camps: Jilava (1940), Caransebes (1942), Vacaresti (August, 1943), Targu Jiu (September, 1943). The bars isolated him from what was happening outside: the agreement between Hitler and Stalin; internal conflicts between communists; the loss of Basarabia and North Ardeal territories; the attempted legionary coup d'etat; the abdication of Carol II; the Antonescu dictatorship. Sealed away from the tumultuous history unravelling in his homeland, the prisoner plotted his own vision for Romania's future.

August 1944 was a crossroads in his – and Romania's – destiny: Ceausescu was released and began his rise to power. The Romanian communist family – the Moscovite faction, the imprisoned generation of Dej, and the veteran covert activists – reunited that autumn in the mansion at No 16, Eliza Filipescu Lane (where the Indian Embassy is housed today). Ceausescu was among them. Under the protective wing of Dej, whose favorite he had become while in prison, Ceausescu struggled, flattered, adapted, worked, raised himself up, step by step, tenaciously, stubbornly, and with a real instinct for power:

- at 27 he was the leader of the Communist Youth Organization (UTC) and, later, of the Central Committee (CC) of the Romanian Workers' Party (PMR);
- at 28 – party instructor in Constanta and Oltenia;
- at 29 – deputy in the Grand National Assembly (after he had mobilized motorized troops in the electoral precinct to 'convince' electors to place ballots in the urns which had already been filled by the communists ahead of time);
- at 30 – Sub-Secretary of State in the Ministry of Agriculture (where the forced collectivization began);
- at 31 – Co-Minister of Defense, political head of the army, then

politruk with a specialization in Moscow;
- at 36 – secretary of the Central Committee (a key position in the Communist Party, dealing with the organization of the Party);
- at 37, during the second Romanian Workers' Party congress, he was accepted as a member of the Politburo, where his duty was to supervise the internal affairs of the party within the Ministries of the Interior, Securitate, the Armed Forces, the Magistracy, and Justice (he used this position to create a network of connections, installing his people in the Party's key positions).

III November 5, 1957. An IL-14 airplane carrying a delegation of thirteen Romanian Workers' Party members, on its way to Moscow for the October anniversary of the Great Socialist Revolution crashed upon landing at the Vnukovo airport, at 17:48, due to a piloting error. The Foreign Minister, Grigore Preoteasa, and three members of his delegation died. The other passengers suffered serious injuries. Nicolae Ceausescu, the secretary of the Central Committee of the Romanian Workers' Party, was luckier. The medical record released in Moscow states: 'Trauma to the outer right hemithorax and to the left calf. Scratch wounds on the face, hands, and feet. Temperature: 37.5 degrees, general state: satisfactory'. But fate had still been close to playing the most cruel joke on this ambitious young man, when he was just steps away from grasping power.

A few years later, on March 19, 1965, 17: 45, when Gheorghiu Dej died surrounded by the leading team of the Romanian Workers' Party, Nicolae Ceausescu was the first to bend over and kiss him. The three veteran members of the Politburo, friends of Dej who were qualified to replace him, were not well suited for the job because of their 'unhealthy origins': Ion Gheorghe Maurer was German, Emil Botnaras – Ukrainian, Dumitru Coliu – Bulgarian. (According to Paul Niculescu-Mizil, former member of the Central Committee, the three prerequisites for the future leader were: 1. to be Romanian, 2. to be an activist, 3. to be part of the working class). The desire of this triumvirate of the old guard to promote a docile young man to the head of a collective leadership converted Ceausescu's defects into strengths. They pulled the strings for the junior member of the Politburo whom they considered the easiest to manipulate.

At the congress of July 19 – 24 meant to validate the Politburo elections, the 1357 delegates voted Ceausescu not as Prime Secretary, but as Secretary General, a title not used in the eastern Bloc since the death of Stalin. Ceausescu, 47 years old, Europe's youngest political leader to date, launched his mandate at full strength: the PMR returned to its old name, the Romanian Communist Party. After only one month, the name of the country changed too: Romania went from being a Popular Republic to being a Socialist Republic. The honeymoon of the first steps in this seemingly modest and tolerant young dynamo's governing career did not in any way foreshadow the bitter years of its end.

In the beginning, Ceausescu successfully focused on four goals:
- the liberalization of internal politics;
- the wellbeing of Romanians;
- more power for himself (under the pretext of rehabilitation for the victims of the Dej period, he pulled the strings to replace the team that had promoted him and with whom he was supposed to share power, with the younger members from his entourage);
- an offensive strategy of seduction of the West, playing the rebel son of the Warsaw Pact family, while careful not to upset the USSR too much.

Romanians lived better and they were proud of their President. Frustrated by history, they saw in Ceausescu one of their own, who was on equal standing with the world's bigger players. When he condemned the military intervention in Czechoslovakia (on the night of August 20-21, 1968), Romanian enthusiasm was spontaneous. This act of defiance against Moscow brought him the respect of the entire world. But August 1968 was just the tip of the iceberg: Ceausescu consistently cultivated his aura of atypical communist leader:
- he was the first to stabilize diplomatic relations with the Federal Republic of Germany (1967);
- the only one who did not break off relations with Israel after the Six-Day War (June 1967);

- the only head of state who allowed Jewish citizens in his country to leave for Israel (it cost $2,000 – $5,000 per person, as the Securitate general Mihai Pacepa would reveal);
- the first Romanian President to visit the United States at a time when relations between the USSR and the US were extremely tense (1970);
- the first to refuse to align himself with the oil cartel founded by the General Plan of Comecon (1971);
- the leader of the only socialist country that was a member of the World Bank and the IMF (1972), etc.

IV In less than a decade, following the withdrawal of Soviet troops in 1956, the Romania of Gheorghiu Dej went from servility towards Moscow to a more autonomous foreign policy. Dej and his successor, Ceausescu, were both Stalinist wolves who, out of necessity, wore the pro-western sheepskin of a national-liberal kind of communism, reacting to Khrushchev's attempt to reform the eastern Bloc. It was a defensive move that made them as popular at home as they were abroad. The West thought they had found in Ceausescu the Trojan horse of the eastern Bloc, and they issued him a carte blanche for almost two decades. Some western observers exalted him, comparing him to Kennedy or predicting that Romania would become a kind of Switzerland. His fame as a stubborn, strong-headed nationalist with a special role in the Warsaw Pact opened almost every door for him. And Ceausescu proved to be a born mediator, extremely tolerant in his foreign policy (the polar opposite of the fanaticism that he exemplified in his internal affairs) – he was capable of making a pact with the devil himself.

'Ceausescu was a tyrant when it came to politics, an economic disaster, but in his foreign policy he had a spark of genius', said Silviu Brucan, former editor-in-chief of Scanteia, and later one of the main actors of the events in 1989. 'Although uneducated, he was smart, a wily, peasant sort of smart'. Soon, political tourism in Romania was in style. Richard Nixon, the future president of the US, was the one who opened the season in 1967. That year, Corneliu Manescu, the

Romanian Foreign Affairs Minister, became the president of the UN General Assembly. Ceausescu returned the visits. 1973 was the apogee of his trips abroad: Iran, Pakistan, the Netherlands, Italy, the Federal Republic of Germany, Yugoslavia, the US, the Vatican, the USSR, Morocco, and several countries in South America.

Pope Paul VI told him in the Vatican (May 26, 1973): 'Excellency, we ask Heaven to bless your activity, which we follow with great interest, and we ask you to consider us humble supporters of your policies of independence and sovereignty, which you are executing with such consistency'.

Ceausescu collected a considerable number of friends, medals, orders, and academic titles, a list of which would fill up 30 pages of this book. They vary from the French Legion of Honor to Luxembourg's Order of the Gold Lion of the House of Nassau, from the Order of the White Rose of Finland to the National Order of the Leopard of Zaire, from the British Order of the Bath to a handful of Orders of Lenin, of Karl Marx, and of the Red Banner from communist countries. He was the contemporary of six American presidents; he got along with all of them, and was friends with Nixon (they visited each other in Washington and Bucharest twice). Most of the time, he cultivated his good relations with the United States, which were tested in 1970 when Romania suffered floods (38 out of 39 provinces were affected, 600,000 people were evacuated) and America sent more than $11.6 million in aid, and culminated on July 25, 1975 when Romania obtained Most Favored Nation status (renewed annually until 1988).

Moscow had gotten used to the grandeur of Ceausescu's foreign policy: they probably considered him an original, yet harmless, clown. He, however, took himself seriously: in July 1973, at a meeting of the eastern European Communist Party leaders, the Romanian spoke heresy: he asked for collaboration with the Social Democrats (considered traitors of communism), called for the abolition of the two military blocs – NATO and Warsaw –, defended China in the quarrel with the USSR, and criticized Brezhnev for not doing more to avoid a nuclear war.

International tensions cooled down for a few years, and his double play was no longer necessary: the West discarded Ceausescu. Between 1974 and 1976, Ceausescu only traveled to the West twice. The number of western visits to Romania decreased as well. In 1974 no one came. Feeling betrayed by the West, Ceausescu turned to the Russians, whom he needed to help turn Romania into a modern, industrialized state.

In a private conversation in August 1976, Erich Honecker, leader of the German Democratic Republic, then on vacation in Crimea, told Leonid Brezhnev, the head of the USSR: 'Ceausescu keeps nagging me to go visit Romania. In general he's been acting better than usual. This is good. We'll catch him again in the Warsaw Pact'. During the same period, Ceausescu oriented himself towards the Third World (Africa, South America, the Arab states). He posed – proving his political instinct – as the European promoter of national independence. He approved million dollar credits, considered investments for the future, cooperated in the exploitation of underground riches and the exportation of industrial products and weapons.

V Nicolae Ceausescu met Lenuta Petrescu in 1939 at a protest at the Workers' Cultural Center. It was love at first sight; Lenuta was young, beautiful, two years older than him, and a member of the Communist youth organization – she was responsible for Sector two of Bucharest under her alias, Florica. Seven years later they were married; they would have three children (Valentin, Zoe, and Nicu) and stay together for 50 years.

'They were very close, they held hands. Ceausescu would not disobey her, and she would take great care of him, making sure he ate, had everything he needed and was satisfied. They would eat in the garden and they would have a good time together. He liked the music of Ioana Radu and Mia Braia and, after they ate, he would sing, they would play backgammon, and she would cheat. He would say: you cheated again, I'm not playing anymore. She would say: come on, Nicu, I won't cheat anymore... And that's how they had their family fun', says Suzana Andreias, head of personnel at the Ceausescu family residence in Snagov for almost three decades.

Ceausescu liked chess, pool, and volleyball. Based on the verse he would read at party Conventions, it seems he read Romanian literature, primarily the poetry of Eminescu. He was not a picky eater and had rustic tastes. He discovered movies when he was 35 years old. After 1955, he took up hunting, first invited by local party leaders whom he controlled at the time as member of the Central Committee politburo. Since 1965, it became a rule: he would go no Sunday of the season without hunting. In 25 years, he killed over 7,000 animals.

In 1966, after finishing the **Academy of Economic Sciences** (ASE) in the evening class section, he presented his thesis: *Selected Problems of Romania's Development in the 19th Century*. The real author is unknown. Starting in 1968, his speeches were typed; they make up 33 volumes.

In the last ten years of his life, he suffered from diabetes. As he grew older, he became more and more fearful. From 1972 on, he did not wear any article of clothing for longer than one day. The Fifth Directorate of the Securitate founded a tailor's workshop just for him: it produced office wear, Lenin caps, Mao jackets, English tweed pants, Soviet style heavy padded coats and German style hunting suits.

He was pedantic and obsessed with punctuality. Every morning, at 8.00 sharp, a line of cars escorted him to the office. He ate lunch at 13:00 sharp. He used Badedas shower gel and shaved with Gillette. He liked Odobesti white wine and red sparkling wine.

VI Between 1950 and 1989, and especially after 1965, industrial production in Romania increased by a factor of 44. Ironically, the driving force behind this Stalinist industrialization was a fear of Moscow. Nikita Khrushchev wanted to transform Comecon into a multinational planning organization. Gheorghiu-Dej refused the role of granary for the Warsaw Pact countries, which would have fallen upon Romania, preferring to turn to the forced industrialization of the country. Ceausescu stepped on the gas, benefiting from his role as 'Trojan horse of the East' and taking advantage of western financing (especially from the US and the Federal Republic of Germany). His authoritarian style of governing transformed Romania from a mainly agricultural country into one that registered production in almost all industrial branches.

In 1973, he approved the founding of joint ventures with the participation of western capital. From the first year, there were 20 such enterprises. The volume of commercial exchange with the West almost doubled: from 28% in 1965 to 45% in 1974. Between 1971 and 1975, Romania registered an 11.3% annual increase in GDP, never again surpassed. Whole towns became construction sites, and the propaganda couldn't keep up with the inauguration of factories and plants that popped up like mushrooms after the rain of western capital. It was a hasty process though, usually using outdated technology, without taking into account the effectiveness or the cost of further investments. Ceausescu banked on quantity, not quality. He was obsessed with the country's high investment rate – over one third of the national income – which, for him, was 'the only remedy against underdevelopment', while industrialization was 'a decisive factor for maintaining national independence and sovereignty'.

But the economy was not profitable. The state enterprises, most of which were overstaffed, led to poverty, suffering from the diseases of planned economy in its most acute, Romanian form: disorganization, nepotism, corruption, negligence and theft. The average GDP growth rate in Romania decreased from 11.3% (between 1971 and 1975) to 9.6% (1976-1980), then to 1.8% (1981-1982).

The galloping industrialization lead to a 10% increase in urban population over a decade: in 1977, almost half of Romania's population of 20 million lived in cities. Collectivization left the village workforce unemployed, while accelerated industrialization created jobs in the city. The state launched an extensive construction program for peasants who had headed to the city in hopes of gaining a better life. For them, the leap from a small room, with one table and benches on which parents, children, and grandparents slept, to apartments with bedroom, dining room, kitchen and bathroom was real and can be considered one of Ceausescu's accomplishments. Apartment blocks were built in great numbers: from 1981 to 1985, 750,000 apartments with central heating and hot water opened their doors to their occupants. Between 1965 and 1970, migration from the country to the city as a side effect of industrialization was considered a phenomenon to be desired. In only a few years, because of the imbalance created by this migration, restrictions were put into place for those who wanted to settle in the big cities.

Forced industrialization plunged Romania into debt. Between 1971 and 1982 the foreign debt grew from $1.2 billion dollars to almost $13 billion. The oil crisis of 1978-1981 was like an earthquake for this economy built on sand. In 1982, Romania's foreign trade income decreased by 17% compared to the previous year. Ceausescu found himself in the situation of not being able to pay back his western creditors. The country's inability to pay was formally declared. Disgusted by his western friends, Ceausescu ordered the foreign debt to be paid without taking out new loans. This was another proclamation of national independence, his obsession. Seven years later, Romania was out of debt, paying the price with unprecedented poverty.

In 1984 the Danube – Black Sea canal was inaugurated, after nine years of construction. The canal, which measures 64 kilometers (40 miles) and shortens the trip to the Black Sea by 400 kilometers (248 miles), had too high taxes to be attractive for navigators ($1 for every ton of cargo) and was yet another act asserting independence from the USSR, with whom Romania shared the Danube Delta.

Construction on the People's House, which was to become the headquarters of the Party and seat of the Government, began in 1985. The head architect, Anca Petrescu, had a team of 400 architects under her direction. Three neighborhoods were leveled – Uranus, Antim, and part of Rahova, along with 17 churches. Every day, over 20,000 builders worked in three shifts. Within five years, the second largest administrative building in the world (second only to the Pentagon outside of Washington, D.C.) rose from the ground with a volume of 2,500,000 cubic meters (88,287,000 cubic feet) and over 7,000 rooms, some of them the size of stadiums. The bill: circa $2 billion.

The grandeur of his economic plans, his obsession with paying off the national debt and his ignoring of the consumer needs of his population all pushed Ceausescu toward a reckoning. Catastrophe was not far off. The generous politics of the '60s and '70s were replaced by one of strict saving in the '80s. Standing in line to buy food became the public occupation. Buildings had central heating, but it was no longer used; medical assistance was free, but it was lacking medicine and technology, and the doctors took bribes. The population's energy consumption was reduced by 20% in 1979, 20% in 1982, 50% in 1983, and another 50% in 1985, each measurement based on the already reduced numbers of the previous years. In 1981, food rationing was reintroduced. There were ration cards for oil, milk, butter, and sugar. The meat on the market was whatever had been rejected for export. Between 1985 and 1988 food exports doubled. To mask the food crisis, Iulian Mincu, Ceausescu's personal doctor, invented a rationed diet plan on the grounds that it was not healthy for an adult to consume more than 3,000 calories per day. In 1983, Ceausescu went even further below his nutritionist's recommendations, fixing per capita rations: *39.12 kg of meat, 73 kg of milk and dairy products, 42.54 kg of potatoes, 66.08 kg of vegetables, 27.49 kg of fruit.* Students, teachers and soldiers were forced to participate in agricultural work. In 1984, the energy crisis started: enterprises were closed due to lack of electricity and raw materials; electricity, gas, streetlights, and heat were cut off daily; gas had become a rarity; on Sundays, driving was limited (one Sunday was only for cars with even-number license plates, the next – only for odd numbers).

In 1985, Mikhail Gorbachev, newly elected Secretary General of the Politburo of the Communist Party of the Soviet Union (CPSU), compared the Romanian economy to an 'old horse ridden by a cruel horseman'. Romanians were doing badly: only 5% of the population had cars, 19% had TVs, 14.7% had washing machines, and 17.6% had refrigerators. Ceausescu was familiar with the numbers of his weak economy. After 1989, at one of his beachside villas, two versions of documents detailing the last harvests were found, one with the real numbers and the other with the fabricated numbers for propaganda.

According to German-Romanian author Richard Wagner, who left the country in the'80s, 'the only people left in his entourage were relatives, lackeys, and criminals ready to do anything. They ran the country like a bunch of demented leaseholders.'

VII The cult of personality inflated as reality worsened. In 1980, when the 'Year of the Dacians' was celebrated, Ceausescu himself was celebrated as a descendent of Burebista's legacy. On TV, there were only two hours of broadcast: between 8.00 and 10.00 P.M. Here is a list of programs from January 26, 1987: 8 o'clock – news, 8: 20 – 'We Praise the Leader of the Country – Poems, an Anthology of Venerations; 8: 40 –'A Documentary Devoted to the Theoretical Activity of Comrade Nicolae Ceausescu', 9 o'clock – 'The Veneration of the Supreme Commander', a made-for-TV play accomplished with the help of the artistic assembly of the army; 9: 30 – news, end of broadcast.

In November 1984, the penultimate Romanian Communist Party (PCR) Convention was held. Hunger haunted the country, while in the convention room, Nicolae Ceausescu, interrupted by ovations – 'Ceausescu – heroism, Romania –communism! Our esteem and our pride, Ceausescu Romania!' – reported on the 'strong development of the food industry' to his party members.

This cult of personality started in 1970-1973 with his visit to Asia. Inspired by Mao Zedong in China and Kim Il Sung in North Korea, Ceausescu presented his theses on his own small cultural revolution in July 1971, 'with the aim of forming a new kind of man', through which he sought to transform Romania into a Korean-style beehive. The bees didn't let out the slightest buzz. In 1910, academic Constantin Radulescu Motru wrote: 'Romanians have a herd instinct and mimic everything they see around them, like sheep'.

On March 25, 1974, Ceausescu was elected President of the Socialist Republic of Romania, a position created especially for him. The eastern Bloc had never seen a communist President before. Ceausescu had become an institution: he was the President par excellence – of the State, of the State Council, of the National Defense Council, of the United Socialist Front, of the Supreme Council of Economic and Social Development, of the Permanent Bureau of the Executive Political Committee, of the Ideological Commission of the Romanian Communist Party, and other commissions and committees.

In 1968, when he condemned the invasion of Czechoslovakia, Romanians spontaneously praised him. Immediately, at the 10 th Romanian Communist Party convention, his yes-men brought him homage, which he rejected: 'We do not need idols or flag wavers. We do not need to make standard bearers out of people. Our idol is Marxism-Leninism and its concepts about the world and the life of the proletariat'. After his visits to China and North Korea, he changed his tune. His election to the position of president meant the beginning of probably the most shameless cult of personality in Europe since Hitler and Mussolini. Ceausescu became an idol in only a few years; he was no longer just the Comrade but titan among titans, the Oak from Scornicesti, strategist of luck, guarantor of Romania's richness, sun, the measure of all things, hawk, the Transfagarasan of our soul, the best worker/soldier/peasant/miner/railway/worker/hunter of the country, all-knowing, beloved leader, earthly god, prince charming, the peak that rises above the country, beloved father.

Since 1970, Romanians, predisposed to accepting authoritarian forms of government, participated, at least formally, in the leader's cult. The cult quickly developed its own dynamic, at first a snowball – the nucleus made up of toadies he had resisted several years earlier – that rapidly began rolling, growing with opportunism and the herd mentality, until it finally reached its extreme form in the '80s, becoming a sort of schizophrenia shared by the entire population. His birthday became a national holiday. On each of his birthdays, a new Homage program would come out, heavy with praise and anthems.

'We love him because he has hunger in his heart/ For work, so that we may have a better life/ All our voivodes hold his arm tightly/ And all our forefathers whisper words of wisdoms in his ear/ He is a man like any other, a man, a man, the man.' read the Homage for Ceausescu's 60 th birthday, by the regime's number one poet, Adrian Paunescu, a Social Democratic Party (PSD) senator in the post-communist regime.

In an interview with his French biographer, Michel-Pierre Hamelet, Ceausescu defined the personality cult organized around him in Romania as 'a problem of organization and clear-sightedness'.

One last protest: 83 year-old Romanian Communist Party veteran Constantin Parvulescu stood up in the middle of the 7 th Romanian Communist Party convention in November 1979 and stated that he did not support Ceausescu, whom he accused of putting his own interest above that of the Party. It was an isolated incident: the leader was reelected and 80,000 Bucharestians gathered for a mega-rally. Students got the day off, and enterprises halted work. Visits around the country made Ceausescu popular in the first years of his government. Then, local activists started building Potemkin villages for him. Before his arrival, a commando would mask reality: healthy cows popped up in the landscapes, pine trees on the side of the road, apples were tied onto trees with wires, and plastic grapes topped the tables at exhibitions. Everything he said was taken as a valuable order to be executed in full. For example, in the 80s, when he found out that Westerners were producing huge quantities of corn per hectare (the secret being the production density of 50 – 60,000 plants per hectare), Ceausescu brought the task back to Romania. One fall, in a county in Transylvania, the comrade visited a representative farm unit. Since they had not been able to achieve the desired density on any field, local specialists stuffed the lot with corn cobs cut from another field. Excited by the explanations given to him on the side of the field where an exhibition of produce, display boards, and graphics had been strategically placed, Ceausescu walked onto the field, peeled a corn cob, and ended up with one of the cobs that had been put there for show in his hand. He realized it had been a farce, he huffed and puffed, and then he forgot about it.

Surrounded by hypocrites, Ceausescu lost all sense of limitations, and increasingly took delight in his role as a feudal despot. French president Valéry Giscard d'Estaing, who visited Romania in March 1979, found a Ceausescu who was 'arrogant, disagreeable, and surrounded by corrupt idiots'. Ceausescu lived his whole life in fear that all those around him could betray him. After Pacepa's flight, his distrust of his close collaborators increased. He turned to all kinds of solutions: he took the reins of the Party and promoted his relatives to key positions. In time, he dismissed almost all of his intelligent and upright collaborators. The noose of power tightened more and more. His most trusted advisors, who had fought each other to get ahead, competed in shielding him from unpleasant information. The Second Office, lead by his wife, filtered all information that reached him. Slowly, the court of Bucharest was overrun by an elite of servants who didn't have the courage to tell him the truth, even at the bitter end.

VIII Elena Ceausescu became number two in the government, the first female vice president in Romania. Born Petrescu on November 17, 1916 in Petresti, Dambovita, daughter of peasants, Elena did not finish fourth grade. She made it to Bucharest where she worked in a textile factory, and met Nicolae in 1939. Considered by many a fatal Rasputin, Ceausescu's wife collected academic titles and bylines for books written by others. 'His biggest mistake was that he listened too much to what mother told him. Even a history written today should point out that mother had an ill-fated influence over him', said the son Nicu Ceausescu in 1991 in Jilava prison, in an interview with writers George Galloway and Bob Wylie.Elena became interested in politics in 1972. In 1985, her massive personality cult began. 'In his egomaniacal evolution, Nicolae Ceausescu was, first of all, supported by his wife Elena. She successfully played several roles in his life. On the one hand, she became his surrogate mother taking the place of a real mother who, in the reality of his emotional life, never supported him enough.

Elena succeeded in protecting her husband, accepting him for what he was. But she nurtured a relationship of sick and immature dependency within the couple. She would take care of his health; she would make sure he ate and felt well. She helped him control his stuttering. Throughout these actions, however, she would satisfy her need to control their relationship. She would often manifest this control through the decisions that were made. Nicolae had given her so much power that, towards the end of the Golden Age, she was the one making all the decisions', says psychologist Roxana Dobri.

IX After the Russian invasion of Afghanistan in 1979, Ceausescu once again got into the good graces of the West. He started getting state visit invitations and he was visited as well. In November 1980, he raised the bar at the CSCE conference in Madrid, presenting his plan for a united Europe, from the Pyrenees to the Carpathians, a common European home without the USSR. In 1982, Leonid Brezhnev, leader of the USSR, died. For two years he was replaced by Yuri Andropov, who was 68 years old, a former KGB head, lover of reform, and who didn't see Ceausescu with good eyes. Andropov was succeeded by 73 year-old Constantin Chernenko who was insignificant, senile, very much to Ceausescu's taste.

During this period of Moscow's increased weakness, Ceausescu let himself be talked into extending the Warsaw Pact, having claimed that NATO and Warsaw both seemed unnecessary to him. Furthermore, in 1984, Romania was the only country in the eastern Bloc that participated in the Summer Olympics in Los Angeles. Unfortunately for Ceausescu, in March 1985, Chernenko was replaced by the dynamic reformer, Mikhail Gorbachev. It was the beginning of the end for Ceausescu and the socialist camp.

In March 1986, Gorbachev presented his perestroika and glasnost theses to the 27 th Communist Party of the Soviet Union (PCUS) convention in Moscow. 'The actions of the Party's organizations and of the State have fallen behind the times. Indolence, the rigid method of governing, low productivity, a growing bureaucracy, all of these have cost us greatly', he said. He continued, offering up ideas for which Ceausescu had fought all his life: 'Each nation should choose its own path and decide the fate of its own territory and resources'.

Ceausescu 'the dissident' saw his role as Trojan horse usurped. He, who had been the favorite child of the West, found himself falling in their general disfavor. 'Betrayed' by the West for the third time, Ceausescu once again turned his back on them, fighting tenaciously against the reforms that threatened his socialist world. But he became more and more isolated. Soon he had only one friend – the other old man of communism, the German Democratic Republic's Erich Honecker. For them, the reforms in Poland and Hungary were a nightmare, and they were the only ones to praise the repression of democratic demonstrations in China in June 1989.

Between the 25 th and 27 th of May 1987, Mikhail Gorbachev and his wife Raisa came to Romania. A pompous welcome was prepared for them. Hundreds of thousands of people lined up along the side of the road from the airport to the prepared residence. On the last evening, the Ceausescus had dinner with the Gorbachevs in a distinctive atmosphere. The men ended up arguing. Ceausescu told Gorbachev that he would be better off quitting international politics and worrying about the internal problems of the USSR. Gorbachev accused him of keeping his country in a state of fear after having isolated it from the world.

Also in 1987, 'Red Horizons', the confessions of one of Ceausescu's lieutenants and the Securitate General, Mihai Pacepa, was published. Ronald Regan, the President of the United States, called it 'my Bible for relations with communist dictators'. Radio Free Europe broadcast 'Red Horizons', in episodes, bringing the scandals of the Ceausescu household into Romanian homes.

X Pacepa's betrayal, in July 28, 1978 caused a stir in the Securitate. Ninety percent of the Romanians who worked abroad were spies. Now, they were in danger. Ceausescu was livid. Pacepa made his secrets public, describing him as 'a pygmy in a perpetual state of agitation who would grimace in order to hide his stuttering, spitting on those around him when he spoke. He would only shake his inferiors' hands with three weak fingers, while his eagle eye sized them up'. Heads rolled not only in the Securitate (all those who had had connections with Pacepa), but also in related fields. The entire Foreign Intelligence Service was restructured. Pacepa's reasons for deserting remain unclear, but it seems that he had heard that he would be accused of corruption. He fled to the US and the CIA took care of him.

On March 10, 1989, the New York Times published the Letter of the six communists of the old guard: Constantin Parvulescu, Gheorghe Apostol, Corneliu Manescu, Silviu Brucan, Grigore Raceanu, and Alexandru Barladeanu, in which they asked Ceausescu to change his domestic policies. They blamed him for not respecting the Constitution, for his village-urbanization program, for building the People's House, for his repressiveness in domestic policy, and for ruining the national economy. 'The conspirators' (whose average age was 80) were placed under house arrest.

On October 25, 1989, Gennadi Gerasimov, spokesman of the Foreign Minister of the USSR, announced a switch in doctrine, from the Brezhnev doctrine to the Sinatra doctrine ('I did it my way'). The events in Eastern Europe quickly came tumbling down: the Berlin wall fell (November 10), Todor Jivkov was dethroned in Bulgaria (November 10), the 'citizen's forum' was founded in Czechoslovakia (November 20). In Romania, at the 14th Romanian Communist Party convention (November 22-24), all was well. Ceausescu's five-hour speech was interrupted 55 times by comrades who stood up to applaud him.

On December 4th, Ceausescu left for Moscow in an attempt to save himself. Gorbachev couldn't stand the arrogant Romanian. 'His lips were perpetually smirking to show his conversation partner that he could read his thoughts and that he did not value him. This impertinence and his lack of value for others took on a grotesque form over the years. He transferred these traits, maybe without realizing it, from his courtiers to his partners who usually were the same rank as him or higher', wrote Gorbachev in his memoirs.

Old Ceausescu returned home and began preparing to defend his power. His plans for suppressing a coup d'etat, kept in his drawer, were known only by a restricted circle. Work on these plans had begun back in the 1970s. Two days after he gave a speech condemning the suppression of the Prague Spring, Ceausescu met with Josip Broz Tito, who told him: 'For your own safety, be careful in Romania'. Ceausescu was afraid that the Russians would come after him: he requested safe houses and escape routes, and a radio transmitter to be able to address his people from any location. In 1970, a special unit of the Securitate came up with a secret plan, Rovine IS-70, which involved an escape abroad in case of emergency. At first, the Securitate oversaw the communist leadership and foreign visitors. Its tentacles extended throughout the whole country, as Ceausescu grew older and more paranoid. In 1965, there was a central phone-tapping center and eleven regional ones. Thirteen years later, there were 248 centers and 1,000 portable stations. By the 1980s, the Securitate had become one of the most feared secret police organizations in the world. In 1989 it had 14,259 employees, of which 8,159 were officers. According to Pacepa, each officer had to have 50 collaborators (members of the Romanian Communist Party) and 50 informants (outside of the Romanian

Communist Party). The result was the constant surveillance of the population. In 1971, after a visit to China, Ceausescu called for the establishment of U.M.0920, a special counter-informative unit, whose mission was to protect him against a Soviet coup d'etat. This unit found out about the Dniester operation, initiated in July 1969, a few days after which, contrary to Moscow's recommendation, Ceausescu visited Nixon. Brezhnev, irritated by Ceausescu's nationalism, considered replacing the Romanian. By 1978, U.M.0920 had identified nine Army and Securitate generals whom the Russian First Chief Directorate (PGU) wanted to use in a coup d'etat against Ceausescu. According to Pacepa, many agents recruited by Moscow from the Romanian Communist Party for the Dniester operation were released of their duties, and then repeatedly rotated lest they take political roots or be contacted by Soviet informants.

Also according to Pacepa, the highest ranking victim of U.M.0920 was Ion Ilici Iliescu, one of Ceausescu's favorites. Ruling over the party's vast propaganda machine and national misinformation operations, Iliescu was an intelligent young man who had studied in Moscow, gaining a thorough Marxist education. Ion Iliescu was named Ilici after Vladimir Ilici Lenin, whom his extremist father idolized. Pacepa says Iliescu preferred not to report to his mentor an allusion made by a member of an 'ideological' delegation (and recorded on tape), according to which 'the Kremlin would be happier with Iliescu as the head of the Romanian Communist Party'. In Iliescu's version, Ceausescu would have dismissed him because he had not agreed with his 'little cultural revolution'.

Other victims of U.M.0920: Valter Roman (father of Petre Roman, the future Prime Minister) and Silviu Brucan.

XI In December 16, 1989, the Timisoara revolt began. 1,000 people gathered in the center of town, shouting 'Down with Ceausescu'. A state of emergency was declared. In the middle of the crisis, Ceausescu accused Army and Securitate generals: 'You should be sent before the execution squad. That's what you deserve, because what you have done means fraternizing with the enemy'. Tired and disappointed, Ceausescu threatened to resign. A wave of cries from the Central Committee members for him to change his mind followed; a few women broke down in tears. In the end, Elena persuaded him. 'OK, shall we try again, comrades?' he asked those around him. Before leaving for Iran, he forbade anyone from entering the country if they were not from North Korea, China, or Cuba, convinced that the coup d'etats that had taken place in the German Democratic Republic, Bulgaria, and Czechoslovakia were due to outside help. On December 17, the platoons fired at random into the crowd. The next day, it was quiet in a city under siege.

In December 20, Ceausescu held a telephone conference with the secretaries of each county: he told them that spies were working in Timisoara, accusing the US and the USSR of having made an agreement regarding Romania. That evening on TV, he told the country about the hooligans in Timisoara. The next day, he called a meeting in Bucharest where he promised an increase in salaries and rations. He was booed. The people came out to protest in Bucharest, too; Barricades. The army fired. On December 22, 162 people had already died. The day after the failed meeting in Bucharest, the masses gathered once again in front of the Central Committee, where the Ceausescus had remained overnight. In the morning, the Minister of Defense, Vasile Milea, was found dead in his office.

Ceausescu once again appeared on the balcony before the crowds. Booing ensued again. General Stanculescu, newly appointed Minister of Defense, called a helicopter, pleading with his President to leave the Central Committee building.

'I warned my father that this moment would come and that it would happen this way. The night before he was overthrown, I talked to him for approximately 15 minutes. I implored him to make concessions, to welcome a people's delegation. He was listening but not hearing. Mother told me: Don't be a fool. He always listened to Mother too much', said his son, Valentin Ceausescu to writers George Galloway and Bob Wylie.

The Ceausescu regime's movie was reaching a surrealistic end, and the reel was turning faster and faster. The Ceausescus took the elevator up to the roof. The doors were blocked before the last floor. The bodyguards opened them with blows of their weapons. They climbed onto the Central Committee terrace through a window. They flew to Snagov, where Ceausescu tried to get in touch with the Government, the Army, and the Securitate. Nobody answered. They continued on in the helicopter. The pilot warned them that they could be shot down. They landed on the road in Titu. They stopped a red Dacia, which took them to the village of Vacaresti. They took another car to Targoviste. They stopped at the Aggregate Works of Special Steel where Ceausescu wanted to talk to the workers. They didn't open the gates for him. They went on to the Center for the Protection of Plants in Targoviste. A Militia team came and escorted them to the Inspectorate. The building was surrounded by an angry mob. The Militia car was attacked with stones and followed by several other cars. They fled the city with the two militiamen and hid in the forest near Ratoaia, 20 km outside Targoviste. Only at night were they brought into the Militia building.

Some soldiers took them to the barracks in a white Aro car; they were given military clothes and they were locked in a small, unventilated room. Although they still called him comrade President, comrade Supreme Commander, his tea was sweetened with sugar even though he was a diabetic. Ceausescu was furious. Elena caressed him like a child. On the first night, they slept in the same bed, embracing, and constantly whispering to each other. In the following days, they were locked in a bulletproof TAB vehicle (for their safety, they were told), where they spent their last night.

The former major lieutenant, Iulian Stoica (today an Army Reserve Major), guardian of the Ceausescus between December 22 nd -25 th in the Targoviste garrison, recounts in a TV interview how, on the 24 th of December, Ceausescu verbally attacked his wife (they usually got along very well and took care of each other) when he heard the names of the protagonists of the tele-revolution of 1989. (Stoica had gone out for tea, and he got stuck for 30 minutes in front of the TV that showed incredible things. He told them that he had seen Mircea Dinescu, Sergiu Nicolaescu, Ion Iliescu, etc. in studio 4. Elena, who had the best information cadre, insulted each one of them.) When he heard Ion Iliescu's name, Ceausescu stood up, and started yelling at Elena: 'You didn't let me. You didn't let me do what I should have done. You will see, now he will finish us off, that Soviet spy'.

'It was the first time the two of them had had a confrontation and a heated discussion', says Stoica. He goes on to say that on the night of December 24 th, he thwarted four assassination attempts against the Ceausescus, ordered by colonel Kemenici in hopes of avoiding the embarrassing trial that would follow the next day. Two days after fleeing from the Central Committee building, several members of the National Salvation Front's inner circle gathered around Ion Iliescu in a bathroom at the Ministry of Defense, turned on the faucets so that no one could hear them, and decided what to do with the Ceausescus. On December 25 th, General Victor Stanculescu, with a suite of military personnel and civilians, landed in Targoviste in a helicopter. When Ceausescu saw him, he let out a sigh of relief. 'Don't worry – he told Elena – Stanculescu is here!' Little did he know that the man whom he had named Minister of Defense a few days earlier had betrayed him and had come to prepare his death. The Ceausescus' trial was a masquerade in which even the defense attorneys tried to out-accuse the prosecution. The presidential couple was sentenced to death and lined up with their backs against one of the outhouses in the unit.

Andrei Kemenici, commander of the Targoviste garrison, who had been promoted to General in the meantime (all those who had contributed to this trial were to be rewarded by the new regime), declared in an interview ten years after the trial: 'the hardest part was when I saw the paratroopers trying to tie up Nicolae and Elena. She was begging for mercy and struggling. He didn't struggle. He endured the humiliation. But tears were running down his cheek. He was sobbing. No, he was no longer Ceausescu, he was just a man, and when he was riddled with bullets, I broke down in tears. When he fell, he yelled: Long live the free and independent Socialist Republic of Romania! I don't know if the communist heroes yelled out slogans as they died, as literature would have us think, but Nicolae Ceausescu died exactly like in those books, like in the movies.'

XII 'The Golden Age' Of Nicolae Ceausescu

Four major steps in domestic policy:
The Thaw (1965-1969)
Cultural Revolution (1970-1973)
Romanian Neo-Stalinism (1974-1979)
Decade of Crisis (1980-1989)

Four major steps in foreign policy:
Western political tourism in Romania (1965-1974)
Reorientation towards the USSR and Third World (1974-1977)
Rapprochement with the West (1978-1984)
Anti-perestroika resistance and total isolation (1985-1989)

- 1965 – Nicolae Ceausescu, Secretary General of the Romanian Communist Party at 47, is Europe's youngest political leader to date.
- 1966 – A series of laws prohibit abortion and contraceptives; divorce procedures become more difficult.
- 1967– Corneliu Manescu, Romanian Foreign Minister, becomes president of the UN General Assembly; Richard Nixon becomes the first in a series of western guests to visit Ceausescu during the Cold War.
- 1968 – Defying Moscow, Ceausescu condemns the interference of the Warsaw Pact troops in Czechoslovakia. Wave of enthusiasm in Romania; western interest in 'the Trojan horse of the eastern Bloc'; hypocritical plan of rehabilitation of Dej regime victims, meant to isolate those who propelled him to power.
- 1970 – Catastrophic floods in Romania, 38 out of 39 counties affected, 600,000 people evacuated.
- 1971 – Ceausescu visits Mao Zedong in China and Kim Il Sung in North Korea. He begins to model his cult of personality after theirs; road signs bearing Transylvanian town names in Hungarian and German are prohibited.
- 1971-75 Romania achieves a GDP growth rate of 11.3%, never

again surpassed.
- 1972 – Romania becomes the only socialist country to become a member of the World Bank and the IMF; Ceausescu meets Anwar Sadat, Yasser Arafat, and other members of the Organization for the Liberation of Palestine in Cairo, and begins peace talks concerning war in the Middle East.
- 1973 – The apogee of foreign visits: Iran, Pakistan, the Netherlands, Italy, the Federal Republic of Germany, Yugoslavia, the USSR, several South American countries, Morocco, the US, the Vatican; Romania allows the founding of joint ventures with the participation of western capital (51% Romanian capital).
- 1974 – Ceausescu is elected President of the Socialist Republic of Romania, a position created especially for him; State monopolies seize all rare metals and precious stones.
- 1974-1976 – The West gives up on Ceausescu, who travels there only twice. He reorients himself towards the USSR and the Third World, where he plays the role of credit-lending European.
- 1975 – Romania obtains Most Favored Nation status with the US (renewed yearly until 1988)
- 1976 – The right of settlement in big cities is heavily limited.
- 1977 – In March, a 7.9 magnitude earthquake: 1,570 dead, 11,300 injured, 35,000 households destroyed; in August, the Jiu Valley miners' strike; in October, the new anthem of the Socialist Republic of Romania (based on a text by Ceausescu) and the law that replaced Mister, Mrs, Sir, and Ma'am with comrade or citizen.
- 1978 – The Ceausescus visit Great Britain (June 13-16); the betrayal of the general of the Securitate, Mihai Pacepa (July 28). Foreign Intelligence Service restructured.
- 1979 – At the 7 th Romanian Communist Party (PCR) Convention in November, Constantin Parvulescu, veteran of PCR, 83 years old, rebukes Ceausescu for placing his personal interest above those of the party; cars can be driven every other Sunday, alternating even and odd license plate numbers; The Russian invasion of Afghanistan; Ceausescu is again esteemed by the

West.
- 1979-1981 – The fall of the Shah of Iran; the oil crisis strikes countries with unstable economies, like Romania.
- 1980 – CSCE conference in Madrid in November: Ceausescu presents his plan for a united Europe, from the Pyrenees to the Carpathians; a person may not be in possession of more than one house or apartment.
- 1981– Rationing of staple foods. Drastic measures for energy savings. Gas is scarce; people forced to participate in agricultural work.
- 1982 – Ceausescu orders the rapid payment of foreign debt (almost $13 billion) without taking out new loans; Romania under austere measures without precedent; emigrants' houses and land taken by the state.
- 1983 – Possession of photocopiers prohibited.
- 1984 – The Danube – Black Sea canal is inaugurated, after nine years of construction; any privately owned typewriter must be registered with the Militia; energy crisis; new legal, fiscal, and medical rules for a more efficient enforcement of anti-abortion laws; Romania is the only eastern Bloc country to participate in the Summer Olympics in Los Angeles despite the Soviet boycott.
- 1981-1985 – 750,000 apartments opened for use; the inhabitable surface area per capita is 12 sqm.
- 1985 – Construction begins on the People's House, which was to become the headquarters of the Party and seat of the Government; any conversation between a Romanian and a foreigner must be reported to the Securitate within 24 hours. Romanians are forbidden from hosting foreign citizens if they are not close family.
- 1986 – In March, Mikhail Gorbachev presents his perestroika and glasnost theses in Moscow; minimum wage abolished, payment based on accomplishments.
- 1987 – Mihai Pacepa's book Red Horizon is published, revealing the side scenes of the Ceausescu regime; workers' revolt in Brasov.

- 1988 – Program for the organization of villages; annual per capita rations.
- 1989 – The New York Times (March 10) publishes the letters of the six old guard communists – Parvulescu, Gh. Apostol, C. Manescu, S. Brucan, G. Raceanu and A. Barladeanu – asking Ceausescu to change his domestic policy; the revolt in Timisoara (December 16).; on December 25, the Ceausescus are lined up against the wall of an outhouse and shot by an execution squad in Targoviste.

XIII Psychological profile
By Psychologist Roxana Dobri

His mother did not have enough strength to love and protect him. His alcoholic and irresponsible father's aggressiveness scarred him for life. Nicolae would always avoid this fatherly model, looking for a good father to protect him and offer him security. Since he could not find such a person, he turned into the Romanian people's Father. Because of his parents' relationship, Ceausescu was destined from early childhood to become an ambivalent individual. He was in his element in the conflict between the US and USSR. He defied Russia's authority, in fact defying the paternal authority. He turned into the rebel adolescent who denied his parents – i.e. those who had built Communism in the world, including Romania – in order to throw himself into the arms of a family at odds with his own – i.e. the West. The anger and helplessness that characterized his early years, his youth in capitalist Bucharest were sublimated in the frenzy of grandeur that was going to be sustained progressively by the whole country.

He hid his frustrations and humiliation well, gaining power, gradually but surely, first at home and then on an international level. The system he promoted supported the myth of self-achievement, the rule according to which he overcame his own life history without ever escaping it – promoting peasants' and poor workers' children (like himself). His childhood limitations and poverty probably drove him to the creation of 'the New Man', a humble and ascetic socialist.

Preparing his ascent to the top of the Party, many years before, Nicolae Ceausescu relied on unquestionable qualities. He manifested signs of excellent emotional intelligence abilities that helped him take his destiny into his own hands right from the moment he arrived in Bucharest. Joining the Romanian Communist Party was the only way he could achieve acknowledgement and rapid social ascension. He was servile and submissive to Gheorghe Gheorghiu Dej, who would grant him access to the communist networks of the time. His abilities to negotiate convinced the old Party members that he was the most suitable successor to Dej. His capacity to seduce and convince through humility and submission, to dissimulate, helped him seize power in Romania. In reality, he proved to be emotionally unstable, acting without thinking of the consequences of his own deeds. He was an isolated individual (he had no friends, the only person he relied on being his wife), fierce and angry, critical and evaluating with his employees. His non-verbal behavior during his speeches from the podium or balcony shows a man who is rigid, limited, tormented by his own need to control his speech impediments and his emotions and to be accepted and flattered by the crowd. These were not the personal characteristics of a man who lived the delusive picture of total power and the need to be worshipped, a need satisfied year after year by the millions of people who chanted his name for minutes on end.

Some observers of the time thought that Ceausescu lived in a parallel universe, trying to explain the fact that the hard life of the Romanian people in the '90s was caused by the Party machine and not by the dictator's decisions. I believe that world was the universe that Ceausescu consciously wanted and created – in a socio-political environment that facilitated the delirium of his grandeur – according to the mental pathology with which he lived.

CHAPTER 6

THE NUTCRACKER

How the oldest Romanian seal preserved from feudal times was discovered.

Photo by George Dumitriu

Professor Damian Bogdan was a living legend for the students studying history in Bucharest six decades ago. This famous specialist in Cyrillic and Slavonic languages had an original method of providing documents and ancient objects for his studies. Every holiday he traveled all over the country, plunging into the attics of the villagers, buying old stuff from them. In 1952, while visiting the North of the country, he found in a mill the seal matrix of Alexandru cel Bun, prince of Moldavia (1400-1431). This is the oldest Romanian seal preserved from the middle ages. The miller used it for cracking nuts. The professor bought this precious artifact (photo above) for 10 $ (approximately the cost of twelve loaves of bread). The seal matrix weighted 250 grams and contained 81,5% lead, 14,5% tin and 4% iron. The seal bearing the Moldavian aurochs with a star between its horns was stamped on official documents dating back from

1409 to 1425. Damian Bogdan studied the matrix seal and wrote about it in *Studies and Materials on Middle Age History, vol I, 1956*. In 1970, Romania's National History Museum bought the matrix seal from the professor for 30.000 de lei (the cost of Trabant car), says one of his students, Radu Constantin Coroama, former director at the Romanian National History Museum.

CHAPTER 7

LIFE IN THE SWAMP

Nine true stories about what it's like to be a Gypsy in Romania.

Wherever you are in Romania, – in any city or village –, if you take a 30-minute walk in any direction, you'll find a community of poor Gypsies. Apart from a minority that got rich exploiting barely-legal economic opportunities, for more than two thirds of some one million Romanian Gypsies, the tumultuous years following the fall of communism meant a transition towards hopeless poverty, delinquency and violence. They were among the first laid off during the 1990s restructuring process and many did not manage to get rehired. About 70% of the Gypsies live on a Minimum Income Guarantee (financial aid from the State) and occasional activities. 80% of them have no profession. Like Mocirla ('The Swamp'), almost every poor Gypsy community is affected by the same 'shortages' when it comes to jobs, income, education, access to medical services, identity cards, property titles, and miserable, dirty, over-crowded houses.

This is a story about what it's like to be a Gypsy (Roma) in Romania. A story told by the Gypsies themselves. Over 16 hours of interviews were edited for concision and clarity. Certain regionalisms, flagrant language and grammar mistakes were straightened out, here and there.

II How was Limbos ('Tongue-y') to know that that night would be different? He came down from the hill, talked a bit with some friends by the road, walked into a Cristi Teslaru boutique, the only one in the neighborhood, and stole a pack of underwear. He gave away eight of the pairs to people on the street, like a modern-day Robin Hood, and brought two pairs home to his wife. All this fun cost him two years in prison. Upon his return to Mocirla, he stole a chicken (snapping the neck of another irritating bird and leaving it in the coop) and went back to jail for another year. At 24, Limbos, whose real name is Ciprian Gruia, spent four years in prison and three years in school, two of which he completed in prison. He's a strange young man with quiet, slick, black eyes, a gentle voice that gets caught in his thin mustache, a sandy-blonde curl hanging in the middle of his forehead, a lot of enemies, and restless hands and feet. He had three little children. Now he has one. He found the last one lying dead in bed next to him and buried him.

To the rest of the world, Mocirla is infamous as a thieve nest. To Limbos, it is home. Outsiders who see Mocirla's nearly 200 run-down houses, spread out randomly like a sick swarm of bees on a hill on the outskirts of Buhusi, watching them from their cars while driving to Roman, raise their eyebrows and speed up. Townspeople are afraid to climb up here: most Gypsies have empty bellies, sly gazes, sharp tongues, and quick hands. Every time it rains – and it often does – the mud reaches the knees, and the three roads that climb up from Orbic Street towards the Gypsies, with a 55-degree slope inaccessible to cars, literally turn into mud slides.

None of the nearly 1,000 Roma living on the hill has a job. A few hundred left for Italy and are sending money back home. Those left behind live off stealing, welfare, state child support, and occasional suspicious jobs. Most of the men have been to jail.

Most of the children enrolled in the Buhusi Arts and Crafts school in the Orbic neighborhood are from the Roma community. During the farming season, the majority leave school to work in the fields with their parents. When they come to school, they get bored quickly and leave, unable to be kept in class by any means. Once they reach 16, many abandon school as they're getting married or starting to work.

Until a few years ago, Mocirlans worked in the felt factory in Buhusi. After the factory's restructuring, they were left to get by however they could. They are all waiting for a Messiah with a different face (a second Ceausescu to resuscitate the country, or at least a patron with a lot of money to revive the factory, or an Andreea Marin to bring them on her philanthropic talk show 'Surprises, Surprises' and give them what they need). Mocirla cannot be understood from the outside. You have to go inside. You have to meet the people who live here.

III The Unemployed Man
Vasile Gruia, 56 years old, with nine kids, a wise man among the Gypsies, talkative, charming, a 10 th grade graduate, a former painter in a factory for 31 years. He didn't teach his children Romani because he's convinced it won't help them with anything. He lives on welfare and odd day jobs.

Man, before, in the communist days, if they found out you didn't have a job they'd force one on you! They'd give you a job. You'd have something to live on. But now, nobody asks you, 'Man, where do you get your money from? How do you live? What do you do?' Now people just begin stealing, or do whatever they can. I wouldn't steal, even though I'm tempted by need. Not me, 'cause I don't do that, 'cause I make it on the little I have, but there are families with seven, eight little kids, and when they start crying from hunger, their parent or grandparent or brother will say, 'Come on, man, let's do something, anything, but let's cash in!' And they'll steal something and get seven, eight, ten years in prison.

Here... start at this end of Mocirla and go all the way to the other side, and stop at every house and ask if anyone has a job. No one! What are they supposed to live on? They start stealing 'cause they don't have anything else to do. There's some forest nearby. There are some who have horses. They'll go to the forest and steal a cartful of wood. If it wasn't for them, this whole area you see, and there are another two or three villages – Silistea, Romani, Lipoveni – if it wasn't for them, bringing carts of wood to sell here and there, 'cause they sell it cheaper, I don't even know how these people would heat their houses. Even here, we whine and complain, but there are villages, even farther away from the cities... you should see them. They shake at the sight of a coin. It's hard in this country, really hard!

Don't you see how people with an education, the brighter ones, all leave Romania? To America, to Italy, to Australia... Everywhere! They leave and that's where they end up. 'Cause they didn't know how to value them over here. A doctor here gets five million lei (150 $). And shouldn't he ask you for money when you go to him? Of course he should, 'cause a doctor can't get by on five million (150 $) a month. A policeman gets seven, eight million (240 $) and he has to deal with all those crazies. He can get killed at any time, 'cause there are dangerous people. They'll come out in front of you, and you, as a criminal, say to yourself, 'well, better his mom be the one crying, and not mine', and you kill him. Or he kills you. Here in Mocirla policemen shot people. And what happened to them? Three people were shot. It was fatal, not 'oh, I was defending myself'. He shot straight at them. What happened, man? If it's a law for me then it means it's a law for everyone. 'Cause like they say, the law is everyone's mother...

I was a painter in a factory. And I worked in the factory for 31 years. Can you imagine? 31 years in the same job. Since the day I started until unemployment. They gave us those compensation salaries: they didn't take into account your ability to work; they didn't take into account your qualifications. It only mattered if you were one of the boss' guys. Now I don't even have a pension 'cause I'm not old enough. I have to wait to turn 62. I have that tiny welfare, and, to be honest, without any shame, I'll go here and there and work by the day. There are lots of people that no one will hire; out of fear. They'll say, 'this guy will see what I have in my yard and come and steal it'. So they'll only take people they know have never had any problems with the police. So, you get it. Nothing can get done here. If only there was some company to give them work. If not, it's going to go on like this until the shit hits the fan. The police can't do anything to them, the government can't do anything to them, no one. They'd rather go to jail than hear their hungry kids crying at home.

Look at me: at my age, I tried to work on construction sites. In Bacau and Buhusi, I went to all the construction sites possible. I've been out of a job for two years. No one will take me. I'm over 50. I can't even find any work 'under the counter'. And with the minimum state welfare... why do they even give me those two million? They make me sit around for almost twenty days, and don't give me anything to produce, something that I can benefit from producing, so I can get my minimum wage? There's a guy on the field who clocks you in. But if you go and see the job these boys do there, you'll die laughing. They take a paper from over here, put it over there, hang out over there, and then they send them home and write down four hours.

Give me something to do, man!

IV The Schoolgirl

Let's say her name is Geanina. She climbs a hill, through the mud, and sings soulfully: 'Man, life slips away and all that's waiting for us is a cold grave/Once you're gone, you're forgotten by everyooooooone!' This girl is the devil herself. 'She has green eyes, she's blonde, she loves life, she goes around with boys 10, 15 years older than her', says one of her classmates, Cora, who got married when she was 13. Geanina, an only child, is 14, she's in the sixth grade, and this was probably her last year of school. She's going to get married soon, but only 'with a Gypsy like me, so I have something to talk to him about'. Here, if a girl reaches 9th grade and isn't married, people yell old maid at her. She has had ten boyfriends. She dumped the last one because she saw him with another girl.

I didn't leave him because he's poor. I left him because he doesn't know how to respect me. If he respects me, I'll respect him too. When I got to school, I saw him with another girl. You choose: me or her. And he chose her. But I'm not mad. I'm not his boss. The kid does what he wants. These days I don't go to school much because dad and mom go off and work by the day, and I stay home so no one steals our stuff. Actually, you know, I don't go to school anymore because the boys kidnap you. They kidnap girls around here. If a boy sees a girl he likes, he and his friends kidnap her, they take her somewhere, he sleeps with her, and it's done, the girl is married. They tried to take me once. The boys came to school on horseback, they run us down... He rode in with his friends and took me. I barely got away. I begged him! They dragged me like this. They took me to his house. I was lucky he let me go when my friends Monica and Lacramioara came.

V The Sick Lady

Margareta Avadanei, 49 years old, has a huge tumor on her left leg. She sits in her house like a monstrous doll that her scrawny husband moves from the window to the bed and back. He washes her and takes care of her. She had 400,000 lei (12 $) help from the state that the mayor withdrew when records proved that her husband, Vasile, had received a 200,000 lei (6 $) raise on his pension. She takes a fistful of painkillers, but they don't have any effect anymore. She cries and her voice shakes when she tells her story.

What if I could at least go to the outhouse? What would that be like?! I lie on the bed and I can't do anything. If this good husband of mine turns me over, I turn. If not, I don't. It's hard. I can't go outside. Who will take me out? I stay in the house... my elbows are black from the windowsill. In the morning, he puts me by the window, just like this, all day. I can't take the pain anymore.

I've been like this for 20 years. It started out like a rash. Then it started to grow. And it kept swelling up. Like blisters after you burn your skin. When I'd go to the hospital, they'd treat me, they'd give me some of that spray that heals. But now it doesn't heal anymore. No hospital will even take me anymore. I keep going, but none will take me. They can't do anything for me. And treatments are expensive.

I don't have anything, no pension, no state help. Vasile has a medical pension. Money? From where? I borrowed money from a loan shark, and I'm in debt eight million lei (240 $). I get four, I give back eight. Where am I supposed to get eight million from to pay them back? It's a hard life for me, very hard. Where else can I go? They come and ask me: 'Are you going to give us the money or not?'

Where am I supposed to get it from? Vasile has a hole the size of a coin in his head. And with his stomach, and his bile, the poor guy! For a man to live with this kind of torture every day – it's hard. Another man wouldn't put up with everything I've been through. It'd be hard for him...

Where else can I go? Who else can I talk to? When my parents were alive, I had some support, but now... my parents are dead. Where else can I go? It's hard. They said they'd give me that welfare so I can get treatment. They won't even give me that.

What else can I say, honey, it's hard! I sold everything in the house. I don't have anything left. Open the door over there, so he can see! Everything I had, I sold. What else can I do? If I wasn't indebted to those Gypsies, it'd be different. But now, I can't be thinking about the treatment when they come to my door asking for money. What else can I do? What else can do? I'm dying here.

(*One month after this interview, Margareta Avadanei died.)

VI Il Consigliere

Nae Butuc: A Don Quixote with only three front teeth, thin, and with the ends of his moustache moving up and down with every word. Although he is Romanian, he is the local head of the Roma party and the council member representing the Roma at the mayor's office. You can always find him under his umbrella at one of Buhusi's outdoor cafes. He says he is the protector and friend of the Mocirlans, their link to the mayor and the police. 'A money lender, a loan shark, a crook, and a middleman for departures abroad – for a price', he is described by Buhusi's deputy mayor Vasile Zaharia, and even by some of the Gypsies in the community.

I'm fighting to change our image a little, because there are a lot of untrue stories about Mocirlans. It all starts with poverty. There used to be a community of Roma here, right next to our city who lived with us in the factory. As Buhusi was a monoindustrial city, once the industry fell, everything fell – and from there started the westbound mass migration. I, being Romanian, was working for a company, in supplies and retail, where Gypsies were assigned the lowest-level jobs. That's how I met them. After the Revolution, when the factory began to fall apart and they started to understand hardship, when everyone was creating parties and sub-parties, of course they were open to all those problems and organized their own party. Now I am the Roma's council member at the Buhusi mayor's office, but I come across the same situations as any council member. There is this law, Law 430, forcing mayors to hire us: all community presidents have to be on the mayor's payroll, so we can go to the communities and know how to talk to people in their language, so we can protect their interests… The problem is that mayors are not too sympathetic when it comes to these Roma communities.

It bothers me when I knock on the mayor's door, and I feel he won't help me. But he does help me, because he knows I have the Gypsies backing me and I can very easily start another Hadareni (a violent dispute between Romanians and Gypsies). These people are capable of anything to prove they're right. When they're wrong, they're wrong. I'll give you another example, to base it all on examples: I took five men to jail; five men that had been wanted for three years; after a few talks, they turned themselves in a month later. They went into the chief's office on their own, drank a shot each, and said: 'Chief, take us to jail'. So, it's very painful, but I did that too.

But when they're right, they're right. I have a very good friend who's the manager of a security agency for the Bacau Hydroconstruction Company, that after all the floods, took up a four-year project along the Bistrita River. He asked me to give him 35 people from Mocirla. Last winter, he worked with three of our people and he was satisfied. But these guys have full criminal records. Even in communist times they had trouble with the police. They were the scapegoats. For the times they've been right and for all the injustices committed against them, Hadareni should be a myth.

Their problem is this: what they did was six, eleven, twenty years ago. Romanian law stains you and doesn't clean you. Do you understand, sir? The chief gave me an idea and I think I'll take him up on it, but it's going to be a little hard. Here it is: for everyone who has been in jail, I, as local Roma party leader, have to sue the Romanian government and win their rehabilitation. I have to do this soon. If I want to guarantee these 35 jobs, I have to do it. Thirty-five salaries in their communities mean a great deal. These people are honest by nature. You just have to live among them. To feel them, to understand them. When I'm upset, I come here, I meet up with them, I talk to them, I joke with them, I climb up the hill on this side, they take me with them, I come back down on the other side, and I go home happy.

Mr. Catalin, let me explain to you because I know them best: evil and hate come from inside. For 100 years or more, I don't know how long they've been here, they've been marginalized and stigmatized as Gypsies, Mocirlans, thieves, bandits, wretches, or whatever else they call them. At the factory, the work they did was for much smaller salaries than of the Romanians, because they didn't have an education; very few of them made it. But the authorities didn't take the person into account: Tincoi, or Aurel, or Catalin.

Now we have to be patient, very patient. First of all, I help them become legal. Identity cards, birth certificates, passports for those who want to leave, all those things... from A to Z, starting with the departure. And when they get there, I keep in contact with them, I take their phone numbers. Everything! When they want to come home, they call me, I send a driver, they come back. I have a contract with an agency in Bacau that is especially for them. I work very well with the Police, I go to them almost every week. And when he can, the chief, Mr. Chirilou, who is an extraordinary chief, comes here. If somebody has a problem here, with the mayor, with the police, with anything, I tell them what to do. But I don't just send them there, I go with them personally and take care of it. I am their president. When they make mistakes, I take them to jail. When they don't, I defend them.

(*Three months after this interview, Butuc was beaten up by some Gypsies and was no longer wanted in the Swamp.*)

VII The Young Mother
A woman with inquisitive eyes, with neck length red hair which reveals her round, yellow earrings fluttering in the wind, is sitting at the gate, hands on her hips, half hostile, half gentle. 'It smells like food

here, I just made a stew. It would be nice if I could live in the other house but the water got in and it smells like mould. Just don't say that if you came to the Gypsies, we are less developed and we don't know how to receive guests'. Gabriela Stan, 35 years old, is a tenacious tigress running her own home and her four children (the eldest is in 9t th grade) with an iron hand. She returned from Italy two years ago to take care of her children, her husband is still there and he sends them money every month; she is hoping to leave as soon as possible to Sicily.

Why are those in charge not fixing these roads? I wouldn't want a street like the main road but at least a bit of tarmac so the kids would not get stuck in the mud on their way to school. They should not discriminate us, because we are Gypsies and they are Romanians. We have the same heart, the same eyes; the same mouth. This world is evil. Wherever we go, we don't get priority because we are Gypsies. I used to work at a factory until I got fired in 1998. I got out on a decree. I also received seven million lei (210 $). My husband is still in Italy. I was there for two years. I returned for the children because they are all grown up now and I need to make a future for them. My husband stayed there. But I hope that we can all go back if we find some work for the children. I don't know how we would have managed if we wouldn't have left.

We only got the money from social care three or four times. Everyone would tell me that I have a cow, that I have a horse. I don't know if the cow or the horse gave me money for the basics: meat, potatoes for the children, whatever, if the cow could only say 'here', and put some money in my pocket. People judge badly here. They are very envious. The mayor especially, he upsets everyone. This world is too wicked and I wonder why God is keeping us on the face of the earth. While I was in Sicily, I worked really hard for very little money. Whoever loves to work wouldn't say no, but whoever doesn't... I used to make *formaggio* (cheese), just as you make cheese here, from morning till dawn I was burned by the fire, they were very hospitable people, but very close-fisted.

I got 150 Euros and my husband, Viorel, got 350 as he was

working more. They got paid more. And they wouldn't like to hire one of their Italians, who doesn't work like us, for 500-600 Euros. And I would get a gift every time they saw I was too smart, too clean and too exaggerated, so, in a way they wanted to see if I was Gypsy: but I would tell them my origin, I give you my word that I didn't want them to know. I don't know, someone came with us and told my boss: 'I think this girl is one of those who wear long skirts… And I said: this is not true. They would always ask about the long skirted ones. I said: 'I don't know, I have no idea'. So I was acting smart. Because I worked together with the people in the factory and I know how people are. I wouldn't tell them I was Gypsy because nobody would accept me. Many women left this place and started talking, swearing, doing what you're not supposed to do, selling themselves for five or ten Euros, so…

And they started calling us Gypsies. I was not ashamed that I was Gypsy, but I was afraid of losing my job. If those people found out, they would have fired us on the spot. But the Romanian is still a Romanian. You're looked down upon because you are Romanian, and looked down upon even more because you are Gypsy. When someone came and said 'zingari (Gypsy in Italian) are dangerous, they ammazza persone (kill people)', when I heard that… I thought I would lose my job. And look, to this day, my boss does not know that I am a Gypsy, she calls me at home, she speaks to me, she sends money for the girl. Now my husband sends money, 500 Euros per month, he works on a construction site and does really well, he never imagined he would be able to find such a good job. He has been there for four years and he already makes 1200 Euros per month and we hope he will find something for the children, but something less demanding, I mean, I wouldn't want to work them too hard at such a young age.

Romeo, come here! He is the eldest, in the 9 th grade. I have four children: Romeo is 16, Ionut 15, Cosmin eleven and Bianca 8. I raise my hand at them sometimes, I hit Romeo yesterday. He wants to go out and do whatever he likes, but I don't agree. I don't like seeing him going around, like a bum, being messy, causing trouble. If you want to make a future for yourself you have to work. Romeo is in the 9th grade, he doesn't even know how to write his own signature. I don't even send Ionut to school. He fights with other children, doing crazy things. I told him: you are better off at home. I wouldn't want to break their bones from this age. All that we do, we do for them. We want to lift them up because they are children. I have a husband who's too good to be true and four amazing children. I will work for my children.

My boss, the one I talk to on the phone, she promised me that soon it will be easier with all the paperwork… This is what we hope: to leave.

VIII The Pub Owner

Coming down from Mocirla, a little to the left, there's old Sava's place. It used to be called 'At the Happy Gypsy'. Now everyone just calls it At Sava's. After last night's scene, the pub owner should have bags under his eyes. But morning brings the same calm, rested face. When you see old Sava, a gentle, quiet man of 50, you can't imagine that the night before, he flew out from behind the counter like a hawk among the brawlers and smacked some sense into the fiercest one. Maybe it should be pointed out that many of old Sava's clients are wanted criminals…

I threw them out, the bastards… They're young, I've been in surgery. Otherwise, if I didn't have this hernia surgery, I'd cane them. That's their nature. When there's a scene, Romanians don't come running, but the Gypsies… A Romanian won't jump to save you. Even if someone's about to kill you, they won't get involved. The Gypsies are united, they come running right away, they defend each other, even if they're enemies. When a Romanian beats up a Gypsy, the whole hill comes running.

Well, they don't get drunk every night. But, every now and then, I'll call the police, 'cause that's the only way: they're bad. Last night, my wife called the cops. They were disturbing the peace. They got off easy. They put it on their record and gave them a two million lei (60 $) fine. But then they don't come here anymore. They go up the hill. I told the woman, 'Leave them alone, let them go to hell, 'cause they're dangerous. You'll be one of their enemies. They've been to jail. They're losers. You don't know what to expect from them. They're poor, they don't have anything, but they're mean too, let them go to hell!'

We keep coming down on them... and one day they'll surprise you 'cause they're capable of anything, they have nothing to lose. The woman's brave, but fights mostly with words. She doesn't have a bad heart. But she can't bring them down 'cause they're goddamn fierce.

I've had this booth for about twelve years. Before, I worked as a driver for a merchandise truck, for IRTA. But this new job, ever since I opened the shop, is a lot harder. You saw how easy it is to make trouble.

IX The Old Lady

A handkerchief is pulled over the teary eyes of a tiny, tiny, old lady, with skin like black, cracked clay. At 84, Ioana Gruia is the oldest in Mocirla. At 14, she started working at the Felt Factory in Buhusi and didn't leave until she was old. Her husband died on the Russian war front. She lives alone, she has a four million lei monthly pension, she eats when she's hungry, mostly beans and potatoes. At night, she doesn't sleep much, and cries over the ruined world. It used to be different.

Come on in, honey, come on in. Welcome! Excuse the mess, I can't cope anymore. I say it with fright and shame, honey: I'm weak now. And I don't have anyone to rely on. What am I supposed to do with the four million (120 $) from my husband, dead on the Russian front? You buy food, honey, you buy anything, honey, and, it's hard. In Ceausescu's time it was different. There was bread the size of my head, there was food, salami was nine communist lei (2,5 $) per kilo, fish seven communist lei (2 $) per kilo. Now there's so much hunger, honey. I make a pot of soup today and I'll have it 'till tomorrow. What else can I do? I wake up in the morning, I sweep, I tidy up, I put another pot of beans on the fire 'cause I need to cook myself some food. I send these girls down to the valley sometimes to buy food. I eat beans and potatoes most of the time, 'cause there's no money for anything else. I'll make a bowl of beans and I'll have it for two days. Like I eat a lot?! You can't, when a barrel of wood is two million (60 $). Everything's more expensive. I heard the cigarettes people smoke are 40,000 lei (1,2 $)!

Poor Ceausescu didn't know what else to give, to widows, to orphans. He was good, the poor man. He would see you in a store and ask you: do you have money or not? No? Give her this, give her that; he'd fill your purse. He was good, honey, Ceausescu. I was born in 1921. I was around during Antonescu's time. And when I was born, there were a lot of Gypsies in Mocirla. They worked in the factory. The factory was a pot of gold for all of Mocirla. My parents were at the factory too.

I didn't go to school. I went straight to the factory. When I turned 14, some guy, Cretu (Curly), came to the door, a business man. He went around asking 'You have land? -No. You have land? - No'. He rounded up maybe 100 people, men, women, children and he took them to the factory. The people that didn't have jobs, he took them to the factory. Dad went to the mayor's office, he gave some money, and they wrote me down as 15 years old so I could work. I got into the factory, thank God, the Virgin Mary, and St. Paraschiva.

I got out when I was old. This was my friend – this stick. We would all wait for each other and come home. There weren't cars or buses back then. And we wouldn't go around with boots or shoes in the mud. Nooo, you had your slippers and the men had their moccasins and their pants, honey, and you walked to the factory in the mud, flip-flop, until it drove you crazy.

At five in the morning I would leave home. And I'd be at the factory at six. But I had a good boss. Sometimes I'd come with my feet all wet. You didn't have time to eat. If a pipe was thin, or empty, he'd call you back. I worked 'till I'd burst. But I'd get 1,200 communist lei (360 $). And I built the house on my own, without my husband, 'cause he died in the war. The house is from about 1950.

I worked for 30 years. I didn't steal so much as a string 'cause mom had eight kids and I was afraid of getting fired and starving to death.

And that's how I ended up anyway. But now I'm weak.

If there were factories now – what did that Iliescu do? He disfigured the people – would you see these kids outside? To the factory, honey! But now, where can they go? Where can they go? A bunch of them went to Italy. Gypsies, Jews, Hungarians, all kinds of nationalities left. They leave out of hunger, honey, for work. To the pigs, to the sheep, wherever they can, to the olives, everywhere. You go anywhere out of hunger.

Well, when you get old, you don't sleep like you used to… I can't sleep at night. It's light in the house, I look around, honey, the dog barks at those devils that broke my fence, these criminal kids: they throw rocks, bottles, jars. My fence is their hangout, it's where they meet. From eight to twelve, every night it's a madhouse. They'll break your head if you come between them. You won't even know what hit you when they throw a rock or a bottle or a jar. And they bend over the fence. Crazy kids! It wasn't like this in my day, honey. You couldn't just talk to a girl at night in the street. Her parents would snap your neck! When a boy would come to talk to you, he'd go to your parents first. It's a mess now, honey. My, my, my! They see all that nonsense on TV. I don't have a TV. I don't even want to see or hear any of it.

The world's gone crazy, honey. Girls want to wear their skirts up to their thighs, honey. Well, in my day if you parents saw you like that, or wearing pants, they'd snap your neck like a chicken. My, my, my! It was long skirts, loose, like the Gypsies. It was good. That was the life. You wouldn't see women with their heads uncovered, or with lipstick, or with their nails done. That was the life. A kid of 14, 15 would be in the factory. A boy like you would be a factory boss. The world is ruined, honey! It's not like it used to be. Ask anyone.

X 'The Italian Woman'

She stands next to the table, restless. She taps her fingers on the table or twirls her beautiful hair, dyed red. Cornelia Stan – 31, with two kids, separated from her husband, pretty, vivacious, blue eyed, with a fast tongue – is waiting to go back to Sicily, to her rich, 40 year old Italian. She was there last year, but the carabinieri caught her and sent her back.

If you want to go to Italy, there's Romica Poian with transport. It is more expensive – 300 Euros with customs in Austria and everything – but they take you to your destination. They take care of your passport, here in Buhusi, or wherever you're from. But if you don't have a job secured there, it's better if you just don't leave.

I stayed there six months, and I wouldn't leave the house out of fear of being caught by the carabinieri. As soon as I went out, they caught me. They ask: 'Do you have sogiorno?' If you don't, they put you in a van, they take you to the police station, and ask: mother, father, family, everything? Then they put you in a car and take you to jail. I was in jail for two weeks. It's kind of a migration center with Romanians, Chinese, Italians, Germans, all nationalities. They give you food, clothes, everything. After two weeks, they take you to the airport and they send you back to Bucharest with a ban: you can't go back. But you can go back: you have a civil union with any man and you can pass. On a bus, in two- three days you're there. It's hard. The first time I cried, oh my God! And if you have one of those Italian dictionaries, you pick up the language in no time. It will take you less than a month. Anyway, I'm leaving again. I was there with a 40-year-old Sicilian, and now he calls me, we talk. He has money, and land. He would come here with his car, but he doesn't know his way around and he's afraid of Romania, of being killed. In the end, if he did come, and he had money, I'd kill him myself. I'll find other Italians, now that I know the language. But I'll go to him. I have my man, I don't need money, don't need anything. My mom told me: 'Better a good whore than a bad housewife. If you want to live, girl, go after him. Be smart. Don't leave any tracks, don't leave anything behind'. I'm leaving in a few months. I'll pay the driver and he'll leave me in Tributina, in Rome. From there I'll take a van from Tibutina to Catania. And then, I'll call my Sicilian on the phone and he'll come and get me, ciao, arrividerci.

XI The Teacher

6.30 am. Bundles of smoke-colored fog descend from the surround-

ing ghostly hills. Gabi carefully ponders her every step, zigzagging through fresh cow dung, but her small Cinderella-shoes often sink in the muddy alleyways. Even though she doesn't live in Mocirla but on the neighboring hill, the mud is just as deep. When she gets to the road, she washes her black shoes in a pond and keeps walking towards the school. Gabi Gruia, 29 years old, is a Romani language teacher at the Buhusi Arts and Crafts school. She has a 4,5 million lei salary. She is the only one in the community who went to college, in Bucharest. She lives between two worlds and neither one accepts her completely: she is the intellectual of a Gypsy community with which she cannot identify, while wider society, labels her, even if not openly, as a Gypsy.

Please don't write about me. I don't like it. I usually don't like being praised. I don't want people to look at me like an animal at the zoo just because I am the only one in the community who went to college. What's the big deal? I simply want to be treated like a normal person. My friend, a Romanian language teacher, why doesn't anyone praise her because she finished college? It just feels like something normal to me. I don't dress like a Gypsy, I don't act like a Gypsy. But sir, I am a Gypsy! If you want to accept me for who I am, good. If not, that's fine too. I don't have Gypsy friends. Not even the ones I'm friendly with. It'd be normal for me to feel comfortable around my own kind, to be one of them. But I can't. And it's hard for them too, to accept that one of them can rise above. If you rise above them, it's like they have something against you, because you succeeded and they didn't.

They're afraid of me. I can tell when they talk to me that they're holding something back. They think I have a lot of acquaintances and powerful connections. I think that maybe the only solution for these people would be to be displaced, scattered among the Romanians, a family here, another one there, in different cities, among civilized people. For someone to give them jobs, houses, and so on, so they can do what they see their neighbors doing.

Just about everyone around has seven, eight children. In Bistrita, near here, a family named Buhoi has twelve children. The schoolteacher from over there was telling me that she met with their mother, pregnant in the hospital. She had a mangy kid, with snot around his nose. She asked her why she doesn't wash the child. 'Listen lady, instead of washing this one, I'll just make a new, clean one', she answered. We can't change the world. We have to adapt and move on. I'm not an idealist like I used to be. At school, I know I won't be able to help these children. Before, I was different. I thought I could change them, to save them from this swamp. Now, I've given up. This year, after teachers' strike, and with what Prime-minister did to them, I decided to leave the country. I'm going to go to Italy.

XII **Final picture**

Limbos and another seven or eight men were at old Sava's pub again last night, gathered around a 1 $ bottle of liqueur. They were celebrating one of their returns from Italy: a very big guy, with a tight shirt, with a mean face, with expressionless, predatory eyes that looked you right in the brain. Then, another one came down from the hill, with clay on his head, dead tired. He had worked all day at sticking together a house with clay for 3 $. And with that 3 $, he bought everyone drinks: 'Drink up guys, 'cause now I have money!' The conversation that followed was hypothetical – although the most frequently pronounced word was da burli (fuck) – about what was better: to steal and cash in big all at once or to work honestly for almost nothing? Alone the one that came from the clay, the one that defended working, the one that was made fun of, left, bowing his head and saying, more to himself, 'Whatever! Better I stay here and work than take it in the butt from everyone in jail…'

They hang around like this all the time, fierce, joking.

XIII **On Assigment**

Here we are: two city boys from the Capital lost in Bacau's countryside train station in a downpour, waiting and waiting and waiting. 'Call her', photographer Bogdan Croitoru urges me. The phone rings again and again and again… Not a chance. Not only did the lady with whom we've been in contact – and who was supposed to introduce us to the Gypsy community in Mocirla, Buhusi – wasn't waiting for us at the station as agreed, but she also had her phone turned off. Eventually, we bought some rubber boots and raincoats (it was raining so heavily that the water had risen in the streets), and began wandering around the city. I don't know how we got to a school where there was some sort of a craft exhibition by Roma children from various schools in the area.

There we met Gabi, the Roma language teacher at the school in Mocirla. We told her who we were and what we wanted to do and, unbelievably – the previous series of misfortunes proved to be a wonderful chance – Gabi took us to her house and so we were able (when we had no hope left) to enter and be accepted by the community we wanted to study. The great opportunity of this story was that things didn't work out as planned.

I wanted to tell the story of what is it like to be a Roma (Gypsy) in Romania. But to tell the Gypsies' story you have to become one. And in Romania this is easier said than done. When a Romanian calls you 'Gypsy', his lips distort in a contemptuous grimace: he wants to say you're a thief, you're lazy and dirty... Most Romanians are tolerant of foreigners, but the Gypsies are considered inferior, someone you don't want to be around. A recent study shows that 75% of Romanians don't want to live near a Gypsy community. There are five important trends that emerged after Ceausescu's fall in 1989, when the Gypsy issue emerged in a whole new perspective in the Romanian society:

- Rise of an active ethnic and political movement among the Roma,
- Enrichment of a small segment of the Roma population through the use of 'almost' legal economic opportunities,
- The growing impoverishment of the majority of Gypsies without any hope of correction,
- Growing delinquency and violence,
- Outburst of conflict between groups of Romanians and Roma people.

Gypsies were often the first to be laid-off from jobs in the early 1990s, and have been among those most persistently blocked from re-entering the labour force. Labour market exclusion perpetuates the poverty cycle and lowers living standards. Many Roma have limited future opportunities to climb out of poverty due to low development conditions and long-standing discrimination – including lack of education, poor health and limited opportunities for participating in social and political life.

The Gypsies are a very heterogeneous population. There are Roma people in 262 towns and 2.686 townships, in 40 Romanian counties. How can you choose a representative Gypsy community as a model? Yet all the Gypsy communities are affected by the same problems – lack of jobs, income, education, access to medical services, IDs, property rights, overcrowded residential areas, etc. I was convinced that, in a small Gypsy community chosen on scientific sociological criteria, all the issues affecting the larger Gypsy community could be found. For example, from the small village school one can infer the story of the Gypsy education. The rich of the village can stand for that minority of Gypsies who gathered incredible wealth in the troubled years after Ceausescu's fall. The one arrested by the village Police can speak about Gypsy delinquency. And so on.

I ended up choosing Mocirla (the Swamp), on the outskirts of Buhusi, on completely subjective grounds. There are hundreds of cases in Romania in which Gypsies are isolated and isolate themselves. What drew me here was a name that stroked me in a sociological report: one of Mocirla's unofficial leaders was named Catalin Gruia. My name! I took it as a sign that I had to go there. I had to meet 'Bursucu' (The Badger) – the Gypsy Catalin Gruia – and we did not like each other at all. He was on the side of those Mocirlans who were wary of the fact that my name was also Gruia... I forgot to tell you that I was shocked to discover that half of Mocirla is named Gruia. And if at first I thought this matching of names would be an advantage – I quickly became everyone's cousin – during the last few days, it backfired. People at the bar were starting to say that we weren't really journalists – photographer Bogdan Croitoru and me – but spies from Bucharest and that we want to overthrow Nae Butuc, the community's unofficial leader. (Gabi had a smoldering conflict with the informal leaders of the community, who called us to the tavern to find out what was up with us...)

All this happened as some Mocirlans would have liked to find a young Gypsy king with connections in Bucharest to solve their problems. All the prerequisites are in place for such a man to come along, raised in the community or returning from Italy, able to unite them all and transform a bunch of firewood thieves into a real organized mafia.

XIV Gypsy Clans
Why and how are Gypsies divided into clans?

In the past decades, more and more Gypsies have forgotten or have begun to ignore the tribes they belonged to. A third of the Roma in Romania no longer define themselves as members of a particular clan, according to a 1992 study by sociologists Elena Zamfir and Catalin Zamfir. Most of those who still consider themselves part of a clan are: settlers (13,8%), braziers (5,9%), woodworkers (4,5%), tin workers (3,7%), silk weavers (3,2%), bear trainers (2,7%), brick layers (1,5%), Gabors (1,4%), and florists (1,2%). As in India the family profession was, as a rule, inherited and practiced in the family – the secrets of the trade passed down from father to son – the majority of the Roma clans have been formed, some since the migration towards Europe, around various occupations with which Gypsies earned their living. The main Gypsy clans in Romania and their characteristics:

Blacksmiths
Occupation: Manufacturing of iron tools and objects.

History: They held a monopoly over iron manufacturing throughout the Romanian Medieval Ages. In the 20th century, many became farmers, industrial laborers, or construction workers. After 1989, few blacksmiths who remained in the towns still make wagons and tools.

Characteristics: They were wealthy Gypsies, among the first to settle down, but also among the first to lose their language. The majority of their descendants have lost their Gypsy identity.

Tin Workers

Occupation: Tin-coating the pots and dishes of pension owners around whose houses they would periodically settle; begging.

History: After collectivization, the majority became farmers.

Characteristics: They are the descendants of the Turkish Roma. They were among the poorest Gypsies; they traveled in tilt-wagons pulled by oxes.

Bone Carvers

Occupation: They manufactured objects from animal bones (ex. combs, handles, ornaments).

History: After industrialization decreased demand for their products, the bone carvers became mainly trash collectors or dealers of feathers or kitchen plates.

Characteristics: Bone carvers are the descendants of Indian ivory workers.

Braziers

Occupation: Manufacturing of buckets, pans, pots, alembics, glasses, and so on from brass foil or, more recently, from aluminum.

History: From the beginning, they lived in tents, traveling in colored wagons. Many have maintained their traditional lifestyle until very recently. Of all the Gypsy clans, they were the last to settle down.

Characteristics: Among the braziers, the position of *bulibasa* (chief) is maintained and the kris is still practiced by the community elders.

Woodworkers

Occupation: Searching for and working of gold, carving of soft-wood, berry picking.

History: From the end of the 18th century, when finding gold became increasingly difficult, the woodworkers dedicated themselves more and more to wood-carving.

Characteristics: Woodworkers are the descendants of the old

Indian goldsmiths; they are known as bath makers, spoon makers, and dish makers.

Settlers

Occupation: Various jobs for boyar courtyards or monasteries; agriculture.

History: Gypsies of the hearth were tied to the land before slavery abolition and the 1864 agricultural reform. Several decades after the emancipation laws, the notion of settlers became synonymous with sedentarization. Many Gypsies without trades or plots of land entered the settlers' family.

Characteristics: The Roma of the hearth were the first to lose their traditional language and way of life. The settlers are the most integrated within the majority of the population.

Fiddlers

Occupation: Music

History: The fiddlers are a clan that detached themselves from the settlers in the middle of the 20th century.

Characteristics: The fiddlers from rural settings played at celebrations and were farmers by day. In the city, they were more specialized and lived easier lives. Some of the most talented became renowned musicians.

Florists

Occupation: Flower commerce

History: They are a relatively new clan which appeared in the interwar period.

Characteristics: They are the most homogenized, and relatively rich, Roma category.

Bear trainers

Occupation: Training bears.

History: Their forefathers were magicians, trainers, tightrope walkers. During the middle age, they wandered through towns and cities with trained bears, earning a living from shows. After the profession disappeared at the beginning of the last century, bear trainers learned the trades of other clans.

Characteristics: After settling down, they formed relatively compact groups, maintaining their language and tradition.

Gabors

Occupation: Commerce, tinsmithing, modern professions.

History: They are Roma from Ardeal who took their name from the landowner of the estate on which they worked.

Characteristics: They do not have a specific trade.

Copers

Occupation: Commerce with horses.

History: although it almost disappeared, their clan slowly came back to life in the last 15 years, mostly in Arad, Brasov and Braila counties.

Characteristic: They were specialized in the 'youthening' and healing of horses.

Silversmiths

Occupation: Gold and silver decorations manufacturing.

History: Excellent craftsmen, they represented the elite of the Gypsy clans. Today there are very few left in Bucharest, Teleorman, Ialomita, and Tulcea counties.

Characteristics: Within the community, traditional trying and marriage is still practiced.

XV On the Bed of Procust

Throughout the centuries, Romania's faces and society have shaped the Gypsies.

In the middle ages, although enslaved, most Gypsies remained nomads after their arrival in Romanian territory, scouring the country in hoards – on established routes – to win their keep with their crafts. They would spend the winters on their masters' estate and pay an annual tribute. The progressive boyars who freed them through the emancipation laws of the mid 19th century wanted to settle them, turning them into tax-paying peasants. After the 1864 agrarian reforms, Gypsies became small land-owners. Yet many refused the land, taking instead advantage of their newly-acquired freedom to resume to nomadic lifestyles. Between 1942 and 1943, Marshal Ion Antonescu, convinced that he was ridding the country of parasites, deported to Transnistria 25,000 nomadic and sedentary Gypsies with no means of support, or who had been charged with various offences. Only 10,000 survivors returned to Romania in the spring of 1944. The communists wanted – and succeeded for the most part – to turn the Gypsies into laborers, integrating them, sometimes forcefully, into modern lifestyles. Officially, Gypsies were no longer considered a separate ethnicity; they were sent to school, and were guaranteed jobs and houses. The turmoil following 1989 was a crossroad for the Roma population who went in two opposite directions: while some took advantage from the old regime's burial, most of the others slid down a slope of inescapable poverty.

XVI **Short History of the Romanian Gypsies**
- 1385 – The first documented recording of Gypsies on Romanian territory. Dan the First, ruler of Wallachia, gives to the Tismana monastery, among other gifts, 40 homes for the Gypsies.
- 1855-1856 – The abolition of Gypsy slavery, both in Moldova and Wallachia.
- 1855-1880 – A few decades after the emancipation, the seasonal variations of traditional nomadic lifestyle turn into chaotic vagabondage. The second great Gypsy migration towards the West begins.
- 1900-1940 – Traditional Gypsy professions begin to decline, facing competition from advancing industries. A Gypsy intellectual elite emerges, calling for the 'emancipation and reawakening of the Roma people'.
- 1942 – 1944 – 25,000 Gypsies are deported to Transnistria.

- 1977 – 1983 – The last 65,000 nomadic and semi-nomadic Roma are forcibly settled due to a PCR (Romanian Communist Party) program. Local authorities are ordered to secure them with housing and jobs.
- 1980 -1990 – After the economic crisis, a part of the Roma population returns to the traditional way of life, but with a modern twist. These Gypsies become specialists of the black market.
- After 1990 – Ion Cioaba, Octavian Stoica and Nicolae Bobu are the first three Gypsies to be elected to Parliament.

CHAPTER 8

THE GRAPES OF HOPE

The Rebirth of the Romanian Wine.

Much like a student who failed the subject for a century, Romania now rehearses the components of an equation which proved to be successful in the interwar period: favorable natural conditions + solid investment + legislative support + Western technology & knowhow = good wine. Nowadays, in Romania, the EU's fifth wine producer, almost 445,000 acres of vineyards are undergoing a metamorphosis under the watchful eye of local and foreign investors. Yet another interesting phenomenon is taking place in the comet's tail: after half a century during which spritzers with semi-sweet whites reigned supreme, an aspiring segment of the Romanian population is developing a taste for quality wines.

Wine is a sort of litmus test for a population's degree of sophistication. People need time, information and a broad variety of experiences in order to become more refined, to learn, to develop their taste and respect for quality. Communism destroyed almost every aspect of local colour (or terroir). In doing so, it also destroyed the population's taste for quality. Lately, consumers have become able to tell the difference. They experiment, they read up, they learn that a Cabernet Sauvignon with a touch of tannin and a slightly stronger structure is not recommended for salads and should rather be paired with rare steak. Still, the fans of quality wine remain few. If they are at all like me, Romanians who have just converted to the cult of wine are still fumbling, learning, discovering, seeking. Most of us are like children still learning the alphabet: we can't write words of praise to wine, let alone form sentences.

I On a scorching hot late-August afternoon, a young man with hair and pants coloured like wine walks, deep in thought, between thick-trunked vines, lined up on concrete poles with rusty wires. He stops here and there, pecking grapes, smiling oddly, halfheartedly, analyzing them from behind black, thick-framed glasses, on which a film of dust had settled. And his fingers pick grapes automatically, to get homogeneous samples from the plot. It is the fall of 2010 and Ghislain Moritz, the French enologist of the Avincis Winery in Dragasani, is assessing grape maturity in the vineyard, preparing for his first vintage in Romania. He tastes a Feteasca regala grape and an idea sparks into his mind.

Ghislain trained at the Burgundy school, where he worked between 2000 and 2005 and where good wine is at home. But he quickly realized he had to escape from this paradise where things are thoroughly established and a wine professional can remain in the same job until death.

He started sending out his resumé to Romanian wineries, but without success. He went to Portugal on a contract in 2009. Just then he received a reply from baron Jakob Kripp from the Prince Stirbey Winery, who told him he already had a German enologist, but a neighbor from Dragasani was building a new winery. „He gave me the contacts. Mr. Stoi, Stoi-something..." He sent an email to the Stoicas, told them he was just starting a contract in Portugal, apologizing for not being able to come meet them in Romania. The reply came instantly: we, too, are in Portugal, on vacation. „Within 3 days, we were meeting in Lisbon for coffee. Destiny!", he said.

This is how Ghislain Moritz ended up in Dragasani in the spring of 2010. He started studying about the vineyard, about varieties and climate. He spent the next few months talking to locals, wine growers, agronomists from the research stations in the area. He learnt about local varieties, about what had happened there between the wars, about what works and what doesn't. And now, before the magical moment of harvest, here he is assessing grape maturity in the vineyard: he takes a few grapes from each plot and tests them, in order to determine sugar content, grape acidity, etc. And this Feteasca regala grape that burst in his mouth like a Proustian madeleine... The thing that struck him from the very beginning is the concentration of tannins in the skin – very interesting for a white variety. It had a crisp acidity, a sign that there was an elegant structure and a potential to vinify a remarkable product. He decided to vinify it like a Chardonnay from Burgundy. So: nine months of barrel fermentation for a part of the wine, then assemblage with the rest, to balance it, so that it is more than just a barriqued wine. „And, after a while in bottles, it became a fantastic wine, with a floral aroma and a fine taste, like a Romanian summer apple. Unfortunately, there are too few bottles left from this vintage. Feteasca regala was quite neglected during communism and has an undeserved bad image today. But I, for one, whenever I find a bottle and open it, I recall the adventurous beginnings", he says.

Since December 2010, when the Avincis winery was finished in Dragasani, Ghislain has lived here with his Columbian wife. „There are enologists who make wine remotely, by phone, but I prefer to go through every stage of the process."

Ghislain Moritz is part of the new wave of winemakers in Romania, along with Oliver Bauer (of Prince Stirbey), Laurent Pfeffer (Corcova), Mihai Banita (Lacerta), Balla Geza (Minis), Aurel Iancu (SERVE), Lorena Deaconu (Halewood) or Aurelia Visinescu.

Their passion and experiments create a sparkling dynamics which promise to restore domestic wine to its interwar heyday.

II Grapevine is deeply rooted in the Romanian territory. Greek legends say Dionysus was born here. The old Dacians also had a similar god – Sabazios. At the beginning of the first century, the whiny Ovid, exiled to Tomis, wrote to Rome about how he suffered during the terrible winters in Pontus while drunk Dacians were cutting the frozen wine with an ax. Burebista (82-44 B.C.) failed in his attempt to eradicate grapevine and the Romans conquered (101-106 A.D.) a Dacia where grape was celebrated. On the „Dacia Felix,, medal, minted by Trajan in 112, the Roman province of Dacia is personified as a woman with two children holding grapes and ears of wheat.

The tradition of grapevine cultivation continued throughout the next two millennia, the transformed wine often accompanying ritualistically the lives of Romanians from baptism to death.

„The wine transformed into the Holy Eucharist is given to infants at baptism and to people at major holidays. Wine and bread accompany the bride and groom at their wedding, and at the end of life, before the body is received into the bosom the earth, it is sprinkled ritualistically with oil and wine", says Savelovici Rodica Emilia, historian, ethnographer and curator at the „Crama 1777" Museum in Valea Calugareasca.

Local wines were noticed by travelers who arrived here in the Middle Ages. The abundance in Moldavia, where „at harvest time, a bucket is sold for four coins, and in winter - for six or seven", was recorded by Marcus Bandinus, the Catholic missionary, in his 1646 Codex Bandinus. It was also him who noted that the name of the village of Cotnari allegedly came from the first vineyard grower in Moldavia, a Kotnar sent here by the king of Hungary. Bishop Anton Verancsics (1504 - 1573) praised Transylvanian wines: „Whether one wants them strong or weak, harsh or sweet, white or red, they are so pleasant in taste and of such good variety that one no longer desires the wines of Falern or Campania; and even when comparing them to each other, one likes these much more." Frenchman Virgile Doze, after a journey of one month in Moldavia, published in Brussels, in 1857, a book by the same title where he noted: „A few boyars are making wines with much care, rivaling the great wines of Hungary... A small colony of wine growers from around Montpellier brought to Moldavia would immediately perform an entire transformation that would result in an annual income of several million francs."

On the brink of the modern era, medieval vineyards of princes, boyars and monasteries have become the estates of Romanian high society – with manors and holiday residences, vast and cool cellars and fragrant gardens.

Phylloxera (*Daktulosphaira vitifoliae*), a tiny pest that destroys grapevine roots, overturned this patriarchal activity. It reached Romania during the last three decades of the 19th century, more than 20 years after it had ravaged Europe.

In 1877, botanist Dimitrie Ananescu brought a few infested grapevine cuttings from France, which he planted in his vineyard on the Chitorani Hill near Ploiesti. The presence of phylloxera was officially confirmed in 1884, when thousands of hectares of old Romanian vineyard had already been destroyed. They proceeded with rushed enthusiasm to replace the indigenous varieties with various hybrids (which were given Romanian names, by ear: Delaware – *delivara*, Seibel – *zaibar* or Terras – *tereaza*, Isabella – *capsunica*), along with grafting indigenous vines on rootstocks brought from overseas. The great sin of the resistant and highly productive hybrids is that they give wines that are prone to become sour and low in alcohol.

The bohemian epigrammatist and wine expert Pastorel Teodoreanu bitterly noted that „the anarchy of the replanting done according to everyone's fancy, the ignorance and cupidity of producers came to complete the work of destruction..."

In addition to hybrids, French varieties – Pinot noir, Cabernet Sauvignon, Merlot, etc.– with which the vineyards were replanted, as well as information, technology and specialists were massively imported, mainly from France. Many of the rich of those times did as boyar Vintila Bratianu did; he brought August Joseph Ville, one of the most renowned enologists of the time, to his Samburesti estate in 1915. The Frenchman recommended to clear all vineyards and replace them with French noble varieties. No sooner said than done. Replanting the estate was an inspired move: Samburesti was awarded the gold medal at the 1926 World Exhibition held in Paris.

Another positive example is the Crown Estates, the first high performance centre of agriculture, animal husbandry and logging. (In 1884 the Romanian Parliament decided to stop funding the royal house, which in turn received the right to manage 12 of the 1,200 national estates.) During its first 20 years, the Royal Estate of Segarcea played a major role in saving indigenous varieties and European noble varieties whose existence was endangered by the attacks of the *phylloxera*. Until the winery was built in 1908, the grapevine nursery in Segarcea had a crucial contribution in replanting affected vineyards in the southern part of the country. Later becoming a royal vineyard, the estate has been quality-oriented since the beginning. Planting was done scientifically, the varieties being selected to perfectly match the soil and climate. The quality of wines created here led to the recognition of Segarcea as a

Protected Designation of Origin in 1929. Between the two world wars, Romania tightened its relationships with Germany and Austria, from where new varieties, technologies and capital, and also spritzer came. The state supported the wine world with a favorable legislative package, research institutes and more, smoothing the way to more medals in international competitions. Those were the glorious times when prince Anton Bibescu, Marcel Proust and their friends enjoyed the Corcova wines in Paris or when the aszú wine of Minis was the Habsburgs' favorite.

„According to a tradition passed along generations, viticulture in the Romanian regions accentuated its characteristics differentiated by vineyards. Assortments were defined, from varieties well-adapted to local conditions, cultivation practices by region were naturalized, particularly in terms of vine stock training and pruning, the specific features of wines were accentuated. The assortment of the old vineyard of Dragasani included, for instance, the Cramposie, Braghina and Gordan varieties, which were harvested together, producing a wine that was in great demand (they used to say: 'Cramposia yields the strength, Braghina brings the foam and Gordan fills the barrel')" - wrote Mihai Macici in 1996 in his book Vinurile Romaniei (Wines of Romania).

Then came communism which, as of 1948-1950, nationalized the vineyards, destroying all local characteristics or quality differences. The Party was interested in mass production at a low cost. Trucks loaded with grapes from everywhere carried them to some big winemaking complex, where the new wine for the new man came out on the conveyor — table wine, for the masses, neutral, without personality, white or red, just wine, undifferentiated, cheap. This direction was fueled by the thirst of the USSR, where huge amounts were exported in the '60s and '70s. Politics dictated frenzied exports and too few Romanians came to enjoy good wines, getting accustomed to the spritzer made from semi-sweet white wine. However, viticulture made progress during communism too: the regime invested massively in plantations with valuable varieties and research institutes, introduced mechanization and built modern winemaking complexes.

III On his way back from Fintesti, where he had visited a winery, Cristi Pitulice, the owner of a travel agency and wine critique at vinland.ro, stopped by at Lidl supermarket in Mizil, remembering recent online chats. With sunglasses on top of his head, he rummages through the wine stall, stuffing his shopping basket with 2 or 3 bottles of French, a German sparkling wine, six or so from California, five Romanian ones. He found the prices incredible: wine from Gramma – an honest Aligote at 7,99 lei, Alsatian Pinot Blanc at 11,99, Californian Shiraz at 13,9 – due to the wave of joy, he failed to read „half sweet" on the label, a reason for great chagrin later –, Rioja at 29, Chateau d'Eck at 70. After evaluating them again while he arranged them in the trunk of the car, he went back to the store and bought all the sparkling wine from Halewood, which was at about half the usual price. Some 40 bottles in total, for which he paid 640 lei, the equivalent of some 160 $ (only at home did he discover on the receipt a troublesome bottle at 70 lei). The check-out girl was looking at him with such big eyes that he felt compelled to tell her a credible lie: „It's for a christening..." „I'm not at all crazy about Lidl, but in terms of wine offers, they're really OK", he said.

After a heavy drinking spree in college, Cristi Pitulice gave up hard liquor and beer and converted to wine. But not as a layman, but as serious servant of the cult. „Over these years, I've seen in Romania just about every side of the winemaking landscape. From giant estates following the socialist model, from peasants producing some awesome wines after toiling an entire summer on a patch of vine to wineries with state-of-the-art technology, perfectly aligned vineyards and elite winery science."

Cristi represents a generation of young, well-traveled, open-minded individuals willing to learn and discover wine; one of the neophytes who on some Thursday evenings headed for Richard Fox's wine store.

Out of place among the monumental villas on Bucharest's Dacia Boulevard, like a red mushroom popping up randomly in a double row of stubby stumps – the Englishman's store is as small as a communist garage behind an apartment building, but stylish, well-arranged and full of bottles of good beverages. Every Thursday evening, from 6 p.m., free tastings pack the place with wine fanatics.

The teacher will be here – a badger in his den, surrounded by bottles, chatting about wines faster than an Italian; he has the habit of repeating the last three or four words at the end of a phrase. After 12 years in the UK as a wine expert, Richard came to Romania five years ago, with his French wife, and continued doing what he knows best. He started his business at just the right moment: 15 years ago there weren't any of the wines that are found on his shelves now. „Probably more than 75% of Romanians continue to drink house-made wine, produced by them or by relatives from the countryside, but, slowly, more and more have come to buy good premium bottled wine", Richard Fox says. 85% of his clients live close to the store. „I'm estimating they are that top 5% of Romanians who can afford paying an average of ten euros for a bottle." On Thursday evenings, Richard wins more followers, creating a network of future wine lovers. People come to tastings where producers offer the wines and perhaps they leave the store with a bottle, but more importantly for Richard, people come to him for the experience, for the conversation, because they want to discover, to try something new. Every week, the Englishman preaches like the fathers of the church in the early centuries of Christianity. His audience consists mostly of 30-35 olds, very eager to learn, well-off, working good jobs. Their parents have gotten used to the wine made during communism. „This is the reason many older Romanians prefer semi-dry and semi-sweet wine, they grew up with it, it's an acquired taste. A lot of wine was so bad, they used to put sugar in it so they could drink it. But youth is the future", Richard Fox says.

IV In a 2010 interview, dr. Ion Pusca, founder of Vinul Romanesc magazine, complained that while the Western world has replaced hybrids with grafted vineyards, Romania became, after 1989, one of the world's biggest hybrid wine producers. In the interwar period there was a national program for reducing hybrid vineyard areas. The communist law of vineyards and wine of 1972 stipulated the same. From 93,000 ha in 1980, the area occupied by hybrids decreased to 58,000 in 1990. Then the direction reversed and in the first 14 years after the revolution at least 70,000 ha of noble vineyards disappeared. Immediately after 1989, pride and stupidity were endangering precisely the noble varieties.

The post-phylloxera rushed enthusiasm from 130-140 years ago, the thoughtless clearing and replanting of vineyards, was repeated after the fall of communism – those who were well-off went with famous international varieties, those uninformed and unpretentious, with cheap hybrid varieties. Giving back vineyards to their former owners also brought a tsunami of fragmentation and destruction (many of the small areas returned to farmers have been cleared). The bitter legacy of that well-meant measure is that we continue to have about 894,000 grapevine agricultural operations on areas of only 0,20 ha, on average.

At the same time, the big state-owned farms were privatized and became industrial wine producers dominating the internal market: Murfatlar, Jidvei or Cotnari. The orientation toward quality wine only appeared about 15 years ago, with small wineries. The SERVE winery paved the way for quality wine in 1994. Other producers followed, from Dealul Mare, Mehedinti, Recas, Minis or Dragasani. Currently there are about 70 small and medium vineyards focused on quality wine. A small vineyard only survives if it goes with quality; it cannot produce huge amounts at a low price to make a profit. „You need millions of bottles if the aimed profit is one cent per bottle. If you make only 100,000 bottles, you must aim for quality", says baron Jakob Kripp of Prince Stirbey.

The new owners of small vineyards (about half of them are foreigners – French, Italian, Austrian) have imported technology and specialists from the West. Romania – who joined the EU in 2007 with a good variety of grapes, but with technology and equipment that were good for scrap – has several pockets of nature ideal for cultivating grapevine. But in order to make quality wine you need expensive equipment and expertise. Which is not accessible to any farmer working on his backyard vineyard. The initial investment can be excessive. Alfred Michael Beck spent over 7.5 million euros since starting the Liliac winery project in Batos in 2010. The European funds, 42.5 million euros per year allocated to Romanian viticulture between 2009 and 2013 and 47.5 millions between 2014 and 2020, are as welcome an aid as substantial.

V On August 25, 2015, eight international masters of wine met at Valea Verde in the village of Cund, Mures, to assess top-quality wines from Romania and the Republic of Moldova.

Five months earlier, Marinela Vasilica Ardelean, the soul and mind behind this project, began her forays into some 90 wineries from Romania and the Republic of Moldova. She tasted almost 3,000 wines, choosing the best ones. Marinela is a wine expert and is about to become the unofficial ambassador of Romanian wine. Her guests at Cund, three masters of wine – Caroline Gilby, Rod Smith and Luiz Alberto, together with Paul Robert Blom (international wine taster – Netherlands), Helmuth Koecher (president of Merano Wine Festival – Italy), Zoltan Szoverdfi-Szep (President of ROvinHUd – Romania), Cosmin Grozea (international wine taster – Romania), Mi Yeun Hong (journalist and international wine taster – Korea) spent two days in the rustic hall of Valea Verde Resort, split into four teams, each reigning over a table with scores of glasses nicely aligned on white tablecloths; they tasted and assessed approximately 250 wines with points from 3 to 5 (3 = good, 4 = very good, 5 = excellent). Their favorites will go into a 300-page guide to be published in March 2016. „Small wineries were the most successful, and I think this guide will be a real revelation for the Romanian wine industry", said Marinela Ardelean, the young, beautiful president of the jury. The Wine Book of Romania will help us make an informed choice when shopping for good wine.

But as patience is not exactly one of my virtues, and I didn't want to leave empty-handed in anticipation of it, I asked Marinela to give me a personal top 10 of the best Romanian wines of the moment. She didn't agree at first, but in the end I managed to put down the following list:

Revelatio, 2014 - Davino; Feteasca Regala & Pinot Gris, 2013 - Avincis ; Sauvignon Blanc, 2014 – Clos de Colombes; Selected Cramposie, 2013 – Bauer winery; Sweet Tamaioasa Romaneasca, 2013 - Prince Stirbey; Clarus, sparkling wine from Mustoasa de Maderat, 2013 - Wine Princess; Rose Cabernet Sauvignon, 2014 - Cepari; Cuvée Alexandru Cabernet Sauvignon, 2007 – S.E.R.V.E., Principele Radu Merlot anul I, 2010 - Tohani Estates; Pinot Noir

Private Selection, 2013 – Liliac.

VI A vineyard is a long- and very long-term investment that swallows money and calls for patience. Most domestic producers lack both. And they end up using unrealistic prices.

„If I have 20 euros to spend on a bottle, do I give it for a Romanian wine? For that money I can buy a better wine from Spain or France, from an old winery, from well-established winemakers, therefore of a better quality. Fortunately, the local market has been flooded recently with quality imported wines. For 15 lei you can buy an excellent Spanish wine", Richard Fox says. Romania imports at least three times more than it exports. In 2013 367.4 thousand hectoliters, worth 39.8 million euros, entered the country, especially Italian (24%), French (18%) and Spanish (14%) wines. „Imports make local market prices stay fair. However patriotic you may be, you'll want diversity, you can't drink Romanian wine every day", Richard Fox says.

The export market was, of course, larger 20 years ago, but only in quantity, not in turnover. Romania traditionally exported wine in bulk, for 30 cents per liter, sometimes cheaper than water. The wine wasn't necessarily bad, but the dumping price has done great disservice to reputation.

„20 years ago, I remember you could buy in the UK extremely cheap Pinot noir from Romania. It was the type of wine you drink as a student", Richard Fox says. Perception of Romanian wine has improved, but it isn't brilliant. Unfortunately, many Romanian exporting producers want to quickly recover their money. But on the global market competition is enormous. In the UK, where all wine is imported, the consumer has a choice from a huge selection. „Romanians are privileged to be in the EU, but they must be realistic about the price. A long-term strategy is necessary, to be able to lose money in the first years, before taking root, to expect profit sometime around year 7", Richard Fox says.

According to data from the Wine Exporters and Producers Association of Romania (WEPA), approximately a third of exported Romanian wine goes to the UK, a quarter to Germany and 14% to China. In 2013 Romanian wine exports reached 104.3 thousand hectoliters, worth 19.2 million euros, up from past years.

All in all, if it's made lovingly and skillfully, with a label to match – says baron Jakob Kripp – „wine is an emotional item that, in addition to being able to add to the national economy, can also improve Romania's image abroad. Who benefits from selling anonymous wine, in huge tanks, a wine without a story?"

VII As if at a sign, 50 tourists from North Korea collapsed, their heads on the table. And it was only the third sample of the tasting at the Minis Winery. Balla Geza froze! And the interpreter was nowhere to be found. He had to call an ambulance quickly! A stout man, his white hair contrasting with his tanned face, Balla is an enologist with a PhD in horticulture, a lecturer at the Department of Horticulture of the University of Technical and Human Sciences in Targu Mures and the manager of the Minis Vineyard. Meanwhile, the interpreter appeared from the bathroom and reassured them with a laugh: the same had happened to his people the other day at a winery in Moldavia. What can you do, they are untrained! Things are completely different with the noisy Italians, the trained Norsemen or even Romanians whose appetites are whetted only after having tasted 10 wines...

The episode with the Koreans happened five years ago, when wine tourism had already taken some root in Romania. The wine road in the Zarand Mountains area had already established a path on highway DN 7 to Ghioroc, past the Paulis town hall, being quite traveled by good wine enthusiasts. Tourists came here to enjoy the floral character of the Mustoasa de Maderat; the Furmint of Minis, fermented in 500 liter barrels, a little burned on the inside; the manly Cabernet Sauvignon or, from the stone wine selection, the Pinot noir, Kadarka of Minis, beloved by beginners, Blaufränkisch – a wine on the verge of extinction in Romania, from thicker-skinned grapes – or Cadarissima, first produced in Minis in 1740. Maria Theresa was also here twice, in the land of her favorite wine, Kadarka of Minis. The first viticulture school on Romanian territory was founded here in 1881. During communism, the region has regressed.

The enologist from Arad Balla Geza is striving to restore the glory of the Minis-Maderat Vineyard. He started in 1999 with over 1.5 million euros from the SAPARD funds, laying the foundations of the Wine Princess company, which practices his philosophy: „We must make wines that are typical to our vineyard, use the varieties from this region." Today, the vineyard has 75 ha of fruit-bearing grapevine in a landscape of vineyard-covered rolling hills. A few thousand tourists cross the threshold of his medieval cave every year.

But probably the most tourist-friendly vineyard, justly dubbed the Enterprise ship of Romanian enology, is the Lacerta winery of Dealul Mare. On a Saturday evening, I was amazed to find there almost 120 other visitors, most of them foreigners, and a clinking of glasses and a hum of words like in a buzzing and cheerful beehive during harvest. Were it not for the location, a solitary building surrounded by hills as far as the eye can see, like an island lost in a sea of vineyards, you could swear you were in a shopping mall. Together with cellar man Mihai Badea, we moved a little aside, on the futuristic terrace of the winery, around a tall table full of glasses with various samples for tasting. I was listening in very good spirits the explanations of witty Mihai Badea and I can't figure out whether what he was saying was very funny or the heaped series of tastings that day had made me very cheerful. The fact is the world seemed good and beautiful and increasingly red: Mihai Badea had a red nose, a red face, red eyes, a glass with a red drink, the sunset was reddening on the horizon and I was expecting that, at any minute, his black cap would become red...

„We had a peak, too, in around 2010, with over 6,000 tourists, and in the past two years the upward trend has resumed", Claudia Marinache told me in the cellar built in 1922 for the Urlateanu Manor; she is the administrator of the manor bought and restored by Halewood Wineries in 1999, when the wine tourism began in the Dealul Mare area. The old road from Urlati to Ceptura is a sort of frontier between plain and hill: on the left of the highway crops of wheat and corn are sprawling, on the right – as far as the eye can see – grapevine. The southern exposure of these hills with a maximum altitude of 328 m, which provides the strongest insolation in the country – about 1,670 sunny hours per year during vegetation – combined with the ferruginous soil, rich in iron oxides, recommends the rectangle of about 1,000 km2 between Valea Buzaului and Valea Teleajenului as being ideal for viticulture. Now there are some 9,000 ha covered by vineyards at Dealul Mare, as compared to the 28,000 ha from 1975-80.

Cristi Pitulice, the head of Vinland, takes this trip about 20 times a year, when he brings wine loving tourists to the Dealul Mare wineries and knows all the crosses that used to keep watch at regular intervals over the path of carts carrying wine to Bucharest a century ago.

The proximity to Bucharest and an impressive concentration of producers with already famous names – Serve, Lacerta, Rotenberg, Budureasca, 1.000 de chipuri, Basilescu, Oenoterra, Tohani, Comoara Pivnitei, Sahateni, Visinescu, Halewood, Blaga, Davino or Zoresti – offering wine tastings for tourists make Dealul Mare the spearhead of wine tourism in Romania. „Too bad they can't manage to coalesce into an association", says Cristi Pitulice, slightly upset at the wheel of the minibus that he uses to give rides to his tourists on the wine road. „That's what Romanian wine still needs."

VIII For now, the only ones who have formed an association are the producers in Dragasani. „We are 7 or 8 families with 10 to 40 ha and approximately the same philosophy and orientation. We established the Wine Producers Association of Dragasani to promote the region, so we can coordinate more easily the matters regarding visits, trips, wine tasting, accommodation", says baron Jakob Kripp of Prince Stirbey. The baron, a tall gentleman with impeccable suit and manners, bald-headed and thick-browed, came to Romania in 1997, on his honeymoon with his wife, Ileana Kripp-Costinescu, the granddaughter of princess Maria Stirbey, who was returning to her country for the first time in 30 years. The Kripp family has been making wine for 500 years in northern Italy, but Jakob Kripp is a legal expert. After Ileana Kripp regained her estates in 2001, including the vineyards in

Dragasani, they asked for the advice of the baron's brother, who has a 15-hectare vineyard in South Tirol.

His answer, after visiting Dragasani, was quite eloquent: if you don't make wine here, I'll come and make it. The baron was one of the first investors who decided to bet on Romanian wine.

So did Cristiana Stoica after being granted retrocession of 20 ha in Dragasani: she reunited her great-grandfather's estate with another 20 ha, investing in the Avincis Winery, in „resuming tradition". „They drank Cramposia de Dragasani at Ferdinand's coronation dinner in Alba Iulia", she exclaims proudly, looking at the Dambovita river from the fifth floor of the Opera Center building, where the Stoicas' law firm is located. The little girl – raised in Targu Jiu under the wing of her grandmother, who used to tell her stories about the vineyard and the manor of her great-grandfather, a bank manager in Dragasani, about the ox carts carrying the wine to the market – is now a 50-year old woman, as determined as she is charming. „We will come through. So that we'll be again what we were!"

CHAPTER 9

KADIS FOR THE ROMANIAN JEWS

A nearly extinct community.

At her mother's death, Iulia Deleanu requested the Rabbi's permission to pronounce herself the traditional kadis: 'I have no one left'. Her book, *Kadis for my mother* can also be read as a chronicle of departures, to Israel or to a better world, of most of the members of the Jewish Romanian community in the last 55 years. From nearly one million Jews living here in 1940, about half were killed or deported during WWII. Most survivors made Aliyah, leaving for Israel. Romania has less then 7,000 Jews today. Most of them are over 60 years old. Half are concentrated in Bucharest. In the countryside, there are hundreds of Jewish communities without any Jew left. Of some 100 temples, synagogues and praying houses only about a half still function. The rest were closed, sold or leased. 'This is a miracle: look how many children are in here', said enthusiast the Great Rabbi Menahem Hacohen at Hanuca (Jewish Light holiday) at the Coral Temple in Bucharest. In spite of the harsh statistics, he believes that the Romanian Jew community shall rise again.

The migration to Israel

More than two millions Jews from 104 countries returned to Israel in the last 50 years.

Native Romanian Jews have more than 10% descendence from the Jewish population of Israel.

Kadis is the Jewish pray pronounced by the orphans. Normally, only males can say it.

CHAPTER 10
WHO WERE THE DACIANS?

School teachers taught us to love them as our ideal ancestors. Ancient historians described them as a mysterious people, barbarians who knew how to make themselves immortal. The modern 'Dacomaniacs' claim they were the first great civilization of the world. Who were, in fact, these Dacians?

Illustration: Radu Oltean

At Carlomanesti, not far from the mud volcanoes of Buzau, a Dacian inscription (a world rarity) was discovered together with the foundations of a new sanctuary. At a relative elevation of just over 80 feet, a plateau of over 75,000 square feet is the fiefdom of professor Mircea Babes, who for over 40 years has been meticulously unearthing here a dava dating from the last century B.C. Seen from the valley, it looks like the cap of a giant mushroom carved by two ravines in the Arman Hill. It is an easily defendable location without necessarily being inaccessible to a determined besieger. 'Just enough to protect you from thieves or wild beasts', says Babes.

A man in his 60s, imposing without being too tall, with a large beard and his hands buried in the pockets of his short pants, the professor feels like home in the dava of Carlomanesti as well as in everything related to the Geto-Dacian history. 'If we lived in Denmark, we'd probably have had the chance to find a dozen Dacians preserved in peat bogs, with all their clothes intact', says Babes. When it comes to Dacians we are missing one of the greatest feasts of any archaeologist: the cemeteries. 'What may be found in settlements is the garbage, things that people abandon when they leave taking with them all the valuables. On the contrary, in graves one may find the people and all they took with them to the afterworld'. Paradoxically, there are almost no graves from the classical Dacian epoch (centuries 2–1 B.C.) despite the cultural and demographic thrive.

In the mountains of Orastie, over an area of almost 50,000 acres, there are five strongholds and dozens of important settlements, but not a single grave. It seems likely that Dacians incinerated their dead and spread their ashes in rivers. Having no other choice, archaeologists must be content with the remains of settlements – of which there is no shortage: villages, market towns (dave), fortified strongholds, sanctuaries, treasures, a few weapons and a lot of ceramic objects.

Dava-type civil settlements like the one in Carlomanesti were tribal residences – centers of production, religion, social life and trade. The fortified settlements surrounded by stone walls, found mostly in mountain areas, were merely garrisons or residences for military leaders. The sanctuary of Carlomanesti is the third of this site. All of them have their long sides – and sometimes the apses – north-oriented, like the temples of Gradistea Muncelului, Popesti or Racos. Built of wood and clay, they were 165 to 195 feet long and were covered by roofs. We don't know what happened inside, to whom the offerings were addressed and what the cult was like.

Taking into account the mystery that surrounds the Dacians, the discovery of a fragment of a food-pot bearing some Greek characters may be considered the find of the year. This ceramic fragment with only five characters preserved (*leos B*) completed by professor Babes to basileos B... ('the pot of' king B...) is extraordinarily important: it's the second time in the whole Dacia (after the discovery from Ocnita-Buridava in the 1970s) when we learn from an autochthonous written source that the inhabitants of a dava called their leader a king. Although this leader could only have been a small king – ruling over the dava and the surrounding land around the middle course of Buzau River, the site of Carlomanesti, where the diggings may well continue for another ten years or so, proved to be the source of important archaeological findings. Between 1972 and 1975, professor Babes discovered here a unique collection of small zoo- and anthropomorphic ceramic statues and a treasure containing 124 Dacian silver coins that may have been minted at this dava.

II For centuries, Geto-Dacians ruled the land between the Black Sea, the Balkans, and the Tisa and Dniester Rivers. A historian of the 6th century A.D. described them as a nation of savant warriors who used to dedicate themselves to philosophy and other sciences in-between the battles. 'One may see one of them observing the position of stars, another searching for the qualities of herbs and fruits; this one is studying the phases of the moon, the other one – the solar eclipses...' Although he had some valuable ancient sources on Geto-Dacians at hand, Jordanes, a Roman historian of Goth origin, confused the Getae with the Goths and sometimes, like in the quote above, he exaggerated by describing a situation that may only have been applicable to an elite, not to a whole people. In fact, their main occupations were agriculture and cattle ranching.

According to German archeologist Manfred Oppermann, Dacian peasants lived in rural communities working on pieces of land that were common property while the house, the yard and the tools were considered private property. They grew cereals, fruit-bearing trees and vine. They owned large herds of cattle and flocks of sheep, stud farms and beehives. The Greek called these barbarians 'Getai'. The Romans called them 'Dacians'. Two names for a people made up of some 100 tribes that probably spoke the same language. Ancient authors, among them Claudius Ptolemy, mentioned a series of tribes, the best known being those of *Apuli, Buri, Suci, the northern Dacians, Costoboci, Carpi, Calipidi, Crobyzi, Terizi and the Tyragetae.*

To the Ancient Greek and Romans, they were like any other barbarians: the Germans, the Celts or the Scythians. Red or blond-haired, with scruffy hair and beards, white skin and blue eyes – this is the common image described by historical sources. Stout and vigorous, according to archaeologist Ioan Horia Crisan, both men and women had prominent cheek bones and short and straight noses. Common people were called comati – the longhaired ones. Tarabostes, the noblemen, wore a woolen cap as a distinctive sign of their rank. On the column built in the Roman Forum, where the emperor Trajan ordered a depiction of his Dacian wars to be carved in marble, the women are beautiful and slender, tall and strong, with parted hair tied behind in a loop.

According to historian Hadrian Daicoviciu, the Dacians' clothing strongly resembled the Romanian peasants' costumes: men wore a linen shirt laterally split over their tight woolen trousers. They were girded with a wide belt made of leather or fabric. Over the shirt they wore a short, sleeveless mantle or a furred coat. Women wore pleated short-sleeved shirts and skirts. A kerchief covered their hair. For shoes they put on laced moccasins or fabric slippers. 'You can imagine the Dacians wearing these clothes, more or less similar with the Romanian peasant costume. However we shouldn't make such assumptions unless proven by archaeological finds', says professor Babes. Unfortunately, such objects made by organic, perishable matter were not preserved. And Trajans' Column – the main source of plastic depictions of Dacians – is not considered entirely reliable. Ethnographer Florea Bobu Florescu, who published two important books on the Column and the monument of Adamclisi, thought that the bas-reliefs of the Roman sculptors are standardized representations that don't necessarily resemble the native Dacians.

III In the beginning of the 4th century, the Get Dromichaetes, leader of a tribal union from what is now the Romanian region of Muntenia, went to war with Lysimachus, king of Thracia, one of the generals of Alexander the Great. Following the failure of a first expedition against the Getae, the king's son, Agathocles, was captured. Yet, Dromichaetes set him free and sent him home laden with gifts. Far from being grateful, Lysimachus returned with an even greater army, but this one, too, was defeated and the king himself was captured. The ancient author Diodorus Siculus says that Dromichaetes convinced the Getae, who would rather have killed Lysimachus that it was in their best interest to leave him unharmed. A story then became a classical scene: that of Dromichaetes inviting Lysimachus and his noblemen to a banquet set up with the entire pomp typical for Hellenistic courts. Alongside, Dromichaetes and other Dacian leaders ate a modest meal sitting on a straw rug, using ordinary pots, and drank wine from cups made of wood or horn. But this banquet scene is a widespread fable among ancient writers. We find it identically narrated by Herodotus, two centuries before Diodorus, only he states it happened in the 5th century B.C., between the Persians and the Spartans… It is a simple example that illustrates how a critical analysis of literary sources is absolutely required.'Except for three short inscriptions found on pots discovered through the years at Sarmizegetusa, Buridava, and now at Carlomanesti, Dacians did not leave us any evidence of a written culture'. So we have to rely on foreign writers – Greek or Latin – who, in many cases, narrate second-hand stories, passed from one author to the next. Hence the inevitable exaggerations which have to do with a certain philosophy of the Greek or Latin writer: the philosophy of the good barbarian, who has to be pure and honest precisely because he is a barbarian, as opposed to the civilized world, which was corrupt and decadent', says Mircea Babes.

Still, there is no doubt that the war between Dromichaetes and Lysimachus did take place, and that it ended with the victory of the first. Despite this victory, the political and military record of the Getae in the 6th to 4th centuries B.C. is rather negative. The ancient historical sources mention them opposing and being defeated by the Persians of Darius and by the Macedonian army of Alexander the Great. The situation changed radically starting with Burebista, the founder of the Dacian state. Burebista, who become king some time around the year 80 B.C., aided by Great Priest Deceneus, managed to unify for a while almost all the Geto-Dacian tribes. In only a few years, by sword and by word, he created a formidable kingdom that spread from the middle course of the Danube and Morava, to the West, to the Balkans to the South, the Black Sea and Bug River to the East, and the northern Carpathians to the North.

'Becoming the leader of his people, who were tired by the frequent wars – says Strabon – Burebista, the Get, made them stronger through exercise, and imposing moderation and obedience; in only a few years, he was able to build a powerful state and subdued most of the neighboring populations'. But shortly after the assassination of Caesar, his great Roman rival, Burebista was also killed in a coup set up by his noblemen. 'The tribal aristocracy (*tarabostes*) must have had a hard time enduring the obedience imposed by Burebista. As long as his conquests brought them profits they refrained and simply played a military role. When Burebista, foreseeing a confrontation with the Romans, re-oriented his policy towards defense, the tribal aristocracy, frustrated of its spoils, was no longer willing to support the authoritarian king', says historian Florin Constantiniu. After the king's death the 'Great Kingdom' disintegrated. Only the Transylvanian nucleus remained. There, many kings followed; their names were recorded by historical sources but their chronology is still unsure: Deceneus, Comosicus, Scoryllus, Duras and the last Dacian king, Decebal.

IV Ask ten Romanians who the Supreme God of their ancestors was and nine of them will say: 'Zamolxis' – wrong answer! Most probably, the Geto-Dacian pantheon was similar to the Greek one, which may also be found among Thracians and Romans, Celts and Germans, including various deities led by a great God and a Great Goddess whose names remain unknown. Only great priests and aristocrats embraced the cult of Zamolxis. He got his notoriety due to the ancient Greek from the cities established by them on the coast of Pontus Euxinus. They were struck by the resemblance between his doctrine and that of Pythagoras and created the legend of the Getae's slavery in the Isle of Samos and of his return as a rich man among the 'poor and simple-minded' Thracians.

Being already accustomed to Greek practices, Zamolxis invited the leaders of the country to banquets where he taught them that they wouldn't die, but rather go to a certain place where they would live forever and enjoy every luxury. In his account of Persian king Darius' campaign against the Scythians, Herodotus mentioned the Getae, who knew how to become immortal. 'They believe that they do not die and that those who disappear from our world go straight to their daimon, Zamolxis'. The Getae kept in touch with this god by sending him a messenger every five years; the victim was chosen by drawing lots and thrown onto spears stuck point-up into the ground. If the messenger did not die was believed to be an unworthy person. Herodotus and other ancient authors portray Zalmoxis as a historical personality, a reformer priest and lawyer who ended up deified. According to Mircea Eliade, historian of religions, the main features of this cult were mystery-type: Zamolxis would reveal the chance to obtain immortality through an initiation that included a ritual death followed by a rebirth. The religion described by Herodotus is initiatic, belonging to a elite. Few people were ever invited by Zamolxis into his cave. This is the only way we can explain the absence of any proof of this religion in archaeological sites.

Living in inaccessible solitude on the peak of the sacred mountain of Kogaionon, Deceneus, the Great Priest – a prophet and adviser of king Burebista – enjoyed an exceptional prestige. Following his advice the sot Dacians cut down their vineyards and chose to live without wine. Jordanes reports about Deceneus choosing the best nobles and teaching them to worship some deities and to attend some temples. His account, which suggests a certain religious reform of the Geto-Dacians in the first century B.C., was confirmed by archaeological finds. 'In the epoch of Burebista, a large number of very important changes of a cultic-religious nature took place; they are totally new and they disappear immediately after the Roman conquest: the proliferation of human sacrifices, the appearance of some true sanctuaries and the discreet funeral rituals', says professor Babes.

After the arrival of the Romans, the tombs reappear, grouped in big necropolises, and the davas suddenly disappear. And this is valid not only for the conquered province, but also for the whole territory of the former Dacia – a sign that, after the defeat of their gods, the life of the 'free Dacians' from Muntenia, Moldova, Maramures and Crisana underwent dramatic changes.

V In 1980, Romania pompously celebrated 2050 years since the founding of the great barbarian kingdom of Burebista. As Geto-Dacians lived in a territory that overlaps with the one of today's Romania, 'the authorities wanted to show that from the times of the Dacian king until today, one way or another, victoriously or not, Romanians had had a tradition, a state, a permanence on this Carpatho-Danubian-Pontic space', says archaeologist Vlad Vintila Zira, who digs at the dava of Bazdana. On the occasion of this anniversary, a giant project was initiated to restore and conserve the Dacian fortresses in the mountains of Orastie. The works started triumphantly, with bulldozers, but were then abandoned. Today, in the sacred precinct at Sarmizegetusa Regia, huge concrete blocks piled chaotically, desecrate the ruins of the eleven sanctuaries, creating a sad scenery.

In the afternoon I spent there, a solitary cyclist, with black stretch pants and a yellow helmet, lay down for an hour in the center of the great circular sanctuary in an attempt to absorb the cosmic energy that he believed was concentrated in that place. It was also here that nocturnal orgies have been organized by members of a local sect that seeks integration into the absolute.

Destroyed by Romans and rebuilt according to the project – more artistic than scientific – of architect Cristian Calinescu, the great circular sanctuary is the Dacian construction that stirred most controversies. Initially it was believed – and many people, like the cyclist I was telling you about still believe it – that it was a calendar. The groups of 6+1 andesite pillars, placed regularly in a group of 30, suggested a Dacian calendar. However, recent research led to the discovery of new pillars and the initial speculations were abandoned. Today's presentation of the great circular sanctuary only helps to perpetuate the wrong image of 'the calendar'.

Nicolae Ceausescu, the man who was supposed to be impressed by the irresponsible impetus of the works started more that 30-35 years ago, always double-played the 'Dacians card'. In official speeches, willing to maintain good relationships with the neo-Latin countries of the Western Europe and the revolutionary Latin America, he emphasized the double, Dacian and Roman origin of the Romanians. 'At the same time', says Babes, 'these numerous campaigns designed for the internal market were planned to use the glorious Dacian traditions in order to exacerbate national pride and the devotion towards the Ruler'.

VI Out of a need to legitimate themselves or just for national propaganda, some modern politicians and historians took advantage of the mystery that shrouds the Dacians and overestimated them. The national car of Romania was called Dacia, the national sportive competition – Daciada. The Roman conquerors, although longtime seen as imperialists, or even war criminals, were finally forgiven and accepted as forefathers together with the Dacians in recognition of the fact that they brought here a superior language and civilization.

Today, we are witnessing the outbursts of the 'Dacomaniacs' – people who claim Dacia to have been the first civilization of mankind. The inventor of this thesis, Nicolae Densusianu, an archive-type historian deceased in 1911, wrote a book meant to extend Romanian history all the way back into pre-history and mythology. This book, Pre-historic Dacia, a true Bible of the 'Dacomaniacs', makes Dacia the bellybutton of the World. Dacians are held to have spread everywhere, including Rome, where they supposedly brought the Latin language. The Dacian-Roman wars were, thus, nothing more than fratricidal wars. The Atlas was identified in the mountains of Olt. And even the Greek gods were supposed to have been born here... The funeral monticules were considered prototypes of the Egyptian pyramids, while the Dacian strongholds from the times of Burebista were thought to have been a model for the gigantic Mycenaean constructions (which are some 10,000 years older!). Densusianu's book was severely criticized ever since its publication and considered a 'fantasy novel'. Yet his ideas have found fertile ground all over the Internet, where physician Napoleon Savescu and his collaborators reassess and further develop Densusianu's theories.

VII How was I to know that this bearded gentleman with such a kind look would drag me along like a mountain stream? Veteran photographer Kenneth Garrett, a National Geographic legend, for which he illustrated over 57 stories, took photos of the copy of the Column in the National Museum of Romanian History in the spring of 2013. I wanted to be the one who would accompany him around Bucharest for a week – as a porter, translator, and assistant.

Each day, I would carry into the Lapidarium enough metal trolley cases chock-full of equipment to put a news van to shame. Then – such amazing professionalism – the American worked as a madman, morning to evening, as if in a trance, forgetting to eat, taking photos of the bas-reliefs in thousands of ways, from all angles and in all imaginable lights. I witnessed the live proof that, as Edison put it, genius is one percent inspiration and 99 percent perspiration. Also, as a side effect, I grew to know the scenes almost by heart.

Close to the end, we moved to the treasure room to take pictures of the gold bracelets. For a few hours, Ken's spotlights – of all kinds, filters and sizes – turned the room (which I had seen several times before, but always in obscurity) into a bright studio. Ken improvised a small plinth out of a little bench that he overturned with a giant's gesture and then gingerly covered with velvet. The curator deactivated the alarm, unlocked the glass case where the bracelets were and carried them one by one to Ken's operating table. I lent a helping hand, too.

I found the museum man very listless that day – or at least he treated the artifacts as if they were kitchen utensils. He had nothing against it when I asked if I could help. And that's how I got a chance to feel those bracelets, each weighing almost four and a half pounds, with my own two hands. I couldn't stifle a shiver as I thought and wondered: who had been the people who had borne their weight before me?

VIII Around the beginning of the 1st century B.C. (probably during the reign of king Burebista), three smithies near Sarmizegetusa Regia started to work alluvial gold – by cold-forging it like iron – into solid gold bracelets with winged dragon heads. The custom for religious and military leaders in royal Dacia to bring such gold and silver offerings to the gods was only observed for a few decades. Before being deposed into the ground, the bracelets were cut with a sword or dagger. Thus, everyone knew that they no longer belonged to man, but to the gods. How else could you bury such treasure – at least five such ritual offerings were discovered – in shallow ground, about eight to twenty inches deep, in areas which at the time were highly populated, without fear that they would be stolen?

What is certain is that those who ordered them – probably royalty or close to the royal family – do not seem to have lacked raw materials. Lab tests have shown that the gold used in making the bracelets comes from the Aries Valley, from Brad and other mining areas of Transylvania's Gold Quadrate – an area delimited by the towns of Deva, Zlatna, Baia de Aries, and Caraciu.

Greek or Roman master goldsmiths of the time made jewelry out of thin gold sheets. Dacians were amazing blacksmiths, but lacked tradition in goldworking, so they literally hammered out these bracelets weighing two to four pounds! According to the explanations of Dr. E. Oberlander-Tarnoveanu, director of the National Museum of Romanian History, Dacian craftsmen started by molding a gold ingot by the ancient method of synthesis: gold nuggets and gold dust were placed in the forge and brought to a temperature just below the melting point, until the gold became semi-fluid and could be poured. The alloy obtained this way contains gold, as well as small percentages of silver, copper, tin, potassium, barium, antimony etc.

Then they shaped the gold ingot with a wooden hammer, on a hardwood anvil, until they had a thick rod, about 6.5 to ten feet in length, slightly thicker at the ends – which would become the dragons' heads. They then proceeded to shape the dragon (or winged snake) heads, by engraving and embossing with dies hammered onto the metal or with small chisels. At the end, the rods were coiled into an open-ended spiral. The piece was probably finished with a light, delicate sanding. One bracelet done!

It is a primitive technique, requiring amazing skill. Indeed, the tenfoot-long spirals have a deviation of less than 0.04 inches in diameter. Both the gold bracelets (24 of which have been discovered) and the silver bracelets (28 pieces, of which 26 have been found in Romania) show barely noticeable wear, which means they were not meant to be worn, but offered to the gods. Starting from the Neolithic, such sacred treasures were buried in shallow holes, on heights, in sacred groves, rivers, caves, or other places thought to be gates to the other world.

IX It was the autumn of 106 A.D. and Rome was celebrating. Upon his victorious return from Dacia, Roman emperor Trajan made a gift of 650 denarii to each taxpayer, granted a one-year tax exemption and ordered 123 days of games. Based on the information given by Criton, the physician who accompanied Trajan in his campaigns in Dacia, Byzantine historian John the Lydian – who lived in the 5th and 6th centuries A.D. – states, in his work *De Magistratibus*, that Romans brought from Dacia 3,300,000 pounds of gold and 6,620,000 pounds of silver. The myth of the Dacian gold had started to grow as early as the Antiquity. Herodotus said of the Agathyrsi that they were wearers of gold jewelry. Cassius Dio, also taking his information from Criton, tells of how Decebal hid his treasures in the bed of the Sargetia river and of how Bicilis the traitor led the Romans to the spot. On the Column in Rome, in scene 138, at the end of the Dacian wars, one can see mules laden with precious loot.

Erasmus of Rotterdam described Dacian kosons in a letter to the bishop of Breslau in 1520. As for the treasures of the Dacians, Wolfgang Lazius was the first to identify the location of Sarmizegetusa, in the late 15th century. In the 19th century, French historian Jérôme Carcopino struck a zero off the end of the numbers provided by his Byzantine forerunner, John the Lydian. British historian R. Syme thought they looked credible. Until close to the year 2000, except for a few coin treasures discovered by chance, archeologists have found no gold from the classical Dacian period in any diggings in over 150 years. Many specialists, among whom professor Ion Glodariu in Cluj, have explained this paradox by the fact that Dacian kings would have established a gold monopoly, after which the precious metal was taken to Rome following the Roman conquest. Others, such as professor Mircea Babes, believed that the fabulous treasure that Romans captured in Dacia was, in fact, mere imperial propaganda. 'Trajan must have spent a lot of public money with the two wars, and sacrificed the lives of thousands of soldiers hence he had to demonstrate that all those efforts had been worth it. And he couldn't use strategic reasons with Roman plebeians. So, he was forced to say something like: Look, we conquered Dacia and came back loaded with money. 'Romans must have known that there was gold in the mountains of Dacia. Their espionage services were the Antiquity's CIA. The Dacians probably knew it as well, but never had the technology to mine the ore. This is why, after the conquest, the Romans would bring here people from the *Pirustae* and *Baridustae* tribes from distant Illyria to dig mine galleries in the mountains of Rosia Montana – the ancient Alburnus Maior. They simply didn't find specialists there'. The detective story of the discovery, theft, and retrieval of the Dacian bracelets threw off most of these theories.

X When interrogated by the Public Prosecutors of the Court of Appeal of Alba Iulia County, Remus R., a local living in Gradistea Muncelului, told of how the treasure of Caprareata was unearthed (*file no. 172/P/2005, Hunedoara County Court, June 16, 2005*). Remus and his son, Florin, were hired as diggers by a group of treasure hunters in Deva. On Saturday, the 6th of May 2000, a third of a mile east of the sacred enclosure of the citadel at Sarmizegetusa Regia, on the steep slope near the Muchea Capraretei peak, treasure hunters were combing the area with metal detectors. They were almost ten feet down from a large boulder, like a giant's hat, on a 70-degree slope where no sane archeologist would have thought to dig. N.I. registered a strong signal. Florin got down to digging and, at a depth of one and a half feet, he found a rectangular, lid-like tile, 1'1' by 1'7'. They lifted it and saw a yellow object with leaf-like decorations. They uttered a cry of joy, thinking they had found the crown of a Dacian king. They unearthed two entwined bracelets, their ends decorated with leaves and shaped like wolf or snake heads. In the same triangular hole, walled with tiles, they found three pairs of two bracelets each. N.I. swept around again with his metal detector and found another signal. Florin dug again and brought out two more pairs of bracelets, placed at the bottom of a hole.

'We were so stunned we couldn't even speak to each other. N. flung off his tools in joy, so hard he almost hit me', Remus said. The trove, consisting of ten almost identical solid gold spirals, was taken over by another member of the group, who took the bracelets to his apartment in Deva, washed them with shampoo in his bathroom and weighed them on kitchen scales. The loot was shared among the members of the group. Just four days later, the first pair of bracelets, wrapped up in gauze and hidden inside an Opel, left the country through the Nadlac customs point, a few minutes after midnight.

UNESCO discovered Sarmizegetusa Regia in 1999, when it included it in the World Heritage Sites. Organized groups of treasure hunters had discovered and claimed it years earlier – with hi-tech detectors, jeeps, weapons, guard dogs, radio communication. For almost a decade, they ran wild in this no man's land – with zero surveillance from Romanian authorities, in archeological sites totaling over 77 square miles, more than 3,300 feet high, in an area covered in ancient woods. They poked the Orastie mountains full of holes; these were the gold fever years, which devastated the area and fed the antiques black market. The damages to scientific knowledge of the Dacian civilization cannot even be gauged. Any dig destroys something. An archeologist will make note of all his discoveries and publish them. A treasure hunter is only interested in the price he can get from collectors. Over this period, treasure hunters unearthed at least eleven coin treasures and troves of iron ingots. Pieces of jewelry and thousands of silver and gold coins, tools, weapons, and iron ingots left the country illegally. Some of the ingots weighed over a ton and ended up being sold to scrapyards in the area. As early as the summer of 1996, a man in Orastie was offering to sell 400 gold kosons to the director of the National Museum of Romanian History, Dr. E. Oberlander-Tarnoveanu, who stalled for a few years as the museum didn't have the money; meanwhile, other coins were actually sold to the National Bank of Romania. The kosons had been unearthed from Sarmizegetusa Regia, on the Gradistea hill, by the tree called Bodea's Beech (as it turned out after legal inquiries a few years later).

On the 9th of March 2002, Romanians could see the Dacian gold bracelets live, on the OTV Channel: treasure hunters had gone so far as to boast with their discoveries on TV. The General Inspector of the Romanian Police started an inquiry which was quickly swamped by political interests. The mass-media talked of the theft in Orastie, but the state authorities seemed powerless. It is estimated that, between 2001 and 2004, there were brought to light in Sarmizegetusa five to six thousand kosons – the famous Dacian gold coin, probably locally minted, imitating the Roman denarius issued in 54 B.C.: The obverse bears a Roman eagle, and the reverse shows a consul framed by two lictors bearing the symbols of his authority. In 2005, the Public Prosecutors of the Court of Appeal of Alba Iulia County undertook further investigations and, before long, 13 defendants were tried for illegal treasure hunting on archeological sites. On the 3rd of December 2006, the Ministry of Culture and Religious Denominations in Romania announced the start of the efforts to retrieve four Dacian bracelets which had been found in an art gallery in New York. (The Government dug deep into its pockets, spending 300,000 Euros from the budget reserve.) In 2007, nine bracelets were recovered. The treasury room of the National Museum of Romanian History kept getting richer, too. In 2008 came back two more bracelets and a gold treasure consisting of a necklace with pendants and two earrings, stolen in 2003 from the Dacian citadel at Capalna. In 2009 – one bracelet. In 2011 – bracelet number 13. It is estimated that 24 bracelets were taken out of the country. Only in 2013 did the Hunedoara County Council establish an entrance fee and draw up visiting regulations for the Dacian citadel Sarmizegetusa Regia, only allowing tourists access to the site in the designated area and following the marked routes.

XI Inside the archeological reservation of Drobeta Turnu-Severin, I sat by the sad ruin of a bridge pier cast in a concrete casing. Around me, everything was just a desolate desert. But this area must have been boiling in 105, when architect Apollodorus of Damascus built here, over the Danube, the longest bridge of the Roman Empire, considered by some the 'Eighth Wonder of the Ancient World'. Throughout history, the location and method of construction of Trajan's Bridge stirred up many debates and controversies. In 1971, academician Dumitru Tudor compiled in a monumental work all the information available on this subject – some of it no longer accessible today. He concluded that the bridge was constructed on dry land. The Danube was partially deviated by a channel dug on the Serbian bank along an old clogged riverbed. The water level was drastically lowered. Two channels were formed, separated by a dry area. Where the river level could not be lowered, the Romans used box girders fixed in the moist soil. In these huge boxes they put sacks full of clay to absorb all the water. The Romans used hydraulic cement (Pozzolana – a kind of natural concrete from the Vesuvius' baked limestone) for the base of the pier. Then, a platform of shaped stone blocks tided with wooden beams was built. Over this platform there was a masonry made of cracked stones and mortar, and on top of it some brickwork. The pillars were plated with blocks of shaped stones. The bridge was 3,724-foot long, 49-foot wide and 62-foot high.

'The bridge's pillars remained visible at the surface for a very long time, until they were destroyed by modern navigation', says archaeologist Dan Ciobotaru. In 1906, Edgard Duperrex, an engineer from the Polytechnical School of Bucharest, constructed a model of the bridge that can be seen today in the Museum of the 'Iron Gates' Region. The ruins of the Romanian bridgehead are situated in the southeastern area of Drobeta Turnu-Severin, within the precinct of the museum. Today, only a model of this bridge may be seen in the local museum. The construction was ordered by emperor Trajan (98–117 A.D.) who subsequently led out his legions, for the second time, to settle the Dacian problem for good.

XII In a time when the Parthians of the East rose in arms, while the Germanic peoples became increasingly active in Central Europe, the Romans could not afford to tolerate this dangerous enemy across the Danube – an enemy that could possibly unify the whole barbarian world against them. Decebal was an extremely dangerous neighbor whom Romans confronted in several successive wars. Finally, their legions won and Trajan founded the province of Dacia, which would flourish during the 165 years of Roman occupation. According to historian Paul MacKendrick, the Empire made this province thrive – as they did to any other – from an underdeveloped country to one with an advanced civilization. The Romans built cities and fortresses here, exploited the resources of the soil and, especially, those underneath it, built amphitheatres, public baths (termae), aqueducts, sewage systems. 'And, after Rome withdrew its army, in 271 A.D', MacKendrick says. 'the Dacians were freed and they tried to follow the 'Roman way', yet they couldn't advance further and were swallowed by the barbarian invasions'.

XIII Up on the plateau at Blidaru, the best preserved Dacian fortress, archaeologist Mihai Castaianu, a researcher at the Museum of Ethnography and Folk Art in Orastie, served me with roasted ham, onion and plum brandy. He was born and grew up in these mountains and he is as passionate about the Dacians as I am. He showed me the places and we talked for hours about the endless controversies, ideas and hypotheses that animate the specialists in this field. It was a wonderful late-April day. We stopped for lunch under a wild cherry tree whose blossoms scented the glade. All of a sudden I remembered the tree whose growing was stopped, present on the last element of Trajan's Column as a metaphor of the stunted growth of a fully-blossoming state. Here, in the most beautiful Dacian fortress, I felt it was the time for my Dacian adventure to end as well. Yet the biggest of all mysteries, that of the reconciliation between the Dacians and the Romans that led to the long-debated formation of the Romanian people, still remains. But that is another story.

XIV The daco-roman wars

The Dacians crossed the frozen Danube, plundering the Roman province of Moesia in the winter of the years 85/86 A.D. A series of Roman raids over the Danube followed. At the end of the second one, the winning legions stopped at Tapae. Before subduing the Dacians, Domitian wanted to punish the Quadi and Marcomanni, who had refused to help Romans in their war against the Dacians. After the defeat of this expedition, the emperor made peace with the Dacians. Becoming a client of Rome, Decebal used the money and craftsmen regularly given to client kings to strengthen his army, let in Roman deserters and fortify his strongholds. The Dacian king Decebal – reports historian Cassius Dio –'was skilled at war and tough in action, knowing when to invade and when to withdraw, a master of setting traps, brave in battle, knowing how to use a victory and how to get out from defeats'.

The First War (101-102 A.D.)

Tired of paying, year after year, some people whose power and haughtiness was on the rise, emperor Trajan decided to set things straight in Dacia. After some three years of punctilious preparations, the Roman army, under the leadership of the emperor himself, crossed the Danube on a boat bridge. On March 25, 101, the priests of Jupiter in Rome prayed for the emperor's victorious return. The Romans crossed the river and headed towards the Dacian capital, Sarmizegetusa, in three columns. The western one, led by the Emperor, went up across the Banat region and clashed with the Dacians in the battle of Tapae. The eastern one, including the Inferior Moesian army, led by general Laberius Maximus, went across the plain, taking in the eastern part of Dacia. The third army went north along the Olt and Jiu Rivers. At the beginning of the fall of 101, the Romans had already conquered Banat, Oltenia, Muntenia, the south of Moldavia and the south-east of Transylvania. 'The legions marched on in a well thought-out action', writes Cassius Dio, 'building roads, bridges and castra'. In the first war with Decebal, in order to take the capital, Trajan had to break the defense belt – the fortresses at Costesti, Blidaru, Piatra Rosie, Banita, Varful lui Hulpe.

The Moesian Diversion

In order to save himself, Decebal thought of a diversion. Taking advantage of the coming winter, the Dacians, allied with the Roxo-

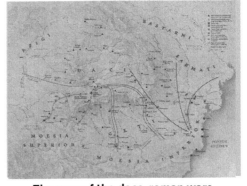

The map of the daco-roman wars.

lani and the Bastarnae, crossed the Danube on the ice that, this time, broke under the weight of horses and riders. A relief on the Column in Rome shows the Dacian riders drowning in the Danube. Still, many of them succeeded in crossing over and attacked the Roman castra on the right bank of the river. The attack was terrible: it is the only time when wounded Roman soldiers are featured on the Column. The emperor embarked many of his troops and hurried to the affected zone. The bloodiest battle took place at Adamclisi. Trajan even sent the Pretorians (his personal guard) into battle. To remember this fight, Trajan ordered the triumphal monument of Adamclisi to be built. Over the spring and summer of the next year Romans moved on in their march towards the capital, defeating the resistance nucleus set up in the Orastie Mountains. Decebal called for peace talks. By the compromise of 102, the Romans kept the conquered territories: Hateg Country, Oltenia, Banat, most of Muntenia and the south of Moldavia. Decebal saved only the northern part of his kingdom and had to move his capital, probably at Piatra Craivii.

The Second War (105-106 A.D.)

When hostilities recommenced in 105, the Romans had already secured positions north of the Danube. The Dacians furiously attacked them. It seems Decebal even plotted to assassinate the emperor – but he failed. Trajan embarked at Brundisium, a port on the Adriatic Sea, and followed the Dalmatian Coast heading to Drobeta.

The legions crossed the bridge and advanced very slowly, at first aiming to stabilize the territories occupied in 102, before launching a general attack. This time most of the troops attacked from the west. The Romans went forward in five columns aiming both at the fortified zone in the Sirianu Mountains and at the new center established by Decebal in the stronghold of Piatra Craivii. Defeated and chased, Decebal committed suicide in 106.

His head was taken first to Ranistorum, to be presented to the emperor, then to Rome, to be thrown on the Gemonian stairs. The settlements in the Orastie Mountains were destroyed and the population was forced to move to the flat areas. The Dacian state was abolished and a great part of its territory became the province of Dacia.

XV Timeline

- 85-86 The Dacian attack on Moesia.
- 87 Cornelius Fuscus' expedition in Dacia. He is defeated and killed.

- 87 Decebal becomes king.
- 88 Tettius Iulianus' expedition in Dacia. Roman victory at Tapae.
- 89 Emperor Domitian makes peace, under conditions which favor the Dacians.
- 98 Trajan becomes emperor.
- 101 The beginning of the first Dacian-Roman war. Trajan's legions victory at Tapae.
- 101-102 (winter) The counter-offensive of the Geto-Dacians and their allies south of the Danube.
- 102 Peace.
- 103-105 The construction of the Drobeta Turnu-Severin bridge.
- 105-106 The Second Dacian War. Trajan's victory.
- 106 Decebal's suicide.
- 106-271 Dacia becomes a Roman province.

XVI When Was Sarmizegetusa Regia Conquered?
A controversy with a predictable answer.

Why would grown-up people lose their time trying to answer childish questions? Pick any schoolkid and they will tell you that the Romans defeated the Dacians in two successive wars, between the years 101–102 and 105–106, respectively; at the end of the latter, they finally conquered Sarmizegetusa Regia and abolished the Dacian state. So it remains written in any history schoolbook. But, in this case, this is exactly where the problem seems to lie...

One of the first heretics who challenged the official view is historian Coriolan Opreanu, who asserted that Sarmizegetusa was conquered as early as the end of the first war, when Trajan hadn't come to conquer Dacia but to teach a lesson to one of his client kings. In fact, priority over this theory should be given to the Roman historian Cassius Dio (155-235 A.D.) who says that, in 102, emperor Trajan returned to Rome leaving in the Dacian capital a Roman garrison (stratopedon) and the king Decebal under the burden of an unbearable peace. Archaeological diggings revealed numerous vestiges of Roman constructions at the site of Sarmizegetusa, famous today for its sacred precinct The Romans destroyed the temples but rebuilt the city and practically doubled its size. 'All we know about the first Dacian War, the directions of the Roman attacks, the tactical and strategic tasks of the legions, not to mention the situation preceding the year 101 (such as the type of relationships between the Roman Empire and the Geto-Dacians, the military presence of the Romans north of the Danube in the first century A.D., the formation of client-king type relationships with local dynasties, the rising of some centers of opposition against Romans on the middle and lower course of the Danube, the changes in military and political visions in Rome during the Flavian epoch), shows that Sarmizegetusa was occupied in 102', says historian Iancu Motu.

No Roman coin newer than 106 was yet found at Sarmizegetusa, a surprising fact if we assume that Roman troops would have been maintained there for five to ten years after the second Dacian war in order to guard the devastated ruins of the capital, as claimed by the partisans of the 106 Conquest. Equally improbable is the hypothesis that Trajan would have stopped only half a mile from Sarmizegetusa, after taking the strongholds of Costesti and Fetele Albe.

At the end of the first war, the Romans occupied the regions of Banat, Oltenia, Muntenia, the south of Moldova and Hateg Country. It is highly improbable that the very residence of Decebal would resist behind the enemy lines. The stationing of an army in the Dacian capital city and the Roman constructions, especially the enlargement of the city, would have been useful only to avoid the violation of the peace of 102; they would have been somehow illogical after the final victory of 106. However, researchers in Cluj continue to claim that all Roman buildings discovered here were built after 106.

'The Daicoviciu School preferred a speculative interpretation: Cassius Dio wouldn't talk about the Dacian royal Sarmizegetusa, but about the future Roman Sarmizegetusa – the Ulpia Traiana. But even in this case, archaeology shows something else: no Dacian remains have been found there – nothing that would justify the stationing of Roman troops in that place in 102. The motivation for these theories that contravene the historical findings and archaeological data is mostly related to patriotic and regional pride', says Mircea Babes. However, this controversy is postponed until all the findings from Sarmizegetusa and from the complex in Orastiei Mountains will be published.

XVIII Trajan's Column

In 2013 we celebrated nineteen centuries since the inauguration of the world's most famous ancient bas relief. Admire the original in Rome and see the plaster casts up close – in Bucharest, London, or Saint-Germain. It was the autumn of 106 A.D., and Rome was celebrating. Upon his victorious return from Dacia, Trajan ordered 123 days of games. A few months later, he ordered architect Apollodorus of Damascus to build the greatest imperial forum. Six years later, in 112, a crowd of people from all over the Empire came to this forum to see the column inaugurated. In ancient times, the scenes depicted on it could be admired up close from the tall terraces of the surrounding structures: two neighboring libraries – the Greek and the Latin one – and the Basilica Ulpia. The scenes that unfold on the marble spindle, like a giant scroll rolled up in 23 full turns, are probably the illustrations of the lost book – De Bello Dacico – in which emperor Marcus Ulpius Traianus recounted his two wars against the Dacians (101-102 and 105-106 A.D.). The sculpted strip measures 625 feet in length and between 35 and 49 inches in width – widening towards the top. The craftsmen, most likely from Syria, placed about 2,500 figurines in 124 vividly-colored scenes. Some of the weapons held by the warriors were painted, others – particularly spears and javelins – were made of copper wire. The top was crowned by a colossal bronze statue of Trajan – replaced in 1598 with one of Saint Peter, by order of Pope Sixtus V. In time, the colors faded, many details became eroded and the metal bits were lost, but the monumental Columna, about 125 feet tall, remains intact after almost 2,000 years and can be seen in Trajan's Forum in Rome. Those who want to pore over its scenes more closely, though, can choose any of the five museums hosting plaster casts from the 19th and 20th centuries – far more 'legible' than the original, worn down by the pollution that has beset

Italy's capital over the last decades.

In 1861, master craftsmen Alessandro and Leopoldo Malpieri made three plaster casts of the Column in Rome, upon the order of Napoleon III (who wanted to erect a copy of the structure in one of Paris' squares). One cast was taken to Paris to be remolded in galvanized copper at the Oudry mill. The French copy was exposed in the Louvre in the summer of 1864. Meanwhile, the idea of building a Column in Paris was abandoned, and in 1870 the parts were moved into storage at the Gallo-Roman Museum in Saint-Germain. Nowadays, in the *Musée d'Archéologie Nationale de Saint-Germain-en-Laye* (near Paris), you can see a galvanized copper copy of the base section of the Column, exposed in the dry moat of the Saint-Germain-en-Laye chateau.

The other copy, donated by Napoleon III to Pope Pius IX, was first placed in the *Lateran Museum*. Another Roman pope, Pius XII, gave it to the *Museo della Civiltà Romana* in 1951. Today, the 125 cast pieces can be seen in Room LI.

The Louvre keeps the Column's base and about a third of the frieze in its collection of plaster casts at *Petites Écuries de Versailles*. In London, *Victoria and Albert Museum's Cast Courts* are dominated by the cast of the column – made around 1864 – cut in two. The height of the gallery did not allow for the monument to be exposed in one piece. After half a century of indecision, the Romanian government ordered a full-scale copy of the column from the Vatican in 1939. Master craftsman Francesco Mercatalli and his team cast it in reinforced white concrete mixed with marble powder. The casts came to Bucharest 28 years later and, after spending several years in the Museum of the Romanian Communist Party, were installed in the newly-opened *National Museum of Romanian History* (in the former Central Post Office). The Lapidarium, a modern building of over 18,000 square feet, was specially built to house it in 1972, in the patio of the National Museum of Romanian History.

A regular visit

From the central lobby, you can enter the Lapidarium. Right at the entrance – on the left wall when facing the base of the Column – an 18-century intaglio plate shows the monument as it first looked, with Trajan's statue at the top.

Across from it, another intaglio, made by Piranesi, shows the column with the statue of Saint Peter on top. Follow the banister until you are about a dozen feet from the plinth, which is a perfect copy of the original in Rome, and stop to take a close look at the first scenes (one to six) from the spiral winding around the monument. The side stairs lead to the lower level. Another, lower central space allows access to the plinth and to bas-reliefs seven through 19, which are exposed all around. In 2013, the base of the column got a new bronze door. Right on its left you can see the plan of Trajan's Forum in Rome. Watch the scenes unraveling on the right, as they continue around the column. As a bonus, the upper level of the Lapidarium hosts many stone monuments discovered in Romania and dating from the Ancient Greek, Roman, Roman-Byzantine and Medieval ages.

A few key scenes

Historian Lucia Teposu Marinescu advises that you should reserve one hour for an unhurried visit of the Lapidarium. No matter the hurry, you must not miss bas-reliefs 17 (the battle of Tapae in 101 A.D. and the portrait of Decebal), 64, 65 (the scene showing the peace agreement at the end of the first war), 85 (the bridge built over the Danube by Apollodorus of Damascus), 102 (the sharing of the last water supplies in the mountains) and 122 (the taking of the Dacian treasures), as well as Decebal's suicide in scene 116.

Lapidarium din MNIR. Foto: Cătălin Gruia

CHAPTER 11

THE CIUC SCOUTS' BIG GAME

How to turn a gathering of jaded high school students into a happy team of survivors.

Four explorers were kidnapped from their tents right before sunrise. They were blindfolded and thrown into a van that started suddenly onto a bumpy road. I also lent a hand... From the passenger's seat, I saw through the small back window how they lied there like bags of potatoes. I felt the worst for Didi: a beautiful teenager with top-model looks, modest like a country girl, easy-going, always with smiling, cursing in a strange way (everything she didn't like, she would put an 'of life' on the end of: heat wave of life, rain of life, and so on). We abandoned them on the side of the road without a word, about 35 kilometers away; they were given a compass and an envelope with instructions; they had strict instructions to return to the camp, however they could, before sunset.

After three hours, when the general assembly in the square was called, no one said a word about the absentees; but eyes sparkled with envy. We are in Meresti scout camp, in Harghita (right on the border of Cheile Varghisului Reserve) organized to celebrate the 15th year anniversary of 'Orion' local center in Miercurea Ciuc. Thirty explorers (the scouts are all of high-school age) came to play 'life in the country side' for two weeks (this year's theme). But they will discover that they are the prisoners and guinea pigs of the organizers – 20 older leader scouts (over 18) – transformed over night into 'extraterrestrials' that will perform all kinds of 'experiments' on them, to toughen and unite the explorers.

The kidnapping of the four scouts is the beginning of a rite of passage named totemization.

II One of the movements that inspired scouthood was the *American Indian Woodcraft Movement*, founded by Ernest Thompson Seton. He wanted to reintroduce the youth to the healthy lifestyle of the pioneers through camping, physical education, young people teaching their fellows, through a kind of picturesque 'Native Americanism' (danses, camp fires, hunting). Even before 1914, some troops were already using totems (some taken right from Thompson's writings, others taken from various writers, like Jack London). Not all countries practice totemization – only some associations in Belgium, France, and Luxembourg. In Romania, the local center in Ciuc is the only one that practices totemization. Only the most deserving of the scouts are selected for this ritual. For no more than 24 hours, the chosen ones are subjected to secret trials meant to prepare them, through physical and psychological exhaustion, to form a new 'me' in accordance with their totem (the name of an animal that they each resemble), which they receive at an exclusive ceremony.

III It's getting dark. A ghostly mist rises from the long and already-wet grass. All around are hills covered in almond tree forests and pastures. A brook and a larger river surround the meadow on three edges. The camp – about as big as a soccer field – is split in two: the upper part is the leaders' turf, while the valley is the explorers'. Taguan (the flying squirrel), alias Cristian Grecu, 22 years old, the beta wolf of the leaders' pack, ordered everyone to wait at the tables covered in blue tarp. I watch in awe as many let their heads fall between their knees so as not to see or hear anything. 'Not a word, you maggots!' Taguan would have yelled under normal circumstances, like a sergeant major, from the leader's mound. But this time, he sent his command through whispers, from person to person. Smart, open, communicative, Taguan, the beloved of the sutani (as the leaders call the little ones) is the explorers' main animator. The totemized leaders have retreated and are making plans in low voices. All of a sudden, all glances shift to the entrance of the camp, where the four kidnapped scouts stand: tired and barely dragging their feet under their monstruos backpacks. Tonight, the secret ritual will take place. I am not totemized and cannot participate, even as an observer.

The next day, the new names of the freshly-totemized scouts are announced. Didi Bolog, 17 years old, participating in her third scout camp, became Hirundo (the swallow). 'How was it?' I asked her. 'We aren't allowed to talk about it', she whispered and went away.

IV At only 70 cm deep, the pick already begins to grind. Bobac (the marmot), alias Ovidiu Ciobotariu, puts his hands on his hips and starts bemoaning his sorrow: he has hit a bed of rocks. From the side of the hole, Cherug (the Danubian hawk), alias Petre Eremia, and Sergiu Bucur (not yet totemized) look at each other knowingly. What bad luck fell upon them that they now have to dig the site for this cursed outhouse? Sergiu goes to ask the boss what's to be done.

Suricat, alias Sorin Bota, shouts out orders to the group of boys that are building the table, a few dozen meters away. Although, in theory, all the leaders are equal, Suricat is the alpha male. Authoritarian, harsh (in the mountains, in life or death situations, there's no room for democracy), but also a clown and a windbag in his moments of relaxation, Suricat is a 26-year-old Nero, with curls covering his forehead as a crown of laurels. His answer is brutal: dig somewhere else. But the boys aren't keen on abandoning their work of three hours. A spontaneous, almost scientific discussion arises, that puts everything into the equation – how many people are there, how many days we are staying, how much shit a person produces in a day, at what density (under conditions of heavy effort on the mountain and intense consumption), how much toilet paper, how much soil is used to cover it, how quickly the ground absorbs it, and so on – all in order to find out how big the whole needs to be. 'I know from experience that it's not big enough', Cherug says and goes back to digging.

The girls have already finished the laundry and are getting ready to weave the net that will serve as a tabletop. It's a laborious task, but one that doesn't seem to bother them at all. Although she left Ciuc many years ago for Bucharest, Dolphin, alias Alexandra Groza, remains the alpha female of the tribe. The other girls gather around her and Inermis (the water deer), alias Laura Badut. At 27 years old, she seems as if she refuses to leave her adolescence behind. Quiet, beautiful, with gentle features, she is integrated but elusive. She doesn't have a loud voice – she doesn't feel the need to impose herself. Her power is quiet. At the end of the day, I accompanied Suricat to inspect the constructions (made only of wood and rope): the big table for 20 people with a shelter for sun and rain, the fireplace, the dish washing area, the outhouse, and the mast – a pole made of birch twelve meters high on which the scouts' flag is hoisted. He was satisfied.

On the second day, when the explorers came, they were split up into five units, six kids each, named after Romanian provinces: Banat, Moldova, Oltenia, Oas and Dobrogea. They received their campgrounds, they enclosed them symbolically in poles and rope, and then for the rest of the day, they built miniature versions of the leaders' settlement: every troop with its own table, fireplace, dishwashing area, and outhouse. In the leaders' campgrounds are the comissary tents, where the food and tools are kept.

V The schedule of an ordinary day. The wakeup call is given at 7: 00 am. The night is cold and humid, but it doesn't matter because there are three or four people in a tent. Then follows a run to the toilet, a bath in the spring, and breakfast. The rules of the camp forbid the explorers from stepping inside the leaders' zone. When they need something – tools, food, medicine – they come and ask for it at the leaders' gate. The doorbell is a tin mug on which they beat with a spoon. Around 8: 00-9: 00 it's time for the general assembly around the flagpole in the courtyard (here they yell the names/totems of all those in the group and the chants of each troop for as long as their lungs can take it; then, the schedule of the day is announced). Afterwards, there are workshops, contests, and all kinds of games, as well as endurance and tenacity tests set up by the alien-leaders.

Lunch is served at 2: 00 pm. Each troop cooks for itself and invites several leaders to eat with them. After the meal, more workshops and tests, or free time to bathe in the river. Then, by the time they gather firewood, it is already evening. They prepare their food. After dinner: evaluation of the troops, after which the head of each troop is called to the leaders' table to talk about the day's events. The campfire starts around 10: 00 pm. Everyone sings and sometimes there are even evening games, during which the explorers are cast out from their territory and have to pass a series of tests in order to return. At midnight, it's lights-out, with the song 'It's night time in Madagascar and the whole jungle is asleep'. Only the two who are designated to serve as night guards remain, on watch all night around the fire, regardless of the weather.

VI In 1908, the English Colonel Baden-Powell wrote *Scouting for Boys* after having applied his method a year earlier in a two-week-long experimental camp on the south coast of England. The scouts (undergoing a kind of non-formal education), he maintained, cultivate the youngsters' spirit of adventure, teamwork, and progress by strenghthening themselve. Practical intelligence, courage, character, and the spirit of mind, cannot be learned in school, but through games and life in nature. Baden-Powell had spent a good part of his life in the army, where he had observed that young soldiers, who had been trained only to listen, could not handle themselves in unforseen situations. So he sought to form people with initiative, through training sessions masked as games.

Baden-Powell had no intention of creating a youth organization. But Scouting for Boys was an unexpected success: in Great Britain, groups of kids started organizing themselves based on Baden-Powell's directions. The scholar Gheorghe Munteanu-Murgoci, who happened to visit England in 1911, brought scouting back to Bucharest. He was the main initiator and leader of the first groups of scouts in Romania. On May 12, 1914, the Association of Romanian Scouts was founded. Scouts from one town formed a cohort, and those from a county were a legion. Prince Carol was proclaimed Commander of the Great Legion.

Scouts participated in World War I both on the front lines and most notably in helping the injured. There were two scout camps in Solesti, Vaslui and in Sculeni, Iasi. After the war, the organization underwent a period of development until January 1937, when king Carol II replaced it with the National Guard, in which all children and teachers were obliged to serve. In September 1940, under the fascist dictatorship, the Guard was also disolved. After World War II, hopes of the scouts' rebirth were wiped away by the coming of communism. The era of the pioneers had arrived. Although both the guards and the pioneers borrowed a great deal from the scouts, the foundation was different. The Pioneers and the Guards were indoctrinated and forced to join and strenghten the cult of personality. Scouts by definition are democratic, the youth willingly joining the scouts; they have the right to their own opinion, and politics are strictly forbidden.

Most Romanian scouts enrolled in 1990 in the *Assosciation of Former Girl and Boy Scouts of Romania*, which in the same year, on June 20, was transformed into the Association of Romanian Scouts (ACER). ACER decided to bring together all the other newly founded nuclei of scouting (after 1989, many scout groups formed, such as the *Association of Romanian Girl Guides* or organizations based on ethnicity or religion). ACER opened its first branches in Targu Mures, Sinaia, Deva, and Galati. In 1992, scouting extended throughout half of the counties, and during the summer, 24 camps were organized, bringing together hundreds of scouts. In June 1993, according to an agreement between ACER and other scouting groups, the *National Organization of Romanian Scouts* (ONCR) was created. That same year, in July, it was welcomed, with full rights, into the *Scout Movement Global Organization* (OMMS).

VII The leaders of the Ciuc scouts are a unique tribe, with a precise hierarchy that has developed over time. All gravitate around Chouette (the owl), alias Irina Groza – the matriarch of the tribe, a discrete, empathetic, affectionate 53-year-old woman who exercises her authority sparingly. If it hadn't been for her, nothing would have existed. Everything began with this gym teacher from the Octavian Goga High school in Miercurea Ciuc who felt like there was something missing in her life. Only school and nothing more? She would have liked to do more with and for the children. That's how she found out about the scouts. Along with two other teachers, Vasile and Maria Grecu (totemized Grizzly and Campagnol) and 21 kids, she organized the original group, based in Chouette's own house.

In August 1994, they received permission from the ONCR to found the local center. The first activities – ski tours, sledding, mountain climbing, or environmental protection – were completed with the help of mountain hunters. In 1996, Belgian scouts Paule and Eric le Boulengé came to form a common camp together with the scouts in Ciuc. This was a turning point in the history of the local center. Between 1996 and 1998, the two Belgians acted as scouting teachers to the Ciuc scouts. 'They opened up a new world for us, and we realized that what had been before was just child's play', says Chouette.

In 1998, a decline in the scouting movement on the national level had begun and in Ciuc it was felt as badly as anywhere else. The old gang had broken up and the kids had gone away to college. In 2003, Chouette put her foot down: 'we're doing it right, or we're not doing it at all'. The perspective they gained after their break-up brought them back together. They decided to make a camp on their own terms, straying from the Belgians. Annual camps followed, and society benefited: in 2005, they helped the victims of the floods; between 2006 and 2008, they marked hiking trails in Fagaras mountains (it was a difficult task, almost beyond the abilities of some children, who were carrying pipes on their backs, but everything becomes easier when you are animated by the scouting spirit).

In 2006, they started to extend, with a branch of 'braves' (middle school students), and in 2007, with 'little wolves' (primary school students). There are currently 118 scouts that pay dues, and 18 on the waiting list. Their headquarters is in a classroom at Octavian Goga High School, where principal Doru Dobreanu is a scout-supporter. Once a year, a general assembly schedules the following year's activities. Once a week, the troops meet, and thus learn to work independently.

VIII Everyone gathered in a circle around a blue tarp placed on the ground. Kudu (the kudu antilope), alias Adrian Cotoara, from the Mures local center will start a wrestling workshop, and he will also be a referee. Each troop has a fighter assigned. Everyone will fight everyone: ten matches, two minutes each. Margay (the wild cat), alias Diana Mosoiu, is oiling the shirtless competitors. And to make everything a bit more interesting, she pours plenty of oil onto the tarp as well.

Under the eyes of so many pretty girls, the boys take the fight very seriously. When the button on Lynx's shorts popped from so much muscle flexing, he continued fighting in his underwear, accompanied by screams of encouragement. 'The girls should fight too! Girls too!' an overexcited scout yells. The wrestlers' show is nothing compared to that of the audience. Laughter; taunts; aplause;

This was one of the many workshops organized by the leaders over the course of the camp (mowing, sewing, rock climbing, forestry, ziplining, caving, fire building, bacon frying, sawing, pulling a log with a rope, making cheese, medicinal herbs, pottery, making traditional sandals and masks, weaving bracelets, cutting wood, rafting on plastic bottles rafts). The leaders (most of them students) are exceptional actor-educators dedicated, heart and soul, to scouting. They work for hours on end preparing themselves for the games and presentations they put on for the explorers. Everything is like a play, rehearsed beforehand, planned in every detail, acted with grace and spontaneity, with make-up, costumes, and props.

IX The wake-up call was given late, and we hung around the tent hoping for a day of well-deserved laziness. Around 10: 00 am, in the courtyard, the news hit us like a lightning bolt: we're going on a hike. The hike involves at least one night spent outside the camp; it's a survival trip, maybe one of the most difficult of the tests, the one for which the others have been preparing the scouts. Only the explorers are going, without any leaders. Dangers: bears, ticks, vipers, chaos.

Madalina Pop, from the Mures Local Center – a tough girl 'with a big mouth', yet at the same time motherly and helpful – was named head of the group. She was given a compass, a map, and a one-day walking circuit to the location designated for sleeping overnight under the stars. We received supplies for our survival – three slices of bread to be eaten with paté or with margarine and honey, and 0.75 liters of water per person. Near midday, 30 kids, with their survival equipment on their backs, gathered in a line and left the camp, singing under the merciless sun. After a half an hour, we were drowning in sweat; soon, we lost the trail markings. We found them again with great difficulty.

In a stroke of foresight, Madalina asked Radu to walk a bit ahead and show us the way. This is 19-year-old Radu Bunea's first time as scout, but he is the son of a mountain ranger and himself an attested ranger, and, as such, has more experience on the mountains than all of us put together. Right when the group finds its breath and a rhythm, Silvia collapses. Only then did we see that she was the only one who wasn't wearing boots but sandals, and that she had bandaged feet. When she unwrapped her bandages, we saw that her soles and toes were raw (from a pair of new boots that had given her bruises and blisters, which she had cut with a small pair of scissors). Everyone gave their advice about what should be done, and in the end, Mihaela and Radu took her back to the camp. They would catch up with us later.

After their departure, the atmosphere deteriorated. The singing and count-offs stopped (every half an hour, the head of the line would shout out 1, the next, 2, and so on, until the end, to check that no one was lost); they started grumbling complaints about the leaders; the water had finished. We crossed many springs, but we didn't have courage to drink from them anymore – the past few days, those who had drunk from them had had stomach problems. We came across a shepherd dog who would open up the way for us everywhere and defended us from other sheep-running dogs. We named him Jeghi Price, for how dirty her fur was and for how delicately she ate her food.

It was already 4: 00 pm and Madalina and Radu still hadn't shown up. Our breaks were becoming longer and more frequent. No one was listening to anyone. For a half an hour, the group tried to organize themselves just to eat; orders were raining down but no one did anything. Antonia succeeded in bringing together a small group. Then she spred a tarp on which everyone put their food from their backpacks. The heat had subsided a bit and the wind was starting to blow in gusts, making waves in the tall grass. Little by little, everyone got to savor their food. The morale was high again. The refrain of last year's camp hit song returned to everyone's lips: 'My slice, my love/ you are my whole life'. The group started to walk in a steady rhythm; we would only stop to extract a tick from an unlucky girl. The mountains were echoing with songs: 'Hunger is screaming inside of us', or 'Mother, where are you? Spank me if you want, but come and take me home', or 'I crushed a little mouse at night on the wall/And from his stomach I ate spaghetti'.

Near nightfall, Mihaela and Radu caught up with us. They were bringing four liters of tea from the camp. We continued to walk, our minds empty, hunger and thirst erased by exhaustion. It had gotten dark and we still hadn't arrived at the marked location. The full moon, the fog that lifted from the valleys, the light of the moon that rapidly changed intensity – evrything looked like on a movie set. Madalina sent forward a team of six people to look for a campground and gather wood for the fire. The group came together again after two hours.

Around the fire, happiness returned. *Stop the hearse/ The dead man wants to drink a Cola.* That's how it started – Radu's guitar, cracked and tied with string, unleashed itself. The performance was magical. We sang non-stop and no one was even thinking about sleeping. At night, by the light of the fire and the sparkles in the girls' eyes while watching the guitarist, everything becomes mysterious and possible.

At around 3: 00 in the morning, it started pouring. The boys had spread out a tarp for cover, but it was impossible for it to shield all of us. We ran towards a nearby shepherd's cabin, which Radu had discovered that evening. We took shelter there – 30 people in 50 square meters. Some in the attic, some in the main room in which there were chairs, two beds, a table, washbasins, and pots, all crammed in and heaped on top of each other. It smelled like goats and whey, it was full of dung and mice, but it felt like heaven.

The singing started up again, drowning out the sound of thunder and wind outside. We slept however we could, contorted as if we were playing one big game of Twister. But we slept better than ever. In the morning we each ate our last slice of bread with paté and started again. The whole way, I exchanged stories (we had already become friends at this point) with Ioana Balaj, an introverted high school student, an almost gothic being, but yet still a volunteer and a strong character, once you get to know her. Small and speedy under a giant, broken backpack that hangs somehow to the side, Ioana is the kind of girl that makes hours feel like minutes (like in the commercial). In the end, we exchanged backpacks, as mine was about the size of a small bundle.

There were unexpected incidents on the way back too, but nothing we couldn't handle: the group had bonded, had a rhythm, had luck, and had solutions. We reached the camp around noon. We regrouped and reentered singing triumphantly while the leaders cheered for us.

X The scout method – verified for more than a century – is based on seven elements: respecting the oath and law of the scouts, personal progress, group life (the troop system), learning through action, life in nature, and support from adults. 'The values of the scouts are the same in every corner of the globe. When you meet a scout, you know you are standing in front of a person who is honest, loyal, ready to give you a friendly help in hand at any time, and trying to leave the world a little better than how he found it', says Chouette.

'Scouting is a state of mind', says Baribal (the North American black bear), alias Octav Grecu. It sounds a little bit like the kind of love that makes you want to be a better, more generous person, especially when you experience it in your teenage years, when our souls are the most receptive.

Surrounded by songs, games, youth, generosity, and joy, the two weeks I spent with the Ciuc scouts were among the best of my entire life. When it was over and the kids all left in a military truck, I felt like crying (along with everyone else). And not only because I was saying goodbye to friends, but also because I realized how much more beautiful my own childhood could have been if I had been lucky enough to have a Chouette in my life.

In a Romania facing crises at all levels, with a disintegrating school system, the scouts from Ciuc are a ray of hope that things can be different. I would give anything to be able to turn back time and lose myself again among the explorers, walking at sunset in a straight line through the tall grass, carrying wood for the campfire down the valley on a stretcher, all the while singing loudly: 'Go, viper, go; shoo, snake, shoo!'

XI The history of youth organizations in Romania

- 1907 – Lord Baden-Powell, British colonel, creates the scouting movement.
- 1913 – The first scout troops in Romania appear in Brasov and Bucharest, led by Colonel Grigore Berindei.
- May 12, 1914 – The Association of Romanian Scouts is founded. The association becomes official in 1915, with Prince Carol (the future king Carol II) as Commander; on June 1, 1915 the 'Girl Scouts of Romania' association is founded.
- 1914-1918 – During WWI, the scouts actively participate in helping the injured as well as in the front lines.
- 1919 – The first large camp of Romanian scouts takes place in Brasov, at 'Pietrele lui Solomon'.
- 1920 – The first international jamboree in London. Romania participates with a delegation of 100; scouts from all countries gather every four years at the jamboree (peaceful meetings between tribes, in the Native American dialects) for a celebration of friendship.
- 1922 – The International Organization of Scouts if founded; Romania, through ACER, is a founding member; the first worldwide competition.
- 1930 – The first national jamboree at Sibiu.
- January 24, 1937 – Carol II disintegrated the 'Scouts of Romania'. In order to act as a counterweight to the Legionary Movement, Carol II incorporates the scouts into the National Guard, a paramilitary organization based on the Hitler Jugend.
- 1945 – The Romanian Scouts Association is founded.
- April 30, 1949 – A few hundred children take the scout oath on the grounds of the Giulesti Theatre (then the 'Gh. Gheorghiu-Dej' Palace of Culture).

- 1976 – 'The Eagles of the Nation' appear.
- June 20, 1990 – The Scouts of Romania are founded.
- November 17, 1993 – The association changes its name to ONCR and becomes a member of the Global Organization of the Scout Movement (OMMS) at the International Conference in Bangkok.
- 2009 – The Romanian Scouts National Organization has approximatively 2500 members from 63 branches; worldwide, there are 28 million scouts in 216 countries.

CHAPTER 12

BACK IN THE SADDLE

Cyclists reinvent the wheel along with blocking traffic in Bucharest. They are the sacrifice generation.

During one hot evening, I was one of the drivers suffocating in the cars lined up in endless phalanges of colored snails, yearning for the speed of pedestrians flowing between Piata Romana and Universitate. A cyclist flew by, softly, whistling while the left handlebar of his bicycle almost brushed my right rear-view mirror, like a relaxed acrobat stepping on an imaginary rope between the row of cars and the curb. A little further on, when he could no longer ride on the road, he climbed onto the sidewalk and carried on undisturbed. This is typical Romania: when everyone sits quietly in line, civilized and disciplined, there's always one wise guy who cuts in front. But at the same time, I could catch a glimpse of that man's sensation of freedom, after escaping from the flock. The next day, I bought a bicycle, joining the small group of audacious people forced by traffic jams to take the bicycle by its horns again. The total number of cars in the capital has tripled in the last 25 years, reaching about 1,500,000. At rush hour, one kilometer takes you 10-20 minutes by car, a quarter of an hour on foot and five minutes by bicycle.

II A stuffy guy, having the air of a London motorcycle rider, got swiftly off a Brompton bicycle with small, toy-like wheels; then, in a single gesture, just like you close an umbrella, he folded it down to the dimensions of a briefcase. This is George Culda, the president of *Bate saua sa priceapa iapa*, an association that promotes bicycle riding. A few years ago, George and his group of friends with whom he used to go hiking in the mountains made up their minds to make tourist cycling routes, to mark them, so that people would no longer get lost. That's how the association Bate saua sa priceapa iapa was born in 2004.

'However, I realized that I was talking in vain about wonderful tourist cycling routes to people who no longer had the guts to get back in the saddle. The bike culture has disappeared in Romania and it needs to be reinvented'. Even though bicycle riding is still an underground movement, it is starting to emerge. 'In 2004 it would be weeks before I saw another cyclist in the streets. I was going to work every day by bike and the people were suspiciously looking at me. Today I think there are hundred of thousands of bike owners in Bucharest, tens of thousands of occasional users and thousands of everyday users', says George Culda. Eight years ago, there were only seven bicycle shops in Bucharest. Now there are over 50 (without including the supermarkets). The few small associations that promoted bicycle riding united in the fall of 2007, forming the Romanian Cyclists' Federation.

On the 1st of August 2008, the *MaiMultVerde* ecological association opened the first bicycle rental center in Bucharest, with a total of 100 bicycles. According to the distributors, this market's value is estimated at 40 million Euros a year (approximately 300,000 bicycles sold). The number of road accidents involving cyclists continues to drop slightly as more and more bicycle riders get on the streets and drivers become more careful.

III Ioan Zarnescu, former research and design director at *Tohan Zarnesti* factory from August 1959 until retirement, after the fall of communism, rode a standard Pegas bicycle all his life. At Tohan, they made weapons and bicycles (following a German model) from 1954 until the 1990s. Before the war and until 1954, there had been assembly factories in Medias and Bucharest, but the bicycles were made using imported components. The '6 martie' factory had an average output of 200,000 bicycles per year, 10-20% of which were exported: to Iran (the first exported bicycle), the USA and Canada (foldable and children's bicycles), Yugoslavia (for component exchanges) and so on.

In 1960, a bicycle cost around 750 lei, about half the average wage. In 1981, the price hit 2,100 for a Torpedo – equaling the average wage. Tohan had a capacity for 250,000 bicycles per year. In 1989, Prime Minister Dascalescu wanted to raise production to 600,000 a year. 'The demand was great, they were hard to find. On short distances, the bicycle was the main means of transportation for commuters, peasants and many city dwellers. Everybody went around by bicycle', says Ioan Zarnescu. Russian bicycles were Tohan's competitors – flooding the market with mandatory imports of 200,000 bikes per year between 1980 and 1990, at prices comparable with the ones in Romania. After 1989, the ever more aggressive car culture replaced the two-wheel one. More and more people could afford buying a car and most domestic bicycles became scrap iron.

IV Tudor Smalenic 44, creative director for Harper's Bazaar Romania magazine, has been coming to work by bicycle every day for the last ten years. Back then it seemed like a very weird thing to do, and Tudor, with his blue helmet, looked like a strange sort of pterodactyl. 'Let us see the full half of the glass though, he says. Five years ago, policemen used to stop me on the street and scold me. One of them once told me on Magheru Av.: get out of here, man, you have to pay to ride here'. 'For the cyclists' benefit', in November 2005, the Bucharest Road Police (BRP) and the Technical Circulation Commission within the Municipality prohibited bicycle circulation on Bucharest's main avenues. 'There's no room to build bike tracks on a wide and busy avenue', declared at the time Gheorghe Udriste, executive director of the Road Transport Division, within the General City Hall. The disposition – absurd and primitive – was revoked three days later. Despite the fact that the decision was dropped by the City Hall, a handful of discontented cyclists gathered in Piata Universitatii. It was the first protest of this type in those rough days for bike riders.

The first bike route, between the Regie-Grozavesti student campus and Universitate, was built in 2002, when the general mayor of that time, Traian Basescu, was planning on introducing tracks specifically meant for cycling as a part of the rehabilitation program for the city's main arteries. The initiative was only partially implemented (on the sidewalks of Kogalniceanu and Regina Elisabeta avenues), because Marian Vanghelie, mayor of the 5th city sector, opposed the project.

V A new project (a network meant to cover approximately 46 kilometers, a 1.5 million Euros deal) started in 2006. 'A falsely enthusiastic and superficial start, in the good old-fashioned Romanian way; works were stopped at our insistence. We saw the documentation that the Police had received: on the drawings sent by the design engineer, there are no manholes and no trees whatsoever; those people did no proper on-site checking; they just took a map of Bucharest and drew the lines', says George Culda. Out of the 46 designed kilometers, only 34 have been finalized, adding up to eleven routes. 'I don't know whether we'll be building others. Romanians have a primitive mentality. Haven't you seen...? Bucharest is full of cars and there are very few cyclists', said Adrian Burlacu, engineer at Global Service Proiect, the company in charge with designing the tracks. Former Street Administration director, Claudiu Balan, explained that for these tracks (one meter wide, with insurmountable obstacles and impossible angles on the route), Romanian standards were observed rigorously.

Bucharest City Hall and the Road Police decided that the best solution for the tracks is to be drawn on the sidewalks, to ensure the riders' safety and traffic fluency. Cyclists, discriminated against out of too much care, still have to wait for proper urbanism projects that would separate cars from bicycles on the roadway. Policemen haven't given a single fine for cars parked on bicycle tracks. For the moment, the City Hall has pedestrians arguing with bicycle riders for a space that is often occupied by cars too. But things are moving on. 'We're finally managed to form a working group inside the Bucharest City Hall to come up with proposals and solutions for the bicycle riders', says George Culda.

VI I woke up at midnight on the operating table of the Panduri hospital in Bucharest. Six hours before, I was pedaling home along the endless snake of cars illegally parked on the roadway. The door of a parked white Jeep opened just as I was passing it. It thrust my handlebar forward, swirling me in the air. The driver, who was watching me from the sidewalk, gave me a red towel as a gift to wipe my blood off, and then went on his way. The very next day I left the hospital and bought myself a new bike. And now, almost every evening I'm one of the bicycle riders who pass on softly, whistling, along drivers suffocated in the cars lined up in endless phalanges of colored snails between Piata Romana and Universitate.

VII Short History of the Bicycle in Romania
- 1869 – The first documented mention of cycling in Romania: for a fee, the *Tirul* society makes a few velocipedes available to its members.
- 1954 – Tohan Zarnesti, descendent of the factory built by Malaxa in 1937, produces Victoria, the first Romanian bicycle.
- 1967 – Pionier, the first bicycle for children.
- 1968 – Junior and Pegas, the first bicycles for teenagers.
- 1981 – Romanian multi-speed bicycles are produced.
- 2002 – The first cycling track – between the Regie-Grozavesti student campus and Universitate.
- 2005 – Tohan Zarnesti gives up bicycle production.
- November 2005 – For three days, bicycle circulation is forbidden on the main avenues of the capital.
- 2007 – The Romanian Bicycle Riders' Federation is founded.
- August 1st, 2008 – The MaiMultVerde ecological association opens the first bicycle rental center in Bucharest.
- August 2013 – The first edition of the Cyclist Guide is published. Step by step, year after year, cyclists reconquer the streets of Bucharest.
- January 2014 – The first normal, western looking cycling track in Bucharest: from Buzesti to Uranus streets.

CHAPTER 13

THE LANGUAGE OF THE FOLK COSTUME

Text: Adina Brânciulescu.

Some 70 years ago, a traveling photographer stopped by at the house where I live today. My grandfather, his brother and my great-grandfather had their picture taken wearing the typical folk costume for Ibanesti region, in Mures county. Back then, a person's outfit said a lot about its owner, according to a rigorous code. The costume continuously changed with its owner's age, conveying information about their wealth and marital status. An unmarried lad's costume looked like a blooming tree. With each big crossroad in his life, he lost yet another adorning element, reaching his old age as simple and as stern as an old trunk in winter.

The unmarried young man announced his marital status with his flower-embroidered shirt, and his hat adorned with a long feather and azgardan – a special ornament made of beads. With each major moment in his life, he left something else behind: his feather (upon getting married), his zgardan (when his first child was born), while ornaments embroidered on his sleeves and going from neck down became increasingly discreet, until turning into mere waving lines. A woman's attire respected the same code. As an unmarried girl, she had colored flower motifs (cheita) embroidered along the sleeves of her shirt. She wore nothing on her head, and wore her hair into two braids (which turned into a single one, as she got closer to marriage age). After her wedding, a single decorative stripe remained embroidered on the upper part of her shirt (umar), and she covered her head with a yellow scarf or a big sash decorated with tassels, whenever she went dancing.

'A rich wife would embroider her umar with beads, going all the way down on her sleeve. A poor wife would have a narrower embroidery, with only a few strings of cheite starting from there', says Virgil Chirtes, school headmaster in Ibanesti Padure village. Having given birth to her first child, the woman gave up cheerful colors, and wore the sober black and white costume.

This language of folk costumes is passing away along with the elderly. Youngsters nowadays prefer 'modern' versions, ethnographic pieces adapted to fashion.

CHAPTER 14
TRANSYLVANIA HAY

The treasure in our backyard.
Interview with Rodics Gergely.

34 countries from all over the world ran a 20-page **National Geographic** cover story in July 2013 about a wonderful mysterious land where man and nature, working in symbiosis for hundreds of years, have created 'one of the great treasures of the cultivated world: some of the richest and most botanically diverse hay meadows in Europe'. This unique ecosystem, unfortunately extremely fragile, is right here in Transylvania. Rodics Gergely, director of the *Pogány-havas Regional Association*, is leading a team fighting to save the Transylvanian hay.

Hi Gergely, please give us a short introduction about yourself.
I was born in Budapest, Hungary in a family with quite a few connections to nature and nature conservation. My father – a doctor – is a nature lover, and he taught me a lot about nature during our walks, including most plant and animal names of my hometown. My aunt is a biologist and worked for the Ministry of Environment in Hungary for almost 20 years. It was also my favourite joy to spend as much time in nature as possible: walking, canoeing, and biking. I have a group of twelve friends, the Börzsöny Group, named after the mountain where we had our first outing together when I was 13. I studied rural development and landscape management on the biggest agricultural university in Hungary, and worked later in these domains, along with renewable energy policy and power plant development projects. I love old trees enormously and every time I see local people as well as authorities in our area cutting down

trees older than 40-50 years almost automatically, I get extremely upset. My big dream is to manage a large and beautiful garden or park of an existing or ruined manor house somewhere. I think – like hay meadows – these places express really how humans and nature can create the greatest harmony on Earth, these places are for me almost like the Garden of Eden.

How did you start protecting meadows?

I moved to Transylvania in 2006, when I decided to become director of the **Pogány-havas Regional Association**. I had various reasons, but two of them stood out: the enormous beauty of this area which made me admire the work of these people, and the second, were the people and hospitality I experienced every time I came for a visit to Transylvania. During my first years here, I started putting together development strategies that respect the area's natural and cultural heritage. I thought it was very important not to come here and tell people what to do, because all the visible results of their work are just so much better than those of large scale farming in the rest of Europe. So I started softly, but at the same time we had to be aware of Romania's 2007 European Union accession, which would change a lot of rules on food production and hygiene which I already experienced in Hungary. So the main idea was to help local farmers to get ready for the new rules. In our case this has a very clear link with hay meadow management: if hay is needed, hay meadows will be managed. To increase the need for hay we have to increase cattle numbers, to reach this we have to sell their products for a better price. So we started setting up milk collection points with the farmers' associations, where milk quality could be tested for each farmer, and organized cheese trainings to improve the varieties sold in markets or shops.

In the middle of this process I met a new friend, Demeter László, a biologist from the area, who introduced me to Barbara Knowles, an English biologist who fell in love with Transylvania just like me. She started supporting our work financially, and later she moved to Transylvania and became a colleague, who works with us on a daily basis. Thanks to this, our network of English people and organisations interested in nature and sustainability (small farmers of Romania proved the sustainability of their work by doing it in the last couple of centuries almost the same way) increased a lot. Together with her and László we started our biological research in the meadows which soon proved to be Europe's most biodiverse plant communities; furthermore, Transylvania has one of Europe's last large scale medieval landscapes.

Prince Charles is very interested in this area and he refers to it as 'a library of information which we need for our future survival'. Could you please explain this and why are the Transylvanian meadows and their people so special?

Prince Charles fell in love with Transylvania decades ago. 'Hay meadows provide a huge range of benefits for farming communities and society in general. They create some of Europe's most spectacular scenery and cultural landscapes. Simply to watch this natural, environmental and cultural heritage disappear before our eyes is, surely, not an option we can consider', said HRH the Prince of Wales in a video message during our policy seminar at the European Parliament, held in Brussels in 2012. And indeed, traditional farming here has proved for centuries that it is a sustainable system, where inputs and outputs are in harmony with the rules of nature, and that a lower standard of living doesn't necessarily mean a lower quality of life. Hay meadows are a collection of the plant and insect species of a greater area. They were created by providing optimal living conditions for most plants, mainly by removing the competing taller plants. These places are a concentration of many species. Mountain hay meadows are among the most biodiverse areas in the world. Based on more than twelve years of biological research we discovered:

Altogether 617 plant species in the area:
- 390 species of grasslands
- 81 species in a four by four m quadrat (3rd place in Europe)
- 38 internationally or nationally protected plant species
- 33 red listed plant species
- 12 endemic plant species

Plant habitats create habitats for insects and other animal species. Another interesting example is that the number of butterfly species on one meadow here equals the total butterfly population in the UK, according to research done in 2011. This richness disappeared in Western Europe because of intensive, industrial monocultures. For example, the United Kingdom lost 97% of its species-rich hay meadows since the 1950's. If these countries would ever like to restore their natural habitats, most of their species have to be imported from somewhere else. 'The protection of this native diversity is vital for long-term conservation of the grassland, and has practical applications in plant breeding, species recovery programmes, restocking and enhancement of species and vegetation. The scientific and economic value of ecological and geographical variation in the Transylvanian meadow flora provides a powerful argument for conservation'. – wrote Dr John Akeroyd, a botanist friend of His Royal Highness in his talk abstract for our conference in May 2013.

What threats are they facing?

First of all we have to distinguish between inner and outer meadows. The inner meadows closer to the village are more intensively managed: they are manured, and mown twice a year. Outer – or mountain – hay meadows are far from the village (sometimes 10-20 km away), at higher altitudes and are more extensively managed (not manured, mown only once a year) – these are the very biodiverse ones. The two main trends which make mountain hay meadows disappear on a frightening scale are abandonment and their conversion to pastures. In both cases, species' richness decreases. The reasons are:

- The drop of milk prices during the last decade, which resulted in lower cattle numbers in the area.
- Increased milk hygiene standards, which made many farmers drop their production and sell their cattle.
- Imported milk replaced national consumption of local milk.
- Imported potatoes led to a drop in national prices; therefore local farmers gave up growing potatoes. This created free ploughland near the villages which farmers would frequently turn into intensively-used meadows with few plant species. This decreases the need for mountain hay.
- Mountain meadows are far; production takes more time and is more expensive. Farmers can hardly use tractors and they have to transport hay on a long and risky road. Farmers' children

don't continue farming because of low income levels. European subsidies are equally high for pastures and meadows. Because making hay is a hard job, transport is pricey, most meadow owners agree to let sheep graze on them and get the same subsidy at the end of the year.

What should be done to save them?
In our opinion the main ways of saving them are:
- More cows in the area. This would increase the need for hay. However this isn't enough, as intensive inner meadows can satisfy most or all of the needs.
- New management organs. Meadow management organisations could replace traditional farmers in making, transporting and marketing the mountain hay where the land was abandoned, and could help active farmers with some of these activities. Practically, these could be the villages' common land management organisations. Without subsidies, this work cannot be viable.
- New markets for hay. If hay is not needed for local cattle, it could be sold for other purposes. There is a wide range of opportunities, but these have to be thoroughly investigated. To mention just a few: Quality hay as fodder for high value animals like race horses; hay seeds for overseeding or fodder; producing hay pellets for heating; packaging material for fragile products; tee, hay sculptures and playgrounds and many others.
- Diversified subsidies. As described above, European subsidies provide the same payment for meadows and pastures. Higher subsidy levels for hay meadow management might make a big difference and motivate farmers to continue making mountain hay.
- Nature conservation. In general, we can say that mountain hay meadows should become nature conservation areas at national as well as at European level. Natura 2000 might help to create a top up payment for them.
- Awareness raising and pride. People – farmers as well as city dwellers – should be aware of the outstanding value of these meadows, and they should also be proud of them. If society

recognises the importance of their survival, it will be easier to convince farmers to use them, and to convince policy makers to provide higher subsidies and other support.
- Retuning to a traditional way of life: more and more young, educated people as well as farmers' children start understanding the importance of traditional farming and return to a life involving more physical work and closer to nature. I have to say, this is really just about habits and giving up some of the usual comfort. And at the same time it offers many healthy and uplifting experiences, much better than sitting every morning in a car, jammed in traffic.

What touristic potential does the Transylvanian hay have?

Many biologists and a few sociologists came here and were deeply interested and also very impressed by what they experienced. For biologists the main experience is to see that this type of biodiversity is not just a dream, that this can be created and managed on the long term. We were visited by farmers and managers of protected areas, as well as nature conservation NGOs, who learned about the work we do and the work our farmers do. There is also a less clearly identifiable group of people, seeking new ideas, new impressions about society, nature and sustainability. For them it is sometimes a life changing experience. The things which they learned at university or read in thick, highly appreciated books, here are everyday reality and simply the lifestyle of our farmers. And Transylvanian hay already 'boosted' tourism in some parts of the UK, because after participating at our hay festival, some enthusiastic farmers started reintroducing hand mowing on their own farm, and launched their own hay festivals back home. Lastly, some NGO leaders and university teachers registered for our Hay meadow conference in May 2013 from the Sub Saharan, West Africa area. They were interested in hay meadow management practices and traditional ecological knowledge in our area to reintroduce and teach sustainable and efficient small scale farming techniques in the Fouta Djallo mountain region to reduce food insecurity and malnutrition in their countries.

How many tourists are in your regional association? Where are they from? How much time do they usually stay? How much do they spend? What activities do they enjoy?

We are basically not a tourism organisation, however we do provide guidance and organise daily and weekly programmes for tourists. The conferences we organised so far had between 50 and 130 participants, and we hold an annual event. Our field activities (butterfly or plant research, hay meadow clearing and hay making) gathered between five and 30 participants, and we had about three to six events a year. Participants come from the neighboring area, from other parts of Romania, as well as from abroad.

The largest group of people who came from the eastern part of Romania to learn about Pogány-havas Association's projects counted 50 people; however they only spent a day with us. We also attract one or two groups of interested Hungarians every year. I would say the number of tourists rises to about 100 to 300 on a yearly basis. An average tourist spends daily around 30 $ for accommodation, 20 $ for traveling, 30-60 $ for a guide and probably 30-100 $ for gifts to take home. There are very few opportunities for spending more money on events or places to visit, since the things to see are everywhere around. We provide lifts from and to airports where we try to involve local companies and also travelling by horse and cart or a horse drawn sleigh in the winter. In general our tourists enjoy learning about the landscape and the culture that created it and still preserves it. Therefore meeting locals and having a guide is essential. Still, our most successful event is the hay making festival.

Please tell us the story of the Hay Festival.

The idea of the hay making festival is based on protecting hay meadows from abandonment, to demonstrate to local people that meadows are interesting and valuable for tourists from distant countries and to teach participants the local traditional knowledge of hay making. The venue is the small B&B run by our friend in Ghimes Faget, hosted in his grandfather's traditional house and barn, located in a beautiful mountain landscape. Timing follows the local pattern of mountain hay making. It is in the second half of August and we get up early. For one week, participants can learn and take part in making hay, from mowing to drying, collecting and building hay stacks. There are sometime unexpected extras, like two years ago when one of the neighbors needed help to rescue his nicely dried hay from a thunderstorm; the people involved in the festival did the work quickly, and later in the evening the neighbor appeared with a box of beer; they shared the nice experience and the owner's thankfulness throughout a cheerful evening. Aside from making hay, there are days when we show them how to make traditional cheese, we go to the forest to pick mushrooms and there is also a day when we sit on the bus and learn about the history, the architecture of the area and more about Pogány-havas projects.

The participants come from countries like Norway, UK, Germany, Austria or Hungary. The shared language is therefore English during the day, traditional dance and music in the evening. The programme is doable for all genders and ages, we had participants ranging from a eight year old girl to a 70 year old gentleman. Some of the participants really experienced this week as kind of enlightenment; this quote speaks about it: 'I came to the Festival to find out about and experience traditional haymaking, see the countryside and landscapes and some of its wildlife in a beautiful part of the world I had never been to before, meet some local people and experience a bit of their lifestyle – all of which I did, so it fully reached all those expectations. But the one thing I didn't expect (and the thing I think I will remember the longest) was the truly inspiring people we met.

CHAPTER 15

THE PIPE OF THE MOTI

A nearly extinct tradition.

Isolated in scattered homesteads at the top of the mountains, the old time dwellers of the Apuseni Mountains – the Moti – used the long pipe called tulnic both as a musical instrument and as a sort of mobile phone. Its profound, troubling sounds made up a whole communication code. 'That's how shepherds, or girls and boys talked to each other, each from their own hilltop. And that's how they called men to war', says Paraschiva Petruse, 55, from Patrahaitesti, Alba, one of the few women in the Apuseni Mountains who still know how to play the tulnic. The communication code has been lost and today, Paraschiva only plays her pipe at local weddings.

'The Romanian instrument is related to the Ukrainean or Polish trambitza, the Italian truba, the Scandinavian luur and the Swiss alpenhorn', says Magda Andreescu, curator at the *Romanian Peasant Museum*. The craftsmen who still make tulnics are also very few. Aurel Mocanu, 56, has learned the trade when he was a boy.

'I've learned it from my father who had learned it from his father'. The meter-long pipe can only be made from the wood of a fir tree grown far away from water sources, up, on the top of the mountain. 'The wood is slit lengthways, hollowed out, then glued together and fixed with belts, also made of fir', Mocanu explains.

His craftsmanship could be saved from extinction by the Germans from *Deusche Gesellschaft für Technische Zusammenarbeit*

(GTZ), who founded a touristic network in the Aries region, home to the Moti. More and more tourists come up the mountain, to buy tulnics right from the craftsmen's homes. A big one, two or three metres long, costs around 25-30 $.

CAPITOLUL 16

PETROVAN'S RED LIST

Romania's top ten most endangereds pecies

Thanks to its wilderness and delay in catching up with the West, Romania remains an Ark of biodiversity in Europe. In the new course the country has taken – full sail to economic development at any cost, through the troubled waters of transition – an increasing number of species are getting shoved overboard. I've asked Silviu Petrovan, one of the most competent local biologists, to put together a top of Romania's ten most endangered species. 'The main criteria for the selection are the international statute of each species, the importance of local populations compared to the world population, their potential as umbrella species (protecting the habitats of other species, which are their prey or predator and depend upon the same territory), their uniqueness and the charisma which can turn them into ambassadors for nature protection', says Silviu Petrovan. Though the law is supposed to offer them protection, many of them are facing an uncertain future.

***The ten species on Petrovan's list are protected as Community interest species in Annex IV (species requiring strict protection) in Government Decree 57/2007 and are included in Annex III of the Habitats Directive (species of Community interest requiring designation of special conservation sites).*

European bison *(Bison bonasus)*
Europe's largest terrestrial animal disappeared from Romanian fauna over 250 years ago. 40 to 50 individuals live in captivity. Five of them have been released in March 2012. Recent studies show

that it is possible to create a large, interconnected population in the Carpathian area, between Romania, Ukraine, Poland and Slovakia.

Egyptian vulture *(Neophron percnopterus)*

Vulture populations in the Balkans have been halved between 2003 and 2011. The Egyptian vulture was declared a monument of nature before the fall of communism, as a critically endangered species in Romania; it is also included in Annex III of the Birds Directive.

There are less than 5,000 pairs left in Europe. Their numbers are dwindling. They no longer nest in Romania. One or two individuals appear in Dobrogea from time to time.

A possible return of the Egyptian vulture in Romania could be the first step to bring back the other three vulture species which disappeared from the local fauna in the 20th century.

Red-breasted goose *(Branta rufficolis)*

Disastrous environmental policies in the 1950s have altered the winter migration paths of birds in the Caspian Sea area.

There are only 55,000 red-breasted geese on the planet. Almost 90% of them spend the winter on the coasts of Romania and northern Bulgaria, in a few areas, such as Lake Techirghiol.

They are affected by coastal development and the change in agricultural areas; they are often scared away by hunters (although hunting them is prohibited) from their feeding areas.

Eastern four-lined snake *(Elaphe sauromates)*

Romania's largest snake has always been rare; exceptional specimens measuring over eight feet have been found.

Only a few dozen are left, and the species is labeled as critically endangered on Romania's red list.

Although strictly protected and not only completely harmless, but even useful to humans, the snake is still often killed by locals.

European sturgeon *(Huso huso)*

If, 100 years ago, fishermen used to catch one-ton specimens, currently there are only a few thousands adults left.

The dam at Portile de Fier, pollution in the Danube, poaching and excessive fishing have led to disaster for Europe's largest fresh water fish. Between 1992 and 2007, global populations dropped by 93%. In Romania, its commercial fishing was prohibited by a law passed in 2006. The measure was canceled through a Government Emergency Order in 2009 and reintroduced in 2010.

The state is spending millions of Euros on repopulation. European sturgeons in Romania are the last wild population in the Black Sea.

Javelin sand boa *(Eryx jaculus)*

In September 2011, a team of herpetologists from Oradea found the first javelin sand boa seen since 1986, near the town of Turnu Magurele.

A red-listed, critically endangered species, the javelin sand boa is all but extinct in Romania, which is the northern extreme of its habitat. The last Romanian populations were probably destroyed during the construction of the Danube – Black Sea canal.

It is not threatened in other countries and could be re-introduced in Romania after captive breeding.

Eurasian lynx *(Lynx lynx)*

The Eurasian lynx is the largest European feline. Despite being declared a monument of nature, it is hunted every year in Romania (with legal dispensation) under the excuse that it causes damage to local communities.

Romania has the largest population of Eurasian lynxes in the European Union: about 1,300 specimens. In May 2012, the Minister of the Environment declared that he intends to suspend exemptions from the hunting ban until 2014.

Its effective protection in the Carpathians would also ensure the protection of important forest areas and of many other species.

Marbled polecat *(Vormela peregusna)*

The only marbled polecat population in the European Union is found in Romania; the species lives only in arid and steppe areas. Population: about 500 specimens, in Dobrogea.

They are endangered, red-listed species in Romania, protected since 1993; still, very little is known about its ecology and situation at national level.

European mink (Mustela lutreola)
Hunting and competition from the American mink (escaped from fur farms) have pushed the European mink to the brink of the extinction.

It used to be found in large numbers; until recently, it even lived in the Maramures area. Currently, there are at most 1,000 European minks in Romania, all in the Danube Delta – its last stronghold outside Russia.

Poaching continues, populations are declining.

Romanian hamster *(Mesocricetus newtoni)*
It is a unique specie, endemic to a small area of Dobrogea and northern Bulgaria and widely unknown.

According to estimations, there are about 2,000 specimens in Romania (although there is no recent solid data).

Agricultural development and the destruction of Dobrogea habitats are its most serious threats.

CHAPTER 17

THE JOURNEY OF A ROYAL HEART

The heart of Queen Mary of Romania - kept in a musem.

Photo by George Dumitriu

Queen Mary Alexandra Victoria of Edinburgh passed away in Pelisor Castle on the 18th of July 1938. Respecting her wish, her heart was embalmed and deposited in Stella Maris, the Orthodox Church in the garden of Balcic Palace in the Quadrilateral (Southern Dobruja at the time), on the Black Sea coast. 'My body will rest at Curtea de Arges, next to my beloved husband, king Ferdinand, but I wish my heart to be laid under the slabs of the church I have build.'

First, the heart was placed in a silver octagonal box (444,73 g.) which was wrapped both in the flag of Romania and that of Britain and put inside a second box made of golden silver (7573 g), adorned with 307 precious stones. The box (photo above) is decorated with floral motives and circular shaped medallions bearing Romania's coats of arms. On the lied, under a crown, there are the coats of arms of Romania and Great Britain, and each corner features an allegoric character.

Both boxes were enveloped into the flag that was hoisted every time Queen Mary was on board of Brig Mircea the First, school ship of the Romanian Navy. This was the ship's last journey. All the pieces, together with the Queen's heart arrived in Balcic accompanied by General Gheorghe Mihail. They were put in a white marble funeral urn in Stella Maris church', says Radu Constantin Coroama, former director at the Romanian National History Museum. As parts of the Quadrilateral were to be surrendered to Bulgaria, after the Treaty of Craiova on 7th September 1940, the boxes containing Queen Mary's heart were brought to Cotroceni by her daughter, princess Ileana. 'Then, the princess obtained King Charles the Second's approval to transport the heart to Bran Castle.

In 1968, when communist dictator Nicolae Ceausescu passed by Bran he noticed some purple flowers growing over the crypt's grating across the river. His secret agents immediately chimed in. The very next day, Bran Castle's director noticed that the crypt's metal grating had been forced. Fearing the worst, he decided to unbind the marble urn and to transfer the boxes inside the castle. The bridge and the stone path leading to the place where Queen Mary's heart rested were removed', says Dorina Tomescu, curator at the Romanian National History Museum. After all that wandering, the heart and its royal boxes became part of the National History Museum's treasures.

CHAPTER 18

ANA ASLAN'S ELIXIR

*A story about the aging of this anti-aging medicine.
Text by Adina Brânciulescu.*

Petcu Steluta is 86 years old and has a lot of plans for the future. She especially thinks about the trips she would like to take. She is a small pedantic lady, still displaying traces of her former coquettish look: her deep blue eyes are cheerful and playful; her nails are polished in bright red, and she is wearing her blond dyed hair in a tight bun. She retired only a few years ago and she only calmed down when the others found out her real age and started protecting her too much for her taste. Because you could easily say she is 65. She is lucid, optimistic, her hands are not trembling, and she takes pride in not using a walking stick like some of her friends, while her hair roots and eyebrows betray her naturally dark hair color. She credits Gerovital as the source of her excellent general condition. She has been taking the injectable treatment for 30 years now. 'I have every trus, in these injections!' exclaims Ms Steluta.

II The story of Gerovital starts somewhere around the middle of the 20th century. Ana Aslan, 52 years old at that time, was teaching at the Medical Faculty in Timisoara, and was interested in studying procaine, a well-known local anesthetic. Along the years, a number of doctors had pointed out a few of its surprising effects: sometimes, articular pains vanished; white hair regained its color; and skin quality improved. However, these were mere disparate observations, coming especially from surgeons. Ana Aslan was considering the potential of procaine in the fight against the aging process. She had been using it for some time, treating arterial diseases or problems affecting peripheral circulation, but she also wanted to extend this treatment to rheumatism cases.

In the spring of 1949 she got her chance. 'On April 15th, I met a young medical student suffering of acute arthrisis. His crisis had started three weeks before', she noted. 'His knee was blocked, each and every movement causing him horrendous pain. The prescribed medication had only alleviated his suffering for a short period of time'. She decided to inject him with a solution of 1% procaine in the femoral artery, although there was also the risk of not being able to pinpoint it, as the artery of a young person is very thin. However she succeeded. A few minutes later, the young man raised his leg and bent it several times. He was discharged from hospital shortly after that. 'My shock and interest were so huge, I gave up my university career – although I had dedicated myself heart and soul to it – and I devoted myself to the study of this substance'.

Two years later, Ana Aslan started a long-term experiment on animals, associated with a clinical survey performed on 25 elderly patients, based on injectable procaine – and improved the patients' general condition. One of the examples subsequently demonstrating the efficiency of this treatment was a 110-year-old patient. Following a four year treatment, his hands and head almost stopped shaking, he could walk unsupported, he recovered his appetite, his white hair was regaining its color, and his depressive state was being replaced by a sound psychological condition.

The satisfactory results prompted the professor to look for a mixture that could leverage the benefits of procaine, and she continued her research together with pharmacist Elena Polovrageanu. They lowered the procaine's pH from 4.5 to 3.3, thus stabilizing the substance and prolonging its effect on the body, before initiating the hydrolysis reaction (normally, the substance is eliminated within one hour).

The final compound they got contained 2% procaine, 0.12% benzoic acid, 0.10% potassium metabisulphite, 0.01% disodium phosphate, with the final pH of the mix ranging between three and 4. The ingredients added to procaine were anti-oxidant agents and stabilizers, and the 'H3' mention added to the product – Gerovital – indicated its vitamin-like effect. This was maintained inside the body for more than six hours, and had a much stronger effect than a mere anesthetic. The clinical evaluation of Gerovital on 7,600 patients allowed for the medicine to be patented in 1957. The vial production was initiated, followed by the production of pills, therapy cream and capillary lotion, five years later. In 1980, Ana Aslan and Ion Polovrageanu created a new geriatric product, Aslavital, which was also patented, with mass production initiated shortly afterwards.

Meanwhile, Professor Aslan's presentations and participations in expert sessions and conferences had made Gerovital famous also abroad. This had a significant impact on the medical world, but an incomparably bigger one on those outside it, where this medicine found numerous supporters. In a world feverishly looking for eternal youth, Gerovital set a new trend, much like the recent silicon implants, explains Dr Stelu Petricu, a dermatologist amused by his own comparison. He is one of the people who also know the history of this medicine.

The number of requests for this treatment increased and, since the Institute of Geriatrics was not prepared to handle so many patients, in 1972 the former Otopeni sanatorium, belonging to the Central Committee of the Communist Party, became part of the Institute, under the name of The Otopeni Clinical Department. Legends were built around the names of the people entering the institute. Some of them were Somerset Maugham, Pablo Neruda, Salvador Dali, Miguel Asturias, Charlie Chaplin and Claudia Cardinale. There was a genuinely elitist atmosphere in Otopeni. '90% of the patients were coming from abroad. The whole department was restricted to foreign patients' use, and everybody spoke at least one foreign language. We had a luggage-handler who was fluent in French and Italian', – recalls Dr. Georgeta Popescu, who has been working for more than twenty years in the Otopeni Clinical Department. However, things gradually evolved for the worst: Ana Aslan attracted Elena Ceausescu's aversion (caused by the latter's envy for her University Professor position). On top of that, the lack of hot water, food and proper accommodation – affecting the whole country – had an unfavorable impact on the image of the Institute. In 1978, the Party College requested the Professor to pay 1.5 million lei, the value of hospitalization fees she had not cashed in from her old and poor patients. Following a seven years trial, initiated in 1981, the judges finally ruled in favor of Ana Aslan, only five months before her demise. At that time, her treatment methods were adding to the national budget an annual income of more than 17 million dollars.

III Ana Aslan was born on the 1st of January 1897, in Braila, as the daughter of a large intellectual family (they were five siblings). Her father, Margarit Aslan, died when she was only 13. 'He loved me deeply, because I was the living proof of his long-surviving youth. When I was born, he was 59. I was the youngest child of the family', she recalled later. At 16, she was dreaming of becoming a pilot and she even flew on board of a small plane. Upon graduating from high school, faced with her mother's opposition against her idea of becoming a doctor, she took extreme measures and went on hunger strike. Finally, in 1922, she graduated from The Medical Faculty and afterwards worked in various hospitals. In 1952, supported by one of her mentors, Dr. C. I. Parhon, she was appointed Head of the Institute of Geriatrics in Bucharest. She held this position until the 19th of May 1988, when she died, at the age of 91.

Dr Monica Barsan is a member of the 'Old Guard' in the Institute of Geriatrics and Gerontology, as one of the people who worked with Ana Aslan. She recalls her respectfully, always using the term 'Professor'. 'The Professor was really nice. She had her sense of humor. She knew how to be really tough when that was necessary, and she became really close in private. However, you had to maintain some sort of distance, because otherwise she could dominate you and completely annihilate you. On the other hand, the Professor did not like cheap flattering. She preferred people to keep their opinions to themselves'. The lady doctor nostalgically reminisces about the years when she used to work in the Otopeni Clinical Department: 'Most patients returned on an annual basis for cures, treatments and tests. These procedures were combined with physiotherapy and gymnastics, as well as social programs – trips to Sinaia and the Moldavian monasteries. Everything was different from what we have now. And of course, there was the Professor herself, protecting this working environment. She was ruling with an iron fist, but she was also protecting us. '

She became world famous, and the collection of letters she received at the Institute includes 130,000 pieces from 123 countries (letters used to reach their destination even if the envelope simply read 'Professor Doctor

Ana Aslan, Romania'). Elegant, with impeccable manners and a distinguished attitude despite her older age, Ana Aslan herself was an example for the patients, recalls Dr Barsan. 'I saw her when she was visiting her patients in their wards, following the rules of the traditional medical school. Allow me to say she was wearing heels this high (the gap between her fingers indicates a length of about eight centimeters) and made her rounds in Otopeni three times a week. She was around 80 years old, at that time'.

Throughout her life, she remained faithful to her passions and habits: she used to read Balzac, Dostoievski, Marguerite Yourcenar; she loved the paintings of Luchian and Van Gogh, and Brancusi's Table of Silence. She was visited – on a weekly basis – by a woman reading her fortune in her coffee mug, and she was savoring her champagne cup every morning. She loved fine materials, high-quality furniture, good music and beautiful people. 'Ugliness gives me the shivers; it blocks and annihilates me. I couldn't possibly live in a repulsive ambiance. I hate old age, ugliness and lies', she confessed to Dinu Lipatti. 'She was very exigent, very refined and very well-traveled', says Dr Georgeta Popescu. 'She lived a princess's life'.

IV In the medical circles, opinions regarding Gerovital were divided: there were voices saying Gerovital was one of the most important medical inventions – but there were also voices contesting that. Its most fierce adversaries called the medicine Zerovital. A survey finalized in 1975, under the title 'Effects of a procaine preparation (Gerovital H3) in hospitalized geriatric patients: a double-blind study', showed that following research on a group of 63 patients, ages between 45 and 83, no physical and psychological improvements were revealed. On the other hand, an article published one year later in the American magazine Psychosomatic supported Gerovital. At that time, tests supervised by the FDA (Federal Food and Drug Administration) were performed in order to assess whether Gerovital could be used as anti-depressive medication on the American market. Normally, these tests are performed during a number of increasingly complex stages, but Gerovital only passed the first stage; further tests were stopped due to lacks of funds.

All in all, similar tests would currently cost around four billion US dollars. Anyway, it would be impossible to continue studies regarding Gerovital. 'This is a cheap, old medicine. Nobody is interested in investing in it anymore', explains the Medical Director of INGG, Dr Gabriel Preda.

Today, the mainstream medical view is that the preparation was seriously investigated in the 1960s and discredited, and that any promotion today is quackery. In the United States, the FDA baned Gerovital H3 from interstate commerce as an unapproved drug and, since 1982, has prohibited its importation. However, Ana Aslan and Gerovital are two names that still bring a lot of money, less to the Romanian state but more to the private companies and treatment centers (a spa and treatment center in Eforie Nord, a competitor of INGG, included the name of Ana Aslan in its marketing strategy). Also, Ana Aslan only patented two beauty products (the capillary lotion and the Gerovital H3 cream), to be produced by the companies Farmec in Cluj-Napoca and Miraj, currently Gerovital Cosmetics, in Bucharest. Rivals ever since, the two companies have diversified their range of beauty products, even if the traditional compound, procaine hydrochloride, was eliminated from the formula.

Apart from the two companies, another implicated player is the strong pharmaceutical group Zentiva, owner of the royalties for manufacturing the pharmaceutical products, while the treatment services are provided by the National Institute of Geriatrics and Gerontology.

V The 34 hectares of wood harboring the Otopeni Clinical Department make for a picturesque setting and a surprising oasis of tranquility, next to the capital. Old people are strolling on the paths, among the trees and in the shade of the old, Greek-style decorated building. Some of them are meticulously exploring everything they encounter: the heating unit, the hidden nooks, and the warehouse full of old things. 'Did you see the heating unit? Did you see how big it is?', says one of them, enchantment gleaming in his eyes. The myth of the miraculous cure against aging has gradually turned into a business, and locations providing revolutionary treatments have become regular clinical departments.

The Otopeni Department, formerly so well-known, is not exclusively open to foreign citizens anymore. The reason is simple: they don't come to Romania anymore, since they can find other locations, with better offers and conditions. The good part of all this is that nowadays the two weeks of Gerovital therapy, combined with physiotherapy, massage and kinetic therapy, attract numerous Romanian patients, who need to make reservations in advance.

As the present is not too glamorous in Otopeni, its link with the past has been sacredly guarded. Albums with photos of Ana Aslan and her articles published at that time make for an impressive collection. The ground floor of the main building hosts Apartment No. 4, currently accommodating a 35-year-old young man who is looking for some peace and quiet, rather than the treatment itself. However, this used to be the Professor's Apartment. And this is how everybody still refers to it. The Professor's Apartment.

VI Timeline

- 1st of January 1897 – Ana Aslan is born in Braila.
- 1949 – Ana Aslan uses procaine for the first time in a rheumatism case.
- 1951 – She initiates a long-term experiment on animals, plus a clinical survey on 25 old patients, based on injectable procaine.
- 1952 – Ana Aslan, General Manager of the Institute of Geriatrics, Bucharest, and pharmacist E. Polovrageanu, prepare Gerovital H3.
- 1957 – The medicine 'Gerovital' is patented and its vial production is subsequently initiated.
- 1962 – Gerovital is also produced as pills, cream and capillary lotion.
- 1972 – The former Otopeni sanatorium of the Central Committee of the Romanian Communist Party becomes part of the Institute of Geriatrics, under the name of 'The Otopeni Clinical Department'.
- 1980 – Ana Aslan and Ion Polovrageanu create 'Aslavital'
- 19th of May 1988 – Ana Aslan dies.

CHAPTER 19

THE AVATARS OF OBOR

The mayor's office in Bucharest's second sector has decided to turn Obor – this cheap and Balkan-like market into a western complex.

The largest produce market in the capital is in full metamorphosis – a new one in a long row of transformations going back more than three centuries. First documented in the 17th century, in the paperwork of the Stelea monastery, Obor used to be formerly called 'The Outside Fair' (as it was held on the outskirts of the city). During the reign of Matei Basarab (1632-1654), The Outside Fair was located on the outskirts of Sibilelor slum (currently – the crossroads between Mosilor and Hristo Botev Streets), on the eastern barrier of Bucharest. As the city gradually developed, the fair was being constantly pushed towards East, along with the barrier. According to historian George Potra, the trajectory of the first century of continuous movements of Obor can be reconstructed tracking down the names of the streets that it followed: Olari (Pot-Makers), Calusei (Little Horses), Vaselor (Pots), Buciului, Brasoveni or any other reminder of other trades connected to the fair. At the end of the 18th century, the Outside Fair reached the estate of Colentina, on the exact place where Targul Mosilor (The Old People Fair – the market connected with the ancient holiday of commemorating the dead) was traditionally held. As his estate was nearby, Prince Grigore Ghica (1822 – 1828) established the Obor in its current location, allowing the barrier to be placed beyond the perimeter of the fair. There were repeated attempts of moving The Outside Fair further on, in various locations, but people kept coming to that traditional place. During Cuza's reign, authorities tried to turn Targul Mosilor – by means of a non-finalized law project – into an annual national exhibition for the whole country. This goal was partially accomplished in 1924, when Mosii became an annual exhibition. The city mayor of that time wanted to turn it into a sample fair, following the model of western fairs. During the final decades of the 20th century, Targul Mosilor gradually faded away, and its allotted perimeter became smaller and smaller, thus diminishing the role of the Obor within the city. 'The Obor Halls, designed to become a significant presence in terms of function and architectural qualities, were not given their full value, although the building is a remarkable achievement in the creation of architect Horia Creanga. Moreover, the subsequent architectural and urbane fittings, utterly inadequate, have proven that tradition was being ignored', says art historian Cezara Mucenic, from the History Museum of Bucharest. Obor's location – at the crossroad between Colentina and Pantelimon, two of the main access roads of Bucharest, connecting Moldavia and Dobrogea – was one of the decisive factors contributing to the development of this area. Also, the Hall is connected to the center of the city by Calea Mosilor, and to other areas by the first ring of the Bucharest belt-road – Stefan cel Mare and Mihai Bravu Boulevards – that have become commercial arteries of the city.

'They sell low-quality products, they cheat the buyers, they steal wallets; it's a dirty place, full of dubious characters – but actually all these are triggered by the City's poor management and by a lack of interest for investments and a civilized trade. The 'ambulant market' style of the Obor could actually become a positive note within the urban landscape', says architect Petru Mortu. The City has decided to evacuate the traders from Obor, in order to make room for the new complex, amounting to a total value of more than 100 million Euros. 'You don't like buying good cheap products? Never mind, you'll buy expensive and lame ones', blurted a vendor.

Timeline
- The 17th century – the first official documenting of the Fair, in the paperwork of Stelea monastery, mentioning 'The large road leading to the Outside Fair'
- Approximately 1700 – The Fair is moved next to the Olari (Pot-Makers) Church, at the crossroad between Mosilor and Carol

Boulevards.
- 1702 – The Outside Fair is located on the same field as Targul Mosilor (The Old People Fair), on the Colentina estate.
- 1786 – Ruler Nicolaie Mavrogheni decides for the Obor Fair to be held on Tuesdays and Fridays.
- 1821 – This is the only year when the fair was not held. The 'Eteria' rebel group of Ipsilanti was stationed in Colentina at that time.
- 1822 – The fair is finally settled in the current location of the Obor Halls and the adjacent park. Ruler Grigore Ghica forbids any executions to be held within the fair perimeter.
- 1830 – The first urban project for Bucharest stipulates the founding of six markets in the city and four more – including the Outside Fair – at the end of its main roads.
- 1830 – A (non-finalized) attempt of turning the location of Targul Mosilor into a cemetery.
- 1865 – The first national exhibition at Targul Mosilor (May 20-27), displaying agricultural and industrial products, cattle, flowers and vegetables.
- 1890 – The City of Bucharest purchases the land where Obor was located, from the Church of Saint Dumitru. The main guardian of this church was Prince Scarlat Ghica.
- 1900 – The fair has the shape of concentric circles, intersected by a number of streets converging towards the center. A kiosk with a dome is built there, and the royal family comes to visit it on the Thursday before Easter.
- 1902 – The Communal Council of Bucharest decides to organize an industrial exhibition within the Obor Fair.
- 1930 – The Obor railway station is established on the eastern side of the Obor, in order to supply the commercial market.
- 1950 – The Obor Halls are inaugurated. Construction works had lasted thirteen years, with a complete halt between 1941-1942, caused by the lack of funds.
- 1970 – The Obor General Store is built.
- 2007 – The Municipality of the 2nd Sector turns the Obor Market into a modern complex.

CHAPTER 20

THE ROMANIAN LEU

The ancestor of the leu, Romania's national currency is... Dutch.

Archive photo from Mr. Mircea Manole's personal collection; Euronumisfil Gold.

Nowadays, Romanians are in love with the dollar or the euro. Around the middle of the 17th century, however, the Dutch thaler was so popular in the Balkanic region that, to Romanians, Bulgarians or Albanians, it was superimposed over the very notion of currency.

The tail side of the leeuwendaler bore a lion standing on its hind legs. So deeply was this silver lion rooted in the public conscience that, even after its withdrawal around 1750 and its replacement by the Maria Theresa thaler and the Spanish thaler, Romanians continued to calculate prices in these fictional 'lei' until 1867, when the first national currency was minted.

Key dates in the history of the Romanian leu
- 1860 – the romanat – the national currency which ruler Alexandru Ioan Cuza wanted to introduce – never goes beyond project stage, due to opposition from the Ottoman Empire.
- 1867 – Carol I signs the birth certificate of the Romanian leu: the 'Law for the establishment of a monetary system and the coinage of a national currency'.
- 1877 – the first Romanian banknotes are issued, with face values of 5, 10, 20, 50, 100, and 500 lei.
- 1880 – the National Bank of Romania (BNR) is founded, with one third of the subscribed capital coming from the Romanian state, and the rest from private investors.
- 1916-1917 – Romanian banknotes can no longer be converted to gold; the country is suffocated by war expenses; the BNR keeps issuing uncovered banknotes; hyper-inflation.
- 1917-1918 – the leu and Bucharest fall into the hands of the Germans. BGR, a bank with German capital, issues German lei, with which the Wehrmacht buys its supplies from an occupied Romania.
- 1917 – the Ministry of Finance, now in refuge in Iasi, issues the smallest banknote in the world. The ten bani (one tenth of a leu) banknote, bearing the effigy of king Ferdinand, is no bigger than a postage stamp: 1 x 1.5 inches.
- 1919 – Romania floods the market with printed money in an attempt to cover its deficit and replace the foreign currency still in circulation. The leu collapses. In 1922, a loaf of bread cost 22 times more than before the war.
- 1920-1921 – all foreign currency circulating in Romania – the Austro-Hungarian crown, the Romanov rubles, the ostrubles and the BGR lei – are withdrawn.
- 1929 – BNR-issued banknotes regain gold convertibility. The leu stands for ten milligrams (0.15 grains) of gold with a ratio of 9/10, while the price of one kilogram (2.2 pounds) of gold is 111,111.11 lei.
- 1929-1933 – the great economic crisis. Dark years for the leu.

Living standards take a dramatic dive. Waves of wage cuts: 10-23% in 1930, 15% in 1932, 10% in 1933.
- September 1940 – January 1941: banknotes issued by the new nationalist-fascist state administration, the 'legionaries'.
- 1940-1945 – food shortage. Prices soar. The average salary of a public clerk (350,000 lei) buys 13 gallons of milk. In the period of German victories in the East, the dollar exchange rate in Bucharest is very low (1 USD = 56.9 lei in June 1942); in June 1944, it reaches 169.9 lei for one dollar.
- 1944 – the Red Army prints Soviet lei to pay for supplies during its transit through Romania.
- 1947 – the appearance of the banknote with the highest face value in the history of the BNR: five million lei. The great communist stabilization: the BNR introduces the new leu, worth 20,000 old lei. Farmers can exchange a maximum of five million old lei, employees or old-age pensioners – three millions. Private companies can only exchange the value of salaries for July, while trade companies have no exchange rights, being forced to sell their stocks. Of the 48.5 billion lei in circulation, about half is exchanged.
- 1952 – a new monetary law; the tail side of the new leu of the proletariat celebrates the triumph of industrialization and the mechanization of agriculture; the head side bears revolutionary figures like Tudor Vladimirescu (25 lei) or N. Balcescu (100 lei). The basic recalculation ratio is 20 old lei for one new leu.
- 1955-1963 – substantial growth in industrial and agricultural production. Prices for consumer goods drop (between 4% and 25%) due to an affluence of merchandise in stores and markets.
- 1974-1975 – wages increase, but the growth depends on the type of economic activity. Further income growth between 1977 and 1980.
- 1979-1980 – successive price hikes to 'maximize returns on certain foodstuffs'. The communist regime invests heavily in industry, neglecting the production of consumer goods.
- 1980s – Romania settles into a 'culture of shortages'. The

population struggles for survival.
- 1991 – the BNR issues the first post-communist banknote, dedicated to sculptor Constantin Brancusi. Over the following years, new banknotes bear the faces of Romanian culture personalities, from national poet Mihai Eminescu (1,000 lei in 1991, 1993, 1997; 500 lei in 2005) to playwright I. L. Caragiale (1,000,000 lei in 2003; 100 lei in 2005).
- 1999 – the new 2,000 lei banknote (issued in honor of the total solar eclipse) makes Romania the first European country to use plastic currency.
- 2005 – the monetary reform introduces the new leu, worth 10,000 old lei. Paper banknotes are gradually replaced by polymer money.
- 2012 – the Romanian leu celebrates 145 years.

CHAPTER 21

BELLADONNA'S CULT

It been happening for thousands of years in Romania's forests.

Illustration by **RADU OLTEAN**

It been happening for thousands of years in Romania's forests.
In the dead of full-moon nights, young girls dance naked in frightening, dark forests around the herb 'of life and death'. This is how historian of religion Mircea Eliade called the nightshade (*Atropa belladonna*). In the folk tradition it is called the 'empress', 'the forest's grass', 'the wolf's cherry' or the 'grand dame'.

It grows in the dark, deep forests and blossoms in June and July. Before picking its leaves, girls lie on top of each other, imitating the sexual act. This extremely poisonous plant is credited for its magical virtues: It's connected to love, fertility, wealth, but has a double power that can be directed towards good or bad deeds.

According to Dumitru Iuga, researcher at the Center for Folk Creation in Maramures, this ancient ritual is still practised in Maramures today, where the nightshade is picked up for love, depression, marriage, dancing, or alchoolism.

'The people I investigated were not ready to admit they picked or used the nightshade. Picking and using it has a private character due to the belief that exposure leads to the loss of efficiency and even brings bad luck to the people involved', says professor Nicolae Bot, from Babes Bolyai University. The best time of the year for picking is between Easter and Ascension Day. A ritual in which sexual purity, courtesy, secrecy, loneliness are mandatory dictates how the plant should be dug up. The herb has to be rewarded with salt, sugar, wine and is picked on someone's behalf.

CHAPTER 22

ROMANIAN ... ESCU

Why is Escu the most frequent Romanian surname.

The story of our family names begins with a village founder as an ancestor. Let us take the example given by historian N. A. Constantinescu in his Romanian name dictionary: Around 1820, the entourage of Negoita Diaconul (the Dean) settled and formed a village near the town of Pucioasa. The settlement was named Diaconesti (the adjectival suffix shows possession, the fact that the village belongs to Diaconu's people, who hold shared ownership of the land). Somewhere in the course of the third generation, when the joint ownership was dissolved, one of the descendant families took the name of Diaconescu. This three-step process in the formation of '... escu' names – 1. founding forefather, 2. eponymous village with the plural ending 'esti', 3. family name with the singular 'escu' form – is supported by documents as early as the 14th century (records mention a Dabacescul in 1387, in Wallachia, now southern Romania, and a Serbanescu around 1392, in Moldova) and became widespread in the 15th century.

In the early 19th century, we see a new addition to the great national 'escu' family: many boyars (Romanian nobles) and foreign merchants took the name of the domains which they had bought to settle down in the country. Such is the case of Tudor Vladimirescu – who took his name from the village of Vladimiri, in Jiul de Sus.

'The Romanian suffix -escu, easca is a descendant of Latin -ISCUS, with ancient Indo-European origins (it may also have existed in the Thraco-Dacian language and in paleo-Slavic), and with Romance language correspondents: -esco in Portuguese, -isco in Spanish, -esco in Italian, -iscu in Sardinian', says Domnita Tomescu, author of the book *Numele de persoana la romani. Perspectiva istorica*. Today, the 'escu' suffix is something of a Romanian brand, much like the 'ov' or 'ski' termination for Slavic people, the 'o' particle for the Irish or the 'di' for the Italians.

Sursa: Police Chestor Constantin Mănoloiu.

Another Romanian patronymic suffix: the regional 'onu' suffix, from the Banat and sub-Carpathic Oltenia areas: Ion Patron'u, sometimes turned into '-oiu'.

CHAPTER 23

WHO IS NR TWO?

Most of us are aware that the Palace of Parliament is the biggest and most expensive building in Romania. But does anybody know the runner-up? The winner takes it all. History does not love second places – most often disregarded, forgotten or lost in some archives. However, without the second best, how could you possibly know how tight the race was and how 'first-class' the one ranking first actually is?

The second most expensive communist building
The House of the Free Press
(#1: The Palace of Parliament, 330,000 square meters).

This Stalinist giant inspired by Lomonosov University building in Moscow used to be called 'The House of the Spark' ('Scanteia' – The Spark – was the name of the Romanian Communist Party's official newspaper). It currently hosts dozens of newspaper and magazine offices, publishing and printing houses. Its 23,000 square meters surface includes more than 6,000 rooms and three kilometers of corridors; the building is 104 meters high, including the antenna on top.

The second football team ever created
United Athletic Club Ploiesti was founded in 1906
(#1: Olympia Sport Club, founded in 1904 by German Charles Viereck.)

Olympia Sport Club, United Athletic Club Ploiesti and Colentina used to play in a local championship before WWI, until 1914.

The second deepest cave

The Grind Sinkhole
(#1: Sinkhole V in the Padis area, in the Bihor Mountains, 650 m deep.)
The Grind Sinkhole in the Piatra Craiului Mountains is 530 m deep.

The second most common surname
Popescu
(#1: Popa, 163,391)
According to information from the Department for Population Record and Databases Management of the Administration and Internal Affairs Ministry, 122,449 Romanians have the surname 'Popescu'.

The second largest ethnic minority
The Roma people 535,140.
(#1: Hungarians – 1,431,807.)
According to unofficial estimates, there are more than two million Gypsies living in Romania.

The second highest peak
Negoiu (2,535 m), in Fagaras Mountains.
(#1: Moldoveanu (2,544 m))

The second most frequently purchased car in Romania
Volkswagen: 8,734 cars registered last year
(#1: Dacia: 23,585 registered cars in 2011)

The second favorite immigration destination for Romanians
USA: 1,086 per year*
(#1: Germany: 1,399 per year*)

The second favorite destination for Romanian tourists
Bulgaria: 250,000 Romanian tourists visited this neighboring country last year.
(#1: Greece, with 300,000 Romanian tourists.)

The second highest temperature ever recorded

44.3 Celsius degrees in Calafat – July 2007
(#1: 44.5 Celsius degrees in Ion Sion, in August 1951)

The second smallest county in terms of area
Giurgiu – 3,562 square kilometers
(#1: Ilfov – 1,583 square kilometers)

The second longest reign
Steven the Great (1457 – 1504) reigned over Moldavia for 47 years.
(#1: Carol I of Romania: 48 years)

The second most frequent search of a word on Google in 2013
'movies' – 13.5 million searches
(#1: 'games' – 25 million searches)

The second largest mammal in Romania
The brown bear. Males weigh 265-355 kilograms, with females reaching up to 150-250 kilograms.
(#1: European bison *Bison bonasus*: Males weigh 300-920 kilograms, with females reaching 300-700 kilograms.)

The second largest fish in Romania
The Wels catfish *Silurus glanis* can reach up to 150 kilograms
(#1: The European sturgeon *Huso huso* can reach up to 200-250 kilograms)

The second rarest animal living in the wild, in Romania
European bison *Bison bonasus*, five specimens
(#1: Romanian darter *Romanichthys valsanicola*, aprox 0)

The owner of the second largest forest area in Romania
Harvard University, USA, 35,000 hectares
(#1: Romsilva, 3,3 million hectares)

CHAPTER 24

WHAT'S IN A NAME?

A Barometer of Ideological Instability.

One street in the heart of Bucharest has had its name changed six times in the last 150 years. It was first called *Fountain Street*, as mentioned by a 1878 document – something to do with the water pump at the end of the road. In 1911, it became *Lueger Street* (named after Karl Lueger, an anti-Semitic and anti-Hungarian mayor of Vienna who supported the cause of Romanians in Transylvania). After WWI, Lueger's name was exiled to a smaller street and was replaced by *General Berthelot*, the chief of French operations in the Moldavian region during the 1917 campaign. When Romania became a communist country, the symbol of Russian science, *Popov*, was obviously favored over Berthelot.

Later on, around 1964, as relations with the Soviet Big Brother cooled down, the quiet, winding street got a new label, as neutral as possible: *Water Lilies' Street*. Yet, after the 1989 revolution, it became *General Berthelot Street* once again. The naming of streets is an ideological, highly symbolic gesture. Although by, let's say, British standards, such a situation seems almost implausible, the story of this street is symptomatic for Romania. 'A study of street names all over the country would indicate the historical instability of the Romanian society, where everything is uncertain, fluid, transitory', says historian Lucian Boia.

CHAPTER 25

ROMANIA'S SOILS

Interview with Mihail Dumitru, Head of the Research Institute for Pedology and Agro-Chemistry.

In the spring of 2007, at the **National Geographic** workshop in Washington, I watched the preview of the *Our Good Earth* story. I left the room frightened by our prospects. I came back to Romania with the funny idea of buying a plot and cultivate it with... soil, for 20 or 30 years – and then, in light of this bleak future scenario, to get rich by selling soil by the pound. At the end of the summer, I went to Mr. Mihail Dumitru, Head of the Research Institute for Pedology and Agro-Chemistry, to find out more about the state of our soils. I left his office just as frightened as before. And the idea of cultivating soil is beginning to seem less and less of a venture to me.

What is the status of our soils?
In Romania, 2.5 million hectares (out of 14.7 million hectares of agricultural land) are severely degraded – and in dire need of quick reforestation. (About 5-7,000 hectares are planted every year). We have approximately 6.3 million hectares of land prone to erosion – and zero investments in remedies. In Western Europe, you can't find any hilltop, valley or ravine without a forest covering it. This is the least people can do to protect the soil. On the contrary, in Romania we have even cut those forests that used to play this protective role, and we continue to cut at an amazing speed; the process has become worse and worse. Equally irresponsible, we continue to work our land from hilltop towards the valley, not on its contour. Anyway, the

deeply fragmented land rendered contour ploughing almost impossible. Therefore, our soil is subjected to erosion. The first strong rain will completely wash it away: the organic matter, the nutrients end in the storage lakes, which they silt and eventually clog.

How did we get here?

Especially during the first years after the fall of communism, when plots of land were given back to their former owners, usually on their original locations, the new owners cut the forests (including those growing on hilltops, in valleys and ravines), protective curtains for about 400,000 hectares of sandy soils. They destroyed a large part of the 3.2 million hectares of land fitted with irrigation systems, and the 2.2 million hectares fitted with systems preventing erosion; they started ploughing from hilltop downwards; they pulled off the noble vines they had no idea how to cultivate and they destroyed most of the intensive fruit trees plantations and so on. Within ten years, Romanian soils went one class down on the quality scale – and its decline continues. From 1990 to 2000, areas with low productive soils, poor and very poor in humus, increased by 35% (going from about five million hectares to 7.5 million hectares).

What does 'going one class down' mean?

In agro-chemistry, soils rank depending on their supplies of nutritious elements: the highly productive ones are Class 1; the good ones are Class two – and so on, reaching the low fertility areas, included in Class 5. We are currently included in Class 3, and within 30 years, our soils will get to Class 4. There was a time when we used to be Europe's bread basket, but our current productivity level only reaches about 40% of the European Community average value. At the end of the day, the law that returned the land to its rightful owners turned out to be some kind of Pandora's Box… Theoretically, this was a sound measure. But in practice, returning the plots of lands according to their former locations has only led to the destruction of agriculture. Our land is currently split into more than 40 million tiny plots. 'We are the only nation on this planet who currently spend more on their fuel in order to get to work than on the actual work itself', said N.N. Constantinescu, a member of the Romanian Academy. Approximately 40% of the land given back to their former owners got to be owned by city people, who have nothing to do with agriculture. They only want to sell their land – therefore they keep it just as long as they can get a good price for it. Which generates situations like uncultivated lands or plots leased to unscrupulous people. Many of the lease holders only want to maximize their profit. They simply don't care about the consequences of their actions. This leads to long-term soil erosion. We should also have a soil protection law, forcing people to at least pay attention and not destroy (if they cannot increase) the soil's humus content by using certain technological procedures.

How can we increase the humus content of our soil?

This is simple: by means of fertilizers. Humus is an organic matter with a consistent molecular weight; it is the most precious part of the soil. You can usually find it within the first 30-40 centimeters below the surface. There are a lot of organic factors contributing to humus formation, including residues and microorganisms eight to ten tons of manure can hardly generate one single ton of humus. This is a lengthy process.Once again, in order to get the picture of what is happening: in Romania, the practice of burning the stubble fields after threshing has almost become a general rule. But this is a crime; a total disaster for the soil's superficial layers. It destroys organic matter and the surface-living creatures. The lease holder is thinking: 'This land does not belong to me. I only want to spend as little money as possible on it. Why should I pack the straws in bales and carry them away, when I can burn them right here? This will save me several millions per hectare'. One single centimeter of soil takes some 600 years to build.

Once the communist industry broke down, Romania's natural systems have started to improve, right?

We cannot say the same about soil. On a global level, one of the main causes of soil degradation is over-exploitation. The paradox is that we are dragged downwards by under-exploitation – or better said amateurish land exploitation, based on no genuine knowledge.

I don't understand...

We are dealing with a whole historic process of involution; after 1989, science has completely disappeared from agriculture. Traditional peasants used to approach agriculture based on a system of rules and customs refined throughout hundreds of years: a genuine textbook of sound agricultural practices, generated by the intimate knowledge of the earth. This type of peasants vanished during communism and was replaced by agronomist engineers, managing workers in the farming cooperatives. After 1991, they're place was taken by subsistence farmers (with no material means and knowledge) and lease holders willing to get rich. Who are these subsistence farmers? You know how they used to say during communist: if you don't go to school, you will herd the cows. Well, these are the people who did not go to school. In Western Europe, you can only herd the cows once you have finished your academic studies or at least some technical specialized program.

How did the traditional peasant use to do things? What has the contemporary peasant forgotten?

We are talking about an entirely different education, about knowledge – a different world. For example, the traditional peasant never worked on a plot of land that did not have the appropriate humidity level. He didn't even dare step on it! Today, people have completely forgotten that rule – or maybe they simply ignore it, because there are not enough machines to work the land only during its best moments. We have the smallest number of agricultural machinery per one hundred hectares, in Europe. Therefore I can say, as the proud owner of a tractor: when the land is too dry or too soft, I will not plough my land, but yours – as you have no tractor and no knowledge of such things. You are at my mercy...Working a plot of land that is too dry or too humid harms the soil's structure and makes it subside. When the land is too dry, you get a lot of big lumps; when it is too humid, you get strings – and then you have to disc the land I don't know how many times in order to mince it.

Another example: before, people used to know this very clearly: if you have built your stables uphill, you will never build your fountain downhill, because stable dejections will end in your well. However, this is exactly what people do nowadays: they put their stables up, and their well – down the hill. Transylvania, in the North of the country, is the only region where the correct settings have been preserved. The rest of the country is polluted with nitrates – in amounts considerably exceeding the accepted threshold.

The traditional peasant knew that all hilltops needed to be covered in forests. In certain hill and mountain areas of the country, where communist cooperatives have not penetrated, you cannot find a single unforested ravine. And even after 1989, nobody started cutting those trees.

We have no agricultural machinery. We do not practice intensive agriculture. We only use a few chemical fertilizers. We still plough our land using horses and oxen. Couldn't we say this is eco-friendly agriculture?

Let us settle this once and for all. We have never really used a lot of fertilizers. The European average value is higher than 270 kg per hectare. In Romania, the use of chemical fertilizers has decreased from an average of 86.4 kg/ha in 1986 to 31.3 kg/ha in 2005; the Irish use 16 times more fertilizer per hectare of land. The Netherlands is fiercely negotiating with its farmers, to make them decrease their inputs from 550 kg to 450 kg, given that their compost covers twice their needs. The first agro-chemistry lesson teaches you to give back at least as much as you have taken from the land: the nutrients that enable agricultural production. You should constantly help the soil with organic matter, and feed the microorganisms. But we do not use any organic matter. Anyway, we have the lowest number of farm animals per one hundred hectares, in Europe. If we were to use even the last drop of manure we produce, we could fertilize 700,000 hectares of land. But we do not use it. People have stopped carrying manure into the fields, although this has an extraordinary value. Instead of scattering it into their fields, they dump it in ditches, former irrigation channels, next to highways and any other place – except where they should.

How much does climate change influence soild degradation?

In plains, where the soil is good, the already considerable water deficit has increased within the last 20 years. Traditionally speaking, we used to have one droughty year out of three. However, 80% of the last 20 years have been dry ones. In Romania's southern regions, drought and irrigations with no use of organic fertilizers have diminished the soil's organic content. During dry spells, the soil is exposed. The vegetation that used to protect it withers. Left naked, the soil suffers from insolation: sun rays and excessive heat, combined with irrigation and rainfall, consume organic matter and lead to a fall in productivity. If your land is located in a sloped area, the first rain will destroy the soil, washing it away. The next one to be destroyed is the structure. The binding material built in by organic matter is lost, affecting soil structure. Soil starts pulverizing, blown away by the wind, washed away by the rain.

CHAPTER 26

LIFE BEYOND THE WALLS

What do they do there, in the monastery?

It's deserted, it's cold, and it's dark. You are exhausted when you get to the hermitage, but the monks are in prayer. What should you do? 'You wait for five, ten or 50 minutes, until the sermon is over; anyway, time goes by in a different way over here', says photographer Dragos Lumpan, who came to the *Putna Hermitage* to document monks' life beyond the walls, the paintings and the traditions. The Putna Hermitage is four kilometers of country road away from Putna, and it was promoted to the rank of monastery in 2005.

In the three weeks he spent here – from Lent until after the Resurrection – Dragos was gradually moved over, from a large guests' room into a small den and then right into a monk's cell, as a sign that finally he had somehow become one of them. Dragos was bewitched by the story of Father Leontie, a straightforward man, a robust forger from Ardeal. By 18, he was a lumberjack and had a girlfriend; they went together to the church in a neighboring village, to listen to a monks' sermon. When it ended, his only question was: 'Can I stay here?' And he stayed. His friends kept trying to make him go back into the world, but he remained a monk. He first moved to Putna Monastery, then to Putna Hermitage. The role of a monastery, as Dragos understood it: 'When you are living a normal life, into the world, with your family, you are disturbed by the ongoing background noise of temptations, which can detour you from your way. But here you have a choir who is singing in tune with you, and tugging at your sleeve, should you detour from your way towards God'. Following a life that is as saintly and as enhanced as possible, monks die and then, upon moving into God's kingdom, they become saints. There are many monasteries where, once you are greeted, you are invited in the nave and presented the holy relics you can pray to. In Greece, Dragos talked to the abbot of the Vatoped Monastery. 'People enquire: What is it that you are doing over there, in the monastery? Come to us and we will show you the holy relics that you can pray to. This is what we do: we are a relics factory, we turn people into saints'.

Daily labors. In the sculpture workshop, a monk is carving a monastic cross. Once he has his hair cut so as to become a monk, each man receives this cross for the rest of his life. Monks often perform manual labors. Hired workers deal with the big work, while monks attend the finely detailed projects. The monastery has rooms for sculpting, painting and carpentering, a shop for religious artifacts, and a small farm with animals and land cultivated by the monks.

A different kind of icons. Several monks are kissing the relics of a saint, in the pronaos. Just like the icons, certain relics are permanently exhibited inside the church, while others are only displayed on the day of that specific saint, upon the arrival of certain guests or once new relics are received. Relics are treated with all the honors owed to a saint. Monks deal with them as one would, in the profane world, with a highly respected person: you go over there, shake their hand and ask them something.

Job description. Part of the monastic term of 'obedience gesture' could be translated as 'job description'. Everybody gathers in the church's synaxis, and the abbot distributes a number of 'obedience gestures' to each monk (things that monk has to do during the year). There is a main one – such as working on the farm – while the rest are punctual, auxiliary (for example, waking all the monks up, early in the morning, for prayer).

Training in prayers. Nicolae Steinhart used to say we are some sort of tourists in this world, walking on a mountain path that has easier and more difficult bits. Monastic life is a sort of climbing, a training in prayer, on the abrupt way towards God: you can get up there very fast, but you can also take a horrendous fall. The stairs of sins in Sucevita are painted with saints; although these saints had led a saint life, at a certain point they were tempted and they fell down, much like a climber falling from the peak of the mountain.

Well-disposed people. Monks are perceived as being old, serious and sullen. 'This is not true. The average age of monks at the Hermitage is 30. I've found an atmosphere of joy and youth in almost every monastery where I stayed' – says Dragos Lumpan. This is the place where you have no worries about what you will be doing tomorrow, one year or ten years from now. You always do the same things, you don't have to change anything, and you don't fight against anything (except for the spiritual temptations: the devils).

Moving to Our Lord. A monk is pensively attending a remembrance sermon. Monks are not buried in a casket, but lying straight on the ground, dressed in their monastic habit. Their graves bear wooden crosses, that rot, and then nobody makes other crosses for them. Seven years after their death, their bones are moved into an ossuary. Death is regarded naturally. Anyway, monks go to the monastery in order to die. The most important thing is to die when we are well, in a good relationship with God. You should die with your gear well packed.

CHAPTER 27
A LIBRARY OF STONES
The complete collection of Romanias rocks.

In a huge industrial hall on the outskirts of Bucharest, 55,840 metallic drawers, one meter long each, grouped into 18 parallel sectors guard samples from more than 1,000 boreholes drilled all over the country.

This is the National Lithoteque 'hosting unique scientific evidence retrieved from thousands of meters deep', says Paul Constantin, researcher at the *Romanian Geological Institute*. According to Serban Veliciu, head of the institute, a single 5,000 meters-deep borehole may cost 20 milion dollars.

Obsessed to become independent of imported raw materials, Ceausescu has tolerated the astronomic costs of those drills and ordered a complete X-ray of the Romanian underground in search of natural resources. This was how the National Lithoteque was born in 1983 – as an achievement of the 'Golden Age' due to unprecedented investments in geology. 'This is something that could have been built only in Communism', says Calin Ricman, researcher at the Romanian Geological Institute.

Together, the Geological Museum and the Lithoteque, contain the complete collection of Romania's rocks.

By a trick of fortune, the Lithoteque, one of the most expensive Romanian scientific projects, is falling apart today, due to lack of funds.

CHAPTER 28

THE OTHER SOCCER

A story about the unseen and unglamorous face of the king of sports. 13 girls play their hearts out, in miserable conditions – and lose.

It is almost six o'clock in the morning. In an empty waiting room, disturbed only by the mockery of some rude security guards, the girls of the Smart Bucharest team are waiting for their coach. Loredana has moved into a corner and she is dozing, slightly closing her big blue eyes. She got up at two o'clock in the morning. Worried about the match, she kept tossing and turning in her bed until she woke up 'The Teacher' – this is how the other teammates call Mihaela. Loredana is 18, she is from Clinceni, a village in Ilfov county. Every day, she commutes to her high school in Bucharest. Yesterday, in order to catch the six o'clock train to Constanta, she slept at the Teacher's house. They both left Trafic Greu neighborhood at five o'clock sharp. Some dogs followed the girls who ran almost a kilometer until the bus schedule started and got on the first bus for the North Railway Station. Coach Gheorge Marinescu shows up cheerfully, hugging his girls and declaring: 'We'll defeat them!', although he knows he does not have six of his best players, and their opponents, Santierul Naval Constanta (The Naval Yard Constanta), have become much stronger lately. Uncle Marin – as the players affectionately call him – is an optimistic 60 year old Joly Joker in his eternal blue training suit, chatting and smiling all the time, revealing his new porcelain teeth. After waiting until the last minute for two girls who didn't show up, the group humbly walks to the 6th carriage of the high-speed train number 1681.

The Smart team got up at the crack of dawn to leave for Constanta, as they have no money to pay for a bus or a hotel.

II 'As long as I still have the strength, I will manage', says Rodica Silcovan, smoking thoughtfully under a ficus tree, in the sunny House of Soccer, at FRF (The Romanian Soccer Federation). The 80 years old matriarch of women's soccer has gleaming eyes and elegant moves. She created the Romanian Female Soccer National Championship. The first edition, held in 1990/1991, was preceded by 'The Liberty Cup' – a tournament involving teams from all over Romania. Based on their final score, they were divided into Division A (12 teams) and Division B (30 teams). Romanian girls had started playing soccer for the big state-owned enterprises' teams ever since the 1970s; however they performed unoficially, in friendly good will matches at county level or to open the men's matches.

'Our girls are resilient, they are excellent middle-distance runners. We have the biologic potential. Money will come too', she says, hoping to get – unlike Moses – to see the Promised Land. According to FIFA, women's soccer is globally becoming the sport with the highest growth rate. In Romania however, the very few sponsors who invest in it become bankrupt or abandon these projects, and dismantle the teams after two or three years. The situation became dire starting with 1994, when state-owned factories, supporting the teams, were closed down one by one. For the time being, the championship – divided into two geographical series for the sake of more economic traveling arrangements – includes only eight teams. The South Series includes Smart Bucuresti, Pandurii Targu Jiu, Santierul Naval Constanta and Targoviste, while Clujana, Motorul Oradea, Resita and Targu-Mures play in the North Series. Smart is one of the poorer teams. At the opposite pole, Clujana has only two local players: the others came from all over the country, signing contracts that granted them money and a place to live.

IV The match will begin at eleven o'clock. The girls from Bucharest, who arrived in Constanta much too early, reluctantly climb the stairs of a bar in the railway station. They take over a few of the black squared-tables and after a lethargic while, the hungry girls start taking sandwiches out of their bags. After their meal, they start chatting as 'manele' songs are rising from the speakers, but the coach signals to the girls that it is time to leave. The field is on the other side of the railway tracks and in order to get there they must get across. Unwilling to go around some train carriages, the team crawls under them.

III Daniel Robe earns money from soccer matches: indoor, on small fields and on the beach. But not from feminine soccer matches. He is a member of the FRF Board, in charge with promoting the National Indoors Soccer Championship; he is also the chairman of the Sub-committee for Beach Soccer and the owner of the feminine soccer team Smart Bucuresti. In 2000, Bucharest had two women's soccer teams: F.C. Regal and C.S. IMGB. Regal, the champion at that time, featured professional players, brought from all over the country. The owners were from the Republic of Moldavia and they used to invest a lot of money in this team. Some of the girls were 'raised' at IMGB by coach Gheorghe Marinescu, whose team had become a kind of 'nursery' for Regal. When the Moldavian owners left Romania, Daniel Robe took most of the players from Regal, and created C.S. Smart Sport. For Daniel, this team is a hobby that costs several thousands dolars per year, without him expecting any profit. Matches are played mostly without a public, and the sums paid for players' transfers – in the rare cases when they occur – are very small. 'Benefits can appear indirectly, in terms of image, because the company I use for organizing the matches needs some advertising', he says.

The extended crew of the Smart team includes almost 20 girls, but only ten of them come on a regular basis to the three weekly trainings, on the Soimii Inuc sportsground, rented for 4 $ per hour. At home, official matches are usually played on the stadium of the Spiru Haret University, rented for 120 $ per hour. The girls' sports gear is bought from a Chinese wholesale market, called 'Europe'.

V Sitting on the little fence next to the locker entrance, Pitica (The Dwarf) is crying. She is convinced that Sabina will get to play instead of her. The tougher soccer players hold a grudge against the few 'models' in the team, claiming they don't play at all, but Uncle Marin simply calls them 'for the sake of beauty'. Pitica is the youngest in the team. She is 16, and looks like a stocky, scruffy hedgehog. The coach sees her and, with a verbal kick in the bottom, sends the girl back to the locker room. In there, blue benches stand next to the green walls, while a small table, just big enough for a gear bag, marks the center of the room. Uncle Marin pushes the bag aside, and presents the game strategy using the girls' playing cards. A sunbeam, a golden reminder of summer days, falls on top of the hot radiator, next to which the girls have changed their clothes. But the sun outside is chilly and a sharp wind is blowing.

Global feminine soccer, governed by FIFA and UEFA, tends to become a social phenomenon. The 2003 World Championship final, hosted by the USA – arbitrated by Romanians Cristina Ionescu (referee) and Irina Mart (lineswoman) – was attended by 90,000 spectators. The Smart against SN Contanta match is watched by seven kids, four gentlemen and two young ladies sitting in the stands.

VI Although at first sight uncle Marin seems to fancy the 'laisssez-faire' approach, the warm-up before the game clearly shows that Smart knows its way with the ball. Elena, the team captain, positions her girls in a threatening 'phalange' and gracefully rehearses the troupe movements they have all learned throughout their training practices; it is a real pleasure to watch their quick game, the exchanging of places and their swift passes. However, once the referee blows his whistle, the soccer field starts becoming too big. A demanding spectator, used to the boys' speedy game, would start yawning in boredom at the square field, as if sitting in front of a huge, almost green aquarium, with colorful fish swimming gently and sharks only rarely troubling the water with their attacks. Watched from the bench, the game looks different. Although she's wearing only a T-shirt and shorts, the 'model' Gabi is boiling up in the freezing chill. She is supporting her teammates with all her heart, squirming and kicking an imaginary ball and discussing with the coach.

VII The game was lively, the girls scored, there were good passes, errors, foul plays, thundering passes, a penalty and a red card. The hosts' coach yelled like a maniac throughout the game, objecting against the referees, the opponents, his own players… Uncle Marin also kept shouting throughout the first half of the game, as if he were commenting the match on the radio, going from threats to begging. But during the second half he became silent, and his girls didn't play much. The game finally ended at two to one for Constanta. The girls had no place to take a shower, so they took the train back to Bucharest. In the railway station, before getting on board, the club delegate handed them the money for the game: 7 $ each. 'Why haven't I stayed at home today?', Luminita, the 38 year-old veteran of the team wearily wondered, back on the train. Penniless soccer might be romantic, but is reduced to being a half way game. The girls are playing their hearts out, but without discipline, resources, proper food and a lot of work, one cannot achieve a high level of performance. Once they understand this, many girls abandon the sport. The very young ones play out of passion and dream of becoming a member of the national Romanian team, where somebody might see them and then, who knows, offer them a contract abroad. The best female soccer players have already left the country and are paid thousands of Euros to play in Germany, Spain, Turkey or the northern Europe. The team split up in the North Railway Station, each girl going her way. Two of them got down the subway stairs, carrying a big red bag stuffed with the team's gear. They paused for a second in front of a shop window displaying underwear, then went on, singing and chanting: *ta-ta-ta-da-da-ta-ta, ta-da-ta-ta-ta-da-da* – a song of a band called Scooter, played at thundering volume on the Ghencea Stadium whenever Steaua Bucharest scores.

CHAPTER 29

THE LOST WORLD OF MAGURA-GORGANA

An international team of archaeologists is searching for the inhabitants of Gumelnita.

Ten o'clock pm. All the windows wide open. Beads of sweat on foreheads; sweaty shirts clinging on to skin. After a day's work in the sweltering sun, archaeologists are still sweating in their base camp: the tin roof, so hot during the day, has turned the school in Pietrele, a village in Giurgiu county, into an oven. The classroom seems really high because of the dark. Clouds of cigarette smoke are blurring the yellow light of the big desk lamps. Wooden benches are standing next to the walls, covered by pottery shards and pots in various stages of reconstruction. A dozen of archeologists – Germans, Romanians, Bulgarians, Grusinians, Dutch and Moldavians – are studying. Each school desk they occupy accomodates different piles of artifacts, according to their expertise: pottery, bones, stones, copper and so on. Shortly after midnight, they go to sleep in tents set in the school yard. Six hours later, a dog still wearing a chain around its neck gives them the wake-up call, chasing the Guinea hens in the yard. Morning has broken. Zippers are unzipped and archaeologists start emerging like ants from a multicolored formicary, and begin their routine: bathroom time, washing up using a bottle of water tied to the fence; they fast forward through breakfast and carry their instruments to the van.

II At seven o'clock sharp, they are on the archaeological site located in the middle of the field, halfway between the villages of Pietrele and Puieni, on the Danube terrace, about eight km away from the river. They are part of a decade long international project, started in 2002, aiming to systematically study (a first for Romania) the prehistoric village of Magura-Gorgana, in order to recreate the world of Gumelnita. There are 72 such tells (settlements that have been gradually raised, throughout hundreds of year, inhabited by relatively small village communities) in Southern Romania. Nine have been systematically researched; seven were salvaged; and ten others were analyzed in search of stratigraphic information. Although diggings have started as early as the 1920s, a detailed research of the tells from the Copper Age in the inferior Danube Basin is still a goal to be pursued, and Gumelnita remains 'an unknown civilization'.

'We chose the tell in Pietrele – the Gorgana site, due to the geographical setting of this site within the northern area of the *Gumelnita-Kodzadermen-Karanovo VI* compound, as a connection between South-Eastern and Central Europe. The distance between this site and the Black Sea is approximately 150 km. Varna, in Bulgaria, is located within the same distance and it has a famous cemetery dating back to approximately the same period as Magura Gorgana and reflecting the same dynamic development, with the occurrence of social differences', says the Project Manager, Svend Hansen. 'We are currently trying to find out how our settlement has developed during its 300 to 500 years of existence; which were its various economic strategies; how people used their environment; in order to be able to realize how the social differences first occurred. You can understand this process only if you systematically excavate one of these tells', says Dr. Agathe Reingruber.

A mixture of *Boian Marita* and *Karanovo VI* cultures, the cultural compound of Gumelnita – one of the major prehistoric cultures in this area – lasted from Aeneolithic until the 5th millennium B.C., located between the Black Sea, Central Bulgaria and the Danube Delta, going as far as northern Greece. The decline of the Gulmelnita civilization started when the Cernavoda I tribes arrived on the Danube banks. Many researchers consider these were the first Proto-Europeans. The Gumelnita civilization reached a sudden end in its main habitat, but continued to exist in other areas (Wallachia, Thrace, The Balkans) for at least another century, during its Stage B.

III Nine people perished in an accident that destroyed their home 6,370 ago. According to analyses performed by anthropologist Dr. Joachim Wahl, three generations from a hunter-gatherer family were living under the same roof: an infant; three small children, ages one, two and four; a teenager of around thirteen or 15; a young woman, age 18 to 25; a man, a woman and an old man of approximately 50. The neighbors across the street were a family of weavers; the weights on their loom are among the oldest ones ever discovered in Europe.

Their home, typical to the Magura Gorgana settlement, was a two-storey structure of 9 x 6 meters, covered in reed, with clay walls and floor. A layer of sea-shell fragments, remnants of a meal that never actually took place, is scattered on the ground floor. A flint axe lies under the threshold, with its sharp edge towards the exterior. Stone axes of various shapes and sizes, arrow points, long spear points for hunting bison, harpoons and fishing net weights stand close to the walls. This house is the main source of weapons and wild animal bone fragments found so far. The house used to have an oven on the ground floor and a hearth on the first floor, where the bedroom was most likely set. The ground floor was the functional area, serving as workshop, warehouse and kitchen. We still don't know whether the house fire was started by accident or following an incident that made havoc of the settlement. The villagers never got inside the house again, to bury the nine people.

'We can assume the people of Gumelnita had a different perception of death and human remnants. We found a chisel made of a human tibia here. Although they were already burying their dead in the cemetery next to the tell, probably not all the deceased enjoyed the same treatment. Perhaps some of them were thrown into the Danube, while others were hung in trees. Ethnology shows us many similar examples. Maybe the bones of those nine were used for a ritual, or maybe they were brought into this house later, by dogs or other animals. We hope our anthropologists will clear this issue', says the Project Manager, Svend Hansen.

IV There are about 20 people on the tell: ten locals carrying earth by the bucket, and about ten archaeologists who 'dig' millimeter by millimeter, using their trowel, brush and vacuum cleaner. Patience, care, a lot of previously held discussions, all kinds of measurements with colored bands and tapes, photographs, plans and sketches. 'To excavate is to destroy; this is why we are trying to gather a maximum of information, in order to understand how it was. Our work resembles the efforts of a forensic expert trying to solve a jigsaw puzzle with everything that has happened here during the second half of the 5th millennium B.C.

We are not interesed as much in the objects themselves – as museums are full of beautiful artifacts – but in the context that can add the story of a certain artifact to the whole image of the Gumelnita world', said Dr. Svend Hansen. The professor, wearing an orange scarf on his head and a Leica photo camera around his neck, seems ubiquitous: he gets down on his knees here, digs a bit over there, has brief conversations, takes some photos and moves on. Watching Herr Svend Hansen, manager of the Eurasia Department of the German Archaeology Institute in Berlin, you see everything about him has become pale white, toned down by the sun of the Danube Plain: his hair, his smile and his clothes. He is 46, and leading this camp – where everything seems to be working on its own, in a sort of German tidy style – like the discreet conductor of an exquisitely trained orchestra.

More often than not, the village workers are standing on the edge of the pit, gathered around like waiters with their arms crossed, watching the archaeologists bent down over the red earth. Whenever a new pail has been filled up, they rush to clean it away. They never dig, but simply carry the earth scratched by the archeologists and sift it through a sieve. After almost seven hours under the mad scorching sun, sometimes enduring temperatures of up to 40 degrees, at around three p.m., the team goes back to base. It's the school in Pietrele, which they have rented for the summer. They bring here their daily harvest: approximately 100 such artifacts, plus 1,500 pottery shards. Sometimes, a certain artifact makes quite a stir: it is thoroughly examined, turned inside out and upside down, admired and discussed, either on site or – most often – at the base camp, where all these artifacts are cleaned, counted and put into categories.

The after three o'clock schedule involves a snack – cake and some tea or coffee; some rest; and dinner around seven o'clock in the evening, followed by the study of all the discoveries, going on as late as midnight. The archaeologists go to bed around eleven or twelve at night, and then start it all over again at six in the morning. They have been digging here for five years now, and will be digging for another five. This is what they do every day, during the pupils' summer break, for eight weeks, every year. Some of them come and go when they have finished their studies.

V A small artificial lake is gleaming on the left of the tell. It's the only thing that can still give you a hint about the way this landscape must have looked like, during the second half of the 5th millennium B.C. The prehistoric village was built on a mound, stranded on the edge of a high terrace that abruptly descends towards the Danube Plain. The terrace now covered with vineyards, corn and stubble fields used to be a steppe dotted with clusters of trees, roamed by wild horses, aurochs and deer; the village grazing ground used to be a labyrinth of pools, forests, lakes and channels – a genuine paradise for fish, turtles, snails, wild boars and aquatic birds. Maps made around the turn of the previous century still show a network of channels, ponds and swamps – the formerly large wetland going as far as the Danube that was reclaimed back in the 1960s. One can still see the shapes of former channels – some deeper and some longer – which can be easily identified on satellite maps. However, these traces are not older than 1,000 years, says Prof. Dr. Jurgen Wunderlich from the Institut fur Physische Geographie, University of Frankfurt Am Main, who is leading the geophysical research to recreate the Magura Gorgana landscape as it was back in the time of the Gumelnita people. 17 m deep drillings and geoelectrical measurements going as deep as 50 m have proven that the

Danube Plain used to be ten meters lower back when the tell was inhabited, as the annual flooding did not touch Magura. It was only after 4000 BC, i.e. about 250 years after the tell had been abandoned, that the wide river meadow was completely flooded.

Approximately 28 houses were built up on the tell, arranged on five strings that go from East to West, separated by 1.5 meter-wide lanes. The tell used to have terraces (with the southern string being up to three meters lower than the northern one) and was surrounded by a moat, an approximately five meters wide. Geo-magnetic prospections of the surrounding area revealed a unique situation among the tells of the Lower Danube Plain: houses are also built on both sides of the knoll, covering an area three times bigger than the one on the tell itself. The settlement expanded perhaps as far as the bottom of the knoll, counting over 1,000 inhabitants living in about 120 buildings, during its most prosperous times. The graveyard was located to the south-west of the tell: it has not been excavated yet, but geo-magnetic measurements indicate more than 50 graves. A potential prehistoric fort was built on the terrace, approximately 600 m away from the tell; it has a 160 meter diameter.

'Magura Gorgana was perhaps the ceremonial and commercial center of a large community. People from satellite-villages used to bring their products here, as if at a central market. This hypothesis is also supported by the large number of tools, flint axes and figurines discovered here, as well as by the defense moat surrounding the knoll and the fort on the terrace. Moreover, ceramic bowls painted with sophisticated patterns reveal an exchange of ideas, symbols and messages – undecipherable today – over a large area', says Svend Hansen.

VI The closest neighbors of the Gumelnita people in Magura Gorgana were 20 km away, on the tells from Cascioarele and Ruse (Bulgaria). It is with such neighbors that the people of Magura must have done their most intense exchanges, especially due to marriages: in a small community, where everybody is related to almost everybody, you try to get a wife from another community. However, they were perhaps also fighting: the weapons discovered here were much too sophisticated to have been used for mere hunting. Most likely these people were not organized in tribes ('tribe' is a modern term), and their identity was limited to saying 'we live in Magura Gorgana.'

According to the archaeologists' discoveries, the approximately 1,000 inhabitants of this settlement mainly lived on hunting and fishing: most of the bone fragments discovered here belonged to either wild boars, stags, wild horses and aurochs, or fish, turtles and snails. Hunting was performed by families, but also by larger groups, when hunters spent more days looking for wild horses or aurochs. The second most important occupation was raising domestic animals: beef seemed the favorite item on the menu, so they bred cows, but also dogs, pigs, sheep and goats. Some farmers also had small plots of land on the terrace, close to the tell where they cultivated cereals (charred grains of wheat and barley were found inside the burnt houses); they also gathered wild berries (sloe, hawthorn, raspberries, elder, cornel). Archaeologists recognize houses as concentrations of burnt adobe and reddish spots. Lanes are grayish-green. Some lanes are covered with a concentration of broken pottery, piles of seashells, bones and flint tools, which shows this is where they used to throw their garbage and broken tools.

'Underneath the burnt houses, we have found intact building remnants (for the first time since researching Gumelnita-style settlements), which proves these houses had been built over the old ones, following a certain pattern given by the already existing lanes', says archaeologist Meda Toderas. Two houses have been revealed in the excavated area: the hunters-gatherers' and the weavers'. Fire cases are extremely rare in Gumelnita villages. How is it possible for these adobe houses, with 50 cm-thick walls, to burn down like torches? – have wondered the researchers. They probably contained wood or some other type of fuel inside. Symbolic interpretation has become popular in these last 10-15 years, in archaeology. Led by them, many experts believe in the hypothesis of 'killing homes', by burning them down upon the owner's death, or during some other type of ritual. Professor Svend Hansen has a more down-to-earth explanation: houses covered with reed and built very close to each other can easily be engulfed by flames, especially on a hot summer day, and the mixture of clay and straws used for building the walls is a fuel in itself, as it keeps slowly smouldering down, even after the initial flame.

Many pots were found almost intact in the burnt houses, underneath the collapsed walls. They vary greatly in shape, size and pattern, all of an undeniable artistic refinement. Ceramic figurines – miniature artifacts of anthropomorphic and zoomorphic inspiration, but also depicting houses, ovens or pots – are a sort of keyhole in Time, allowing us to peek into the world of the Gumelnita people. You can find these everywhere – inside the houses, on the lanes or thrown away with the garbage. Most of them show intentional breaking of the head, legs or antlers. Were these toys? Did they have any ceremonial significance? We can only speculate on the religious beliefs of the Gumelnita people. Some experts have suggested that certain figurines could have been miniature copies of prehistoric sanctuaries. Some women figurine could be wearing specific clothes for that time. According to Professor Svend Hansen, the people of Gumelnita must have had certain rituals and ceremonies connected to the seasons, major events in a person's life – birth, death, marriage, initiation ceremonies – celebrated by the community.

The Professor believes they used the figurines during these ceremonies, and afterwards broke them and threw them away. The lanes are full of such pieces.

VII Magura Gorgana used to be a major link in the pan-regional network area between the north of the Aegean Sea and Wallachia, the Black Sea and Oltenia. The people of Magura got their flint from the south of Danube; gold and copper from Bulgaria, Serbia and maybe the Carpathians (no traces of copper processing have yet been found in Magura Gorgana); Spondylus seashells (for bracelets and beads) came from the Mediterranean area; obsidian from Tokai (Hungary), graphite bars from the Balkans. The Danube of that time, flowing stronger and faster than it does today, was a genuine highway of this region. The settlement lies 150 km away, between the Black Sea and the famous Varna cemetery (the most spectacular Gumelnita necropolis, discovered in 1972, when workers were digging a ditch to bury some electric cables, West of Varna. The wealth of some of these graves, located in the central part of the necropolis, is in stark contrast with most of the others, which are rather poor, thus proving social differences have appeared as early as the Copper Age.)

The houses that have been excavated so far in Magura Gorgana are specialized households. Manufacturing pottery and copper goods, as well as cloths, require highly standardized activities. In this type of community, becoming increasingly complex, a few people who organized the various activities gradually got to accumulate power. They started using metals as a symbol of their status. In Neolithic, copper objects were like today's Rolexes – luxury articles acknowledging their owner's social status. In Neolithic cemeteries, malachite beads and copper earrings are often discovered next to other 'luxury' items such as beads made of Spondylus. The Magura graveyard will be excavated in the following years, allowing researchers to put together many of the currently missing pieces of this jigsaw puzzle. In 4350 BC, the Magura Gorgana settlement was abandoned, following a catastrophic fire. At the end of the 5th millennium, all the tell-type settlements had already been abandoned, and the Gumelnita culture disappeared.

'The centralized structure of the Gumelnita culture – this new system of the Copper Age first appeared in Europe as an experiment – collapsed after 300-400 years, to be succeeded by an inferior social structure', says Svend Hansen. Some researchers consider this culture's demise has been caused by the arrival of the Cernavoda I tribes on the Danube banks. Others believe the cause must have been the resettling of the Danube course, following the flooding of the Black Sea by the Mediterranean Sea, approximately 5000-6000 years ago. Perhaps the Gumelnita people did not disappear altogether, but decided to merely relocate and, as they changed their architecture and pottery style, archaeologists can no longer identify them. The Gumelnita culture has been lost, but not entirely: millimeter by millimeter, the efforts of meticulous researchers such as the archaeologists in Magura Gorgana gradually bring it back to light.

CHAPTER 30

THE YEAR OF THE PARKS

Romania's nature protection areas.

In may 2016 we celebrated the centenary of the *Land of the Best* – the April 1916 edition of **National Geographic** dedicated to American national parks. Back then, the editor-in-chief Gilbert H. Grosvenor sent a copy to each member of the US Congress, urging them to support the founding of a governmental organization that would manage the national patrimony of nature. At that time, the United States had 14 national parks, but no unique agency to manage, protect and develop the wilderness patches scattered across the country into one coherent system. Five months later, a federal law was voted to create the US National Park Service.

Since then, throughout this entire century, **National Geographic Society** has obsessively returned to parks by publishing hundreds of stories – with the same formidable mix of inspiration and information – in order to help people understand the high stake of preserving protected areas. In 2016 – proclaimed by National Geographic as „The Year of Parks" – „fully confident that science, exploration and stories have the power to change the world, we are using our global media platforms to draw the public's attention on the importance of these irreplaceable spots", says Chris Johns, *Executive Director of National Geographic Society Centers of Excellence.*

In terms of nature conservation, Romania is once again a state promoting form without content, with a blessed nature, but without the money or urge to protect it. „We are currently the only European country where the Government does not assume direct responsibility in managing the natural patrimony of national interest", says ecologist Florin Stoican in an interview for this edition. We remain an ark of European biodiversity, but if things keep slipping away on the same slope of disinterest for nature preservation, we will soon become one of the civilized countries where authorities start allotting big budgets for parks only after their wilderness spots have almost disappeared...

It so happens that this year, one century later than the American Congress, the Government of Romania also started discussing the opportunity of founding a *National Agency for Protected Natural Areas*. Having already learned Grosvenor's lesson, we sent a copy of this special edition dedicated to parks to each official head of hierarchy in the Romanian State – with a bookmarker set at pages 28-35. And we can only hope that history will repeat itself, 100 years later. When it comes to nature protection, **National Geographic** has already managed to pull off a few miracles, for it seems to have this special magic force of the fairytale plant called white swallow-wort or the "herb of animals", believed to open any locked door or heart, for that matter...

We'd only like to mention President Omar Bongo, who decided to found 13 new national parks in Gabon after having seen the wild heaven in his country in the first *Megatransect story* (NG, October 2000). Or the photographs from *Hawaii's Outer Kingdom* in the October 2005 edition, that prompted President Bush to found The Northwestern Hawaiian Islands Marine National Monument, 8 months later. Or Ecuador's President Rafael Correa, who last month announced the creation of a new marine sanctuary, protecting 40,000 square kilometers of coastal waters around the Galápagos Islands, after NG Explorer Enric Sala had taken there one of the Pristine Seas expeditions, in December 2015.

It is your turn now,
Mr. Klaus Iohannis, President of Romania.
The time has come for Romania to also have an agency for protected areas. Parks are the best part of the heritage we can leave to our children.

Interview with Florin Stoican

Florin Stoican has been fighting for the protection of Romanian nature for over ten years. On all fronts! He initiated and participated in many projects for the conservation of biodiversity and geodiversity, for tourism and for ecological education. He brought about the foundation of the Buila-Vânturarița National Park and spent the next five years laying the groundwork for its management, contributed to the establishment of the Văcărești Nature Park and other protected areas, and currently heads Kogayon Association, which was the co-administrator of the Buila-Vânturarița National Park for ten years and is, since 2015, the custodian of the Muzeul Trovanților – Costești Nature Reserve. He was a member of the commission assigning custody of protected areas in the south-western region of Oltenia and has been involved in most legislative processes concerning nature protection areas in the last few years. Still, all this success left him with a bitter taste, in a country of forms without substance, with a blessed natural wealth but not enough money, willpower or any great sense of urgency for its protection.

Following a parliamentary initiative, last year the former state administration started to draw up a Government Decision for the organisation and functioning of the *National Agency for Nature Protection Areas* (ANANP). The process was interrupted, then continued under the Cioloș administration.

How far have the talks gotten?

The law for the foundation of the ANANP is on the agenda of the Chamber of Deputies, after it was approved by the Senate. The Ministry of the Environment has invited anyone interested to sign up for the workgroup which will draw up and discuss the Government Decision regulating the new institution. I have signed up, together with almost 40 other people who have shown an interest in the matter, and we are now waiting for the Ministry to call us to the first work meeting.

In theory, we're not doing too bad at all: We have 13 national parks, 13 nature parks, two geoparks and a few hundred reserves and protected natural landmarks, the Danube Delta Biosphere Reserve, plus the Natura 2000 sites. In all, these amount to about 23% of the country's surface area. How do things look in the field? Why do we need a National Agency for Nature Protection Areas?

On paper, things do, indeed, look good, but if we subtract the Natura 2000 sites we get a protected surface area of about 8%, though Romania has the richest, most diverse and most valuable natural assets of all European countries. It is a pity that areas such as Făgăraș, Țarcu or Ciucaș have not gone beyond the status of Natura 2000 sites, though there have been projects and proposals for the foundation of national parks. However, the reality looks different: eight large protected areas needing management structures have no administrator, and 61% of the others have no custodian – even after seven successive sessions for the establishment of their administration/custodianship (a kind of auction held by the responsible authority). What is more, 74 custodianship conventions have been terminated only in the last year, which shows that there is a fault in the system.

Such sites are administrated based on management plans created after studies and consultations and approved by the authorities; currently, 15 years after the creation of the network of nature protection areas as we know it today, only 35 protected zones, or 6% of them, have an approved management plan.

Even if such plans existed, they would still be nothing but sheets of paper, as long as there are no resources for their application. And this is not something that can be done with volunteers, function delegation, and money from projects which are here today and potentially gone tomorrow.

We need the ANANP to ensure durable, long-term management, a coherent vision, management evaluation criteria, system monitoring, and the resources necessary for the effective administration of our natural assets.

There has been talk about the ANANP before, in 2008... Still, we now have a management outsourcing system.

There have been discussions about founding the ANANP in 2008, when the situation of protected areas was not much different from now. The current system is a result of the lack of political involvement and of decisionmakers giving too little importance to nature conservation. The State preferred to find others to do its job, and these others have to somehow conjure up personnel, money and other resources to put in the service of preserving the country's natural assets. For a while, this solution was thought to be viable, until its obvious limitations came to light.

What are the problems faced by Romania's nature protection areas and those trying to manage them?

Protected areas have many problems, all of which cause an increase in the anthropic pressure on wildlife refuges. The list is not complete, but the greatest threats are construction and investments of all kinds (roads, micro hydropower plants, quarries, ski runs, cable transport infrastructure, various forms of development); logging (both legal and illegal); unregulated hunting and fishing; poaching, intensive grazing, unregulated picking and collection of berries, mushrooms, medicinal plants, fossils, rocks and minerals, and speleothems; not to mention unregulated tourism. All this leads to the destruction of ecosystems, the perturbation and fragmentation of habitat, the loss of security for the fauna, environment destruction and degradation.

The greatest issues managers are facing are legislative incoherence and stammering, contrary measures taken by other sectors – particularly those investing in infrastructure, forestry, and agriculture –, incompetence and lack of support from the authorities, and the lack of human and financial resources.

Why is the effective management process in the current system based only on reaction?

Because pressure is ever-increasing, while the allocated resources are extremely few and, most of all, volatile. You can't have effective management if you rely only on volunteering or insufficient, unequipped, badly motivated, poorly trained personnel.

What is the approximate budget of a Romanian natural park? How does it compare to more developed countries?

It ranges between one and two hundred thousand euro per year, but the funds are allocated depending on the manager's possibilities and availability, with an average of 14 employees/management body. Compared to more developed parts of the world – including some African countries, which invest a lot more in conservation – we are very far behind. For instance, a national park in Great Britain has an annual budget – securely allocated by the State – of over five million euro and a management body with over 300 employees. And that is considering the peak of their biodiversity consists of foxes, hedgehogs and squirrels, while we, including our authorities and politicians, pride ourselves with almost half of Europe's large carnivore population.

How could the Romanian state make money by investing in nature conservation?

The earnings can be considerable, but they are indirect. Those who think it's possible to make a direct profit out of managing a nature protection area are wrong and turn conservation into an economic activity doomed to fail. The indirect benefits, however, are great and varied, on the one hand to local communities, on the other to visitors of protected areas. This could include ecotourism activities, within and particularly outside of nature protection areas, from accommodation, transportation and dining to specific services related to interpreting and getting to know nature, guiding, equipment rental and so on, or to durable and effective use of the available natural resources, from berries and timber to traditional products and water. And these are only the sources of income; far more important – though harder to quantify – are, maybe, the conservation of habitats and species, the preservation of pristine scenery, the recreational, informational and educational potential, carbon sequestration, oxygen emissions and many others.

All of this must be considered at a regional level, not in the restricted sphere of the nature protection territory. Such borders are human conventions – the bear and the wolf don't really pay attention to current administrative, legal and political limits. The same goes for the benefits. Nature protection areas should be seen as poles of regional development. If preserved, they will ensure the main pillar of local growth. It is not the park management who should turn a profit, and it should not be pilloried if it does not obtain a direct economic gain. But it's only normal that its budget be granted by the State, since its expenses are covered manifold, tenfold, hundredfold by the economic benefits the protected area brings to the region. But that takes vision, determination and resources.I have seen this applied in Germany, where the over 80 partners in the management of a natural park considered it normal to invest five million euro in its administrative body, which, individually, is running a deficit, as long as the indirect income to local communities exceeded 50 million euro per year.

This included all the money spent in the region by park visitors – on transportation, accommodation, meals, souvenirs, equipment, events and others, money which was not paid into the management's accounts, but into the accounts of hundreds of local companies and entrepreneurs, big and small. Financially, destroying the park is like killing the goose that lays the golden eggs.

Since 1989, it has become almost traditional for the Ministry of the Environment to not have a "notable" Minister, backed by a strong team which would fight on nature's side. All Romanian Governments, as well as the Romanian society, have always had other priorities. Why is now a good time?

The Ministry of the Environment, under its many names and leaderships, has been intentionally weak – maybe the weakest of all ministries – and had little influence compared to other priorities and interests. There has never been a team that would fight with all possible means for nature's real needs; a general line of compromise has always been the norm, and any initiative has started off with the defeatist handicap of one who does not try harder because they won't get anything, not even permission, from those who hold the reins – those in finance, law, state administration, agriculture, industry, transports etc. This policy of compromise was adopted not just by the authorities, but also by civil society representatives who set the general tone, which has resulted in some minor victories and limited success, every now and then. Overall, though, things have been going downhill, and the effects are visible for forests, rivers, bio- and geodiversity, whose conservation is declining, faced with the constant increase of threats from all sides.

What gives us a great opening now is that the current Government is under no political pressure or control and could act for the establishment of an ideal ANANP, which would only take into account the real problems and needs of the country's natural assets. It shouldn't matter that we have no budget backing. The lack of funds is a scarecrow: We are talking about almost a quarter of the country's territory, namely the quarter with the most valuable natural assets, whose loss or degradation would have disastrous consequences for our future, not to mention the national budget. If this line of action was taken, I am convinced the authorities would be widely supported by civil society, which would sway current and future decisionmakers to approve the variant which is best for nature, particularly since lately public opinion has been highly sensitive to environmental issues. This is not about political will, but about the will of the technocratic administration (and I hope such an administration will exist), which can lead to a long-term solution to the dire, sad and shameful situation of the country with the most valuable biodiversity in Europe.

A few days after the publication of this interview in the May issue of National Geographic Romania, on the 11th of May, President Klaus Iohannis signed a decree instating the Law for the establishment of the National Agency for Nature Protection Areas.

ACKNOWLEDGEMENTS

I would like to express my special appreciation to Nicolae Paduraru, Daniela Diaconescu, Elisabeth Miller, Mark Beneke, Duncan Light, Charlotte Simsen, Lucian Boia, Radu Vergatti, Constantin Rezachievici, Constantin Balaceanu Stolnici, Sabina Ispas, Petre Moraru – for their lessons about Dracula.

I'd like to say a special thank you to historians Mircea Babes, Ernest Oberlander-Tarnoveanu from whom I've learned a lot about the history of the Dacians.

I'm extremly grateful to Andrei Pandele, Radu Oltean, Bogdan Croitoru, Andreea Campeanu, Dragos Lumpan, George Dumitriu, Adina Branciulescu, The Romanian Soccer Federation, Ioana Popescu, Mircea Manole, Kunsthistorisches Museum Wien, and Muzeul National de Istorie a Romaniei for their unique photos and illustrations.

I would like to express my special appreciation to Adina Branciulescu, Roxana Dobri for contributing to this book with their essays and sidebars.

Also, special thanks to: Radu Oltean, Bogdan Croitoru, Madalina Nan, Pancras Dijk, Alina Alexa, Razvan Pascu, Adina Branciulescu, Cristian Lascu, Roxana Farca, Klaus Birthler, Cezar Dumitru, Gabriela Cocea, Andreea Campeanu, Diana Tret and Anca Popescu for sharing with us their Saxon discoveries.

I owe a great deal to translators Andreea Geambasu, Adriana

Hoanca, Domnica Macri, Anca Barbulescu, Cristina Mitocariu, Ilinca Anghelescu, Silviu Constantin, Cristina Fenia and Cristina Popa.

And thanks to my friends Alexandra Popescu, Dragos Margoi, and Tudor Smalenic who encouraged me and helped make this project happen.

TRANSLATOR'S PAGE

Andreea Geambasu: The Life of Nicolae Ceausescu, Romanian Gypsies, Stone Library, Gypsy Clans, On Procust Bed.

Adriana Hoanca: Why Do the Hill And the Valley Fight Each Other at Ruginoasa?, The Other Soccer, What About Dracula?, The Bear-Carol Singers from Vintileasca, Romania's Soils, The Ciuc Scouts' Big Game, Life Beyond the Walls, The Lost World of Magura-Gorgana, Ana Aslan's Elixir, The Avatars of Obor Market, The Language of The Folk Costume.

Anca Barbulescu: Romanian …Escu, The Danube's Delta Golden Horses, The Rise And Fall of Saxon Transylvania, The Leu And Its Many Faces, Romania's Top Ten Most Endangered Species, Who is Nr Two In Romania?, The Year of the Parks

Domnica Macri: What's In A Name?, The Journey of a Royal Heart, What About Dracula?, Belladonna's Cult, The Pipe of the Moti

Cristina Mitocariu: The Nutcracker.

Ilinca Anghelescu: The First Romanian Mummy

Silviu Constantin: When Was Sarmizegetusa Regia Conquered?

Cristina Popa: Back In The Saddle

ABOUT THE AUTHOR

Catalin Gruia is a veteran journalist who has written and reported for the Romanian edition of National Geographic for over 13 years. He is currently Editor in Chief of *National Geographic Traveler* and *National Geographic Romania*.

INTERNATIONAL AWARDS
First prize (Geographica section) at the International Seminar of National Geographic International Editions, Washington, 2004

Johann Strauss Golden Medal, Vienna, 2010; b2b.wien.info/de/reisebranche/wtk-2010-strauss-medaille

Kinarri Trophy, Friends of Thailand Awards, Bangkok, 2013, www.thaistory.ro/romania-premiata-la-friends-of-thailand-awards-2013/

If you liked this book you might like
Why We Love Vienna
Thailand with a Baby Stroller